A NEO-ARISTOTELIAN THEORY OF SOCIAL JUSTICE

I0886991

For Caitlin, Brighdin, Thomas and Madeleine.

A Neo-Aristotelian Theory of Social Justice

ADRIAN J. WALSH
Department of Philosophy
University of New England
Australia

Routledge
Taylor & Francis Group
LONDON AND NEW YORK

First published 1997 by Ashgate Publishing

Reissued 2018 by Routledge
2 Park Square, Milton Park, Abingdon, Oxon, OX14 4RN
711 Third Avenue, New York, NY 10017, USA

Routledge is an imprint of the Taylor & Francis Group, an informa business

Copyright © A. J. Walsh 1997

All rights reserved. No part of this book may be reprinted or reproduced or utilised in any form or by any electronic, mechanical, or other means, now known or hereafter invented, including photocopying and recording, or in any information storage or retrieval system, without permission in writing from the publishers.

Notice:
Product or corporate names may be trademarks or registered trademarks, and are used only for identification and explanation without intent to infringe.

Publisher's Note
The publisher has gone to great lengths to ensure the quality of this reprint but points out that some imperfections in the original copies may be apparent.

Disclaimer
The publisher has made every effort to trace copyright holders and welcomes correspondence from those they have been unable to contact.

A Library of Congress record exists under LC control number: 97074459

ISBN 13: 978-1-138-60936-5 (hbk)
ISBN 13: 978-1-138-60937-2 (pbk)
ISBN 13: 978-0-429-46466-9 (ebk)

Contents

Acknowledgements

I am especially grateful to Dr. Len O'Neill, Rodney Allen and Dr. Brian Scarlett for their support during the years when I was a post-graduate student at the University of Melbourne, writing the dissertation which eventually became this book. Special thanks also to Andrew Alexandra and Peter McGrath for spending many hours in the intervening years discussing moral, social and political philosophy. This book would have been a much weaker piece of work without those philosophical discussions. I would like to express my gratitude to Richard Norman and Ms Doris Schroeder for their most useful comments on the manuscript. Also thanks to the editorial staff at Ashgate for their assistance. Finally, thanks to Caitlin Morris for her support during the years I have been engrossed in philosophical research.

Preface

The debate over the proper relationship between theories of distributive justice and conceptions of the good has been particularly vigorous over the past decade. Whilst some have argued that the distributively just should be neutral towards the good life, others have argued that such neutrality is impossible. As will soon become apparent, my sympathies lie with the latter camp. In this book, I not only affirm the necessity of conceptions of the good, I take the further step of providing an account of the good to be employed when formulating principles of the distributively just society. It is my hope that this conception of the good is sufficiently broad to avoid many of the criticisms that such approaches have drawn in recent years.

INTRODUCTION

Introduction

This book is primarily a work in political philosophy, or more specifically in distributive theory. Herein I provide a sketch in broad outline of what a just allocation of distributive resources would look like. On my account, a just distribution will be egalitarian in nature, oriented towards realising the well-being of all. I suggest—somewhat controversially—that this goal is best pursued through the employment of a variety of different distributive principles when allocating different categories of distributive goods, i.e. I endorse a form of distributive pluralism which is guided by an egalitarian ideal. How plausible this is as an egalitarian strategy I leave to the reader.

Of course, the egalitarian project has less friends than it might once have had. Many political theorists nowadays are openly hostile towards egalitarian distributive theories. My claim—in defence of egalitarianism—is that if one takes seriously the Kantian dictum that we should always treat persons as ends and never simply as means, and one agrees with the kind of account of the human good I provide below, then egalitarianism necessarily follows. Much depends upon the plausibility of the account of the human good described below.

Probably the most philosophically-contentious aspect of the book is not its egalitarianism, but rather the *internalist* methodology employed, which involves the use of a neo-Aristotelian conception of the good to generate principles of distributive justice. Since the publication of Rawls' *A Theory of Justice*, many liberal theorists have argued that political theory should be neutral towards conceptions of the human good; such neutrality being believed to be a defining element of liberalism. Rawls constructs his account of justice in a way that he believes avoids the use of such contentious elements; he attempts to develop a theory of justice which is axiologically-neutral. If such a methodological device is available, and there is at least some doubt about the virtue or moral standing of internalism, then surely the internalist needs to provide some form of justification for proceeding in such a way. Another subsidiary Rawlsian objection concerns the connection between internalism and certain counter-intuitive sacrifices consequentialist social theory makes possible. With the aim of providing such justification, in section one I discuss the proper role of conceptions of the good in distributive theory. Therein, I provide a transcendental style of response which amounts to the suggestion that a conception of the good is a *necessary condition* of distributive theory. I argue that the practice of distributing resources necessarily requires sacrifice of some kind and that the sacrifice chosen reflects some covert conception of the good.

To be sure, there are a number of other important objections to internalist methodology not covered here. For instance, some critics might object that the human good is pluralist in nature, that its various forms are incommensurable and hence any attempt to provide a unified coherent account must, by necessity, exclude important elements of possible good human lives. Therefore, internalist approaches should be rejected. Alternatively, some critics might argue that accounts of the good have bad consequences in the context of political theory when implemented because they inhibit the human process of free self-determination, and thus internalist projects should once again be rejected. There are, of course, many other grounds for rejecting internalism. However, I only address these Rawlsian critiques. Why? Well, in the first instance, there are limits to the objections which one can effectively respond to in finite space. But why then discuss the Rawlsians objections rather than any other set? I choose the two Rawlsian-inspired objections in preference to other lines of criticism because I take them to be the most significant objections raised thus far against internalism in political philosophy.

However, that said, I do not wish to give the impression that I have no idea whatsoever about how I would deal with the objections mentioned *en passant* or indeed other criticisms. My general strategy—as the reader might glean from my response to the initial Rawlsian-style objection—would be to argue that notions of the good constitute a necessary condition of distributive theory and hence (i) those who would reject conceptions of the good in effect reject the idea of distributive theory *tout court* and (ii) the said axiologically-neutral methods endorsed by those who would provide non-internalist strategies only provide substantive normative imperatives by surreptitiously smuggling in accounts of the good.

Distributive justice

In the *Nicomachean Ethics* Aristotle divides justice into two broad categories: distributive justice and retributive justice.[1] According to Aristotle, distributive justice, concerns justice as exhibited in the distribution of honour, money, rights and privileges among the members of a community; it concerns the distribution of benefits and burdens. Retributive justice, on the other hand, concerns justice as exhibited in the rectification of wrongs committed by members of a community in their transactions with each other.[2] Retributive justice concerns the appropriate mode of dealing with wrongdoing. Additional to these Aristotelian categories, some theorists have wished to add a third category, commutative justice, which describes fair exchange in contracts.[3] In this book, I shall focus on the issue of distributive justice.[4] Thus my central concern shall be with the formulation of general principles for governing the distribution of benefits and burdens; issues of retributive justice and commutative justice will not be addressed.

While the problem of distributive justice was largely ignored by Anglo-American philosophy for much of this century, since the publication of John Rawls' *A Theory of Justice*, and subsequent to that Robert Nozick's *Anarchy, State and Utopia*, distributive justice has become a central issue for Anglophone philosophers.[5] The influence of Rawls and Nozick has been such that much of what has been written recently has been concerned solely with analysis of their works. However, whilst I examine their work—as well as that of a number of other important contemporary political thinkers—the primary purpose of my book is not exegetical. The central aim is to generate a theory of distributive justice: that is, to generate distributive principles for distributive goods. I shall assume that these distributive principles, once formulated, should be taken to be rules which social institutions must act upon, if they are to be considered to be acting justly. We may observe from the foregoing discussion that justice is amongst other things a virtue of social institutions and arrangements.[6] It is this aspect of justice which will be my major object of theoretical concern.

Another issue relating to the characterisation of justice concerns its status as a reason for action. In this book, I shall be content with merely claiming that justice is one virtue of social institutions and arrangements, rather than the *first* virtue. Justice will be treated as but one reason amongst many which should influence the policy decisions of social institutions. We may contrast this approach with that of Rawls, who claims that justice is the *first* virtue of social institutions, just as truth is the first virtue of systems of thought.[7] Rawls believes that questions of justice should not be subordinated to other reasons for action, such as issues of utility.[8] However, the wisdom of defining justice in such a strong way is open to question. While it is important that justice be recognised as a reason for action, whether it should be thought of as the unequivocal primary reason for action is highly dubious. As William Galston notes there seems to be no reason, formal or intuitive, for believing that justice enjoys anything like an absolute priority.[9]

However, here we should be attentive to the fact that Rawls himself vacillates between defining justice as the first virtue and defining it as one virtue amongst many. Whilst he argues in the introduction of *A Theory of Justice* that it is, in fact, the first virtue, it quickly becomes apparent in the main body of the text that other factors are to be taken into account. For instance, in formulating his general conception of justice—which concerns distribution under circumstances of extreme material scarcity—he allows questions of economic utility to take precedence.[10] It would seem then that for Rawls the principles of justice are 'but a part', although the most important part, of what he calls a *social ideal*, which contains an enunciation of all relevant parts, coupled with a specification of their respective weights when they conflict. Rawls' apparent equivocation on this issue provides yet another reason for being wary of characterising justice as the first virtue of social institutions and arrangements.

One important implication of treating justice as a virtue of social institutions is that, in the current context, questions of international justice come to fall outside the scope of our inquiry. If justice is a virtue of social institutions, then in the contemporary world that means it is primarily a virtue of nation states, for most major social institutions are organised at the present time under the aegis of nation states. (This is similar in some respects to the conclusion reached by Rawls. He opposes the application of principles discovered in the original position to questions of justice between nations). Of course, this is not to deny the importance of issues of international justice, but simply to assert that because of current political arrangements, the theoretical focus will be upon the justice of nation states.[11] (We may hope that with time distributive justice will come to encompass issues of international justice.)

As well as avoiding issues of international justice, I do not address the problem of how injustices should be rectified. I shall not be concerned with formulating principles appropriate for dealing with injustice, i.e. I shall not consider what Rawls calls *partial compliance theory*. Partial compliance theory includes such topics as the theory of punishment, the doctrine of just war and the justification of the various ways of opposing unjust regimes. Rawls contrasts this with *ideal theory*, which concerns the principles of justice by which we may judge some regimes to be unjust. However, there are those who believe that the priority accorded ideal theory is wrong-headed. Virginia Held, for instance, claims that if the existence of particular injustice confronts one inescapably, then it would seem that questions of how to deal with it may well be raised before a satisfactory resolution of the problems of ideal theory can be reached.[12]

Held may well be right. In some cases we may be confronted with such inescapable injustice, that attempting to settle pedantic issues associated with ideal theory may seem irresponsible and puerile. Yet, I do not think that we can invoke this notion of urgency to negate the importance of ideal theory: such practical problems are in the long run not going to be dealt with adequately without some attempt to systematise our views. In this I would concur with Rawls who argues that the reason for beginning with ideal theory is that it provides the only basis for the systematic grasp of important moral issues.[13] I shall be concerned, then, with issues of what Rawls calls ideal theory for the very reason that it provides us with grounds for the systematic understanding of the problems of distributive justice.

Internalism and externalism

What exactly is an *internalist* theory of distributive justice and what does it tell us about the role that a conception of the human good plays in the generation of distributive theory? Herein, the terms internalism and externalism will be used to refer to the kinds of conceptual relations which hold between: i) theories of the good and; ii) the principles of distribution which distribute social goods.[14] For an externalist principles of justice cannot be derived from the good. Externalist approaches specify a relation between i) and ii) in which theories of the good and of social justice are to be conceived of independently. Neither alone is adequate, neither is to be derived from the other, each must be given independent grounds. Externalism, then, is essentially a thesis committed to the conceptual independence of the good and the distributively just. It is committed to the idea that the just must not be derived from the good. The most well-known contemporary externalist account of distributive justice is that provided by Rawls. Rawls' idea of 'justice as fairness'—which he outlined in *A Theory of Justice*—consists in the claim that principles of justice should be generated without unnecessary reliance upon accounts of the human good. Rawls argues that in justice as fairness the right is prior to the good. For the Rawls of *A Theory of Justice*, distributive theory can be derived from the decisions of rational agents. Another exponent of externalism is Robert Nozick. Nozick's idea of deriving principles from rights—where rights are conceived of as side constraints upon action—would provide us with another example of an externalist strategy.[15]

While the externalist might concede that the goods which distributive principles distribute may be derived from a theory of the human good (or a theory of human nature), the principles which distribute these distributive goods must be generated independently of the good. Hence, the externalist would argue that distributive principles are to be generated independently of any theory of the human good. This methodological claim is the central tenet of externalism.

Externalists typically make the further claim that theories of distributive justice *should* be derived *independently* of any theory of the good. This we may call the *thesis of axiological neutrality.* Externalists are not only committed to a particular methodology, but generally to a particular justification of it. This is true of, for example, Rawls who endorses both externalism and the thesis of axiological neutrality.

Internalism, on the other hand, is that methodological doctrine which defends the 'conceptual dependence' of the distributively just upon the good. For the internalist, the distributively just is to be derived from the good. Internalism posits an asymmetrical internal relation between the good and the just; asymmetrical because although the just is derived from the good, the good is not derived from the just. (Utilitarianism, then, would be an example of an internalist strategy because a conception of the good is central to utilitarian distributive principles.) I assume that internalism and externalism are exhaustive of the possible strategies which might be employed for generating principles of justice: principles can be generated with reference to the good (internalism) or without reference to it (externalism).

Defending internalism

In defending the internalist thesis against externalist critics, I shall argue that internalism is an appropriate strategy for generating principles of distributive justice, for the simple reason that in the long run it is doubtful whether any other strategies could be successfully pursued. It will be a central theme of my book that it is unlikely that theories of justice could be formulated without a conception of the human good. Externalism, while both logically possible and coherent as an explicit description of a methodological procedure, is unlikely in fact to be practically realised because distributive theories require an account(s) of the good. William Galston puts it this way:

> The theory of justice contains as an indispensable element, an independent theory of the individual human good.[16]

Galston claims that general distributional principles are vacuous without some determinate concept of what benefits and what harms individuals.[17]

However, as I noted in the preamble, many contemporary theorists believe the use of a conception of the good in the construction of political theories to be undesirable. As a matter of fact, there are two main lines of argument here. Firstly, many argue that distributive theory should be neutral toward conceptions of the good (the 'thesis of axiological neutrality').[18] Principles of distributive justice should be derived, they argue, from other non-axiological sources. Secondly, many other theorists, following Rawls, find the connection between conceptions of the good and consequentialism problematic. It has been argued that since consequentialism is a maximising doctrine, when it is applied to issues of social policy this maximising characteristic necessarily occasions a number of counter-intuitive sacrifices which should be prohibited; consequentialist social theory is thus deemed to be problematic because of the sacrifices it countenances. By association, then, it might well be argued that internalist methodology involves the same morally repugnant sacrifices.

The first objection to internalism concerns the relationship between conceptions of the good and principles of justice. In *A Theory of Justice*, Rawls argues that rather than being derived from conceptions of the good, distributive principles should be neutral toward such conceptions; he argues that the 'right' should be given priority over the 'good'. Rawls defends what is essentially an externalist methodology, in which distributive principles are derived from the decisions of rational agents in a hypothetical 'original position'. I shall refer to this neo-Kantian methodology as 'constructivism' and shall discuss it in the chapter 'Distributive justice and the human good'. In that chapter I shall argue that although Rawls explicitly attacks what I have labelled internalism, he in fact employs conceptions of the good. Moreover, such usage should not be thought the result of philosophical weakness of will on Rawls' part, but rather as an inevitable consequence of the fact that a conception of the human good is required if we are to generate principles of distributive justice. The aim of chapter one shall be to cast enough doubt on constructivism to enable us to continue with our internalist project.

It is important here to note that Rawls' rejection of the good is not idiosyncratic. It should more properly be seen within the broader context of liberalism. As I noted at the beginning of this chapter, neutrality toward conceptions of the good has not only been claimed as a virtue by many liberals; but some have seen it as the central tenet of liberalism.[19] Whilst classical liberals—such as J.S. Mill—thought of liberalism as essentially a theory concerned with freedom, many modern liberals have taken neutrality towards the good as one of their doctrine's defining precepts.[20] They have argued both that the state should be neutral towards different conceptions of the good (which might be called the thesis of 'state neutrality[21]), and that principles of justice should not be generated using conceptions of the good (the thesis of 'axiological neutrality').[22]

My central argument against such liberal claims is that in practice the state cannot but help favour particular conceptions of the good because I am doubtful whether principles of distributive justice can be generated without recourse to them.[23] Furthermore, we should not think that conceptions of the good are indefensible.[24] If we employ what Martha Nussbaum terms a 'thick vague conception of the good', then I have a hunch that many of the concerns which people have with accounts of the good life might well disappear.[25]

To be sure, the foregoing identification of liberalism with neutrality towards the human good is controversial, to say the least.[26] We can think of other possible accounts; for instance, some may wish to tie liberalism to freedom, while others may wish to link it with toleration. However, analysis of what is the defining feature or features of liberalism is not a central concern of mine.[27] My main objective is to contest the thesis of axiological neutrality; and while axiological neutrality may be connected to liberalism, the fact that I argue against it does not mean that the book is essentially an attack upon liberalism; rather, in as much as liberalism is tied to axiological neutrality, then, my arguments do comprise an attack upon liberalism. Nonetheless, attacking liberalism is not my primary aim.

The second objection to internalist methodology noted above concerns a more general claim that consequentialist moral theory—when applied to issues of social policy—gives rise to morally abhorrent conclusions. Some philosophers have argued that consequentialist social theory permits counter-intuitive sacrifices of human lives and interests.[28] This objection has been taken to be a central problem of moral and political philosophy in recent years and has led to the current debate over the relative merit of 'agent-relative' as opposed to 'agent-neutral' moral theory. To be sure, for this objection to consequentialism to concern the internalist, we must assume that the employment of the human good in generating principles of distributive justice leads to the formulation of consequentialist distributive principles. For the purposes of discussion, let us assume that internalist methodology does lead to conseqentialist social theory.

I shall explore this second objection to internalist methodology in the chapter 'Distributive justice and the necessity of sacrifice'. Therein, I shall argue that consequentialist moral theory is acceptable because the implementation of any distributive theory necessarily leads to sacrifice and any system of implementation will have the effect of favouring some conception of the good over others. Moreover, I shall argue that if one uses a hierarchically ordered conception of the good, it is possible to construct a consequentialist moral theory which prohibits certain morally abhorrent forms of sacrifice.

These two chapters, then, involve defence of the internalist methodology, by arguing respectively for: (i) the implausibility of alternate projects and; (ii) the *necessity* of conceptions of the good in the practice of generating principles of distributive justice and in the practice of implementing such principles. I argue against both of the central objections to internalism stated above, that employment of conceptions of the good is in fact an acceptable methodology, because in the end, it is the only *feasible* methodology. I shall argue that principles of distributive justice cannot be generated without the employment of conceptions of the good.

Monism and pluralism

Whilst I defend internalism by arguing that a theory of the good is a necessary condition for the generation of distributive principles, it is no part of the doctrine defended here that a theory of the good is sufficient to generate such principles. In order to generate principles of distributive justice, an abstract theory of how people should be treated is also required. I shall derive this account of how the state should treat individuals with respect to distributive problems from a moral rule concerning the external relations of individuals; that is an account of how persons should treat each other.

With this in mind we can expand our definition of the internalism to be defended herein. My internalist strategy involves the formulation of distributive principles via the conjunction of two components; a theory of the human good and an abstract account of how people should be treated. Distributive principles must be derived from a conjunction of these two component principles. However, this definition gives rise to another question; from where should we derive our abstract account of how people should be treated?

There are two conspicuous answers to this question; i) it may be derived from the conception of the human good (monism), or (ii) it might be derived from moral grounds other than the conception of the human good (pluralism).[29] For the monist internalist, the abstract answer to the problem of how people should be treated is to be derived from a conception of the good. Hence, for the monist, not only is a theory of the good employed in the conjunctive process outlined above, but it is also used to answer the question of how people should be treated. Therefore all of distributive justice is to be derived from the account of the human good. For the monist internalist a conception of the human good is both a necessary and a sufficient condition for the generation of principles of distributive justice.

Monistic internalism involves the following argumentative strategy: firstly, distributive principles are to be derived from the conjunction of a theory of the human good and a theory of how people should be treated and secondly, the abstract theory of how people should be treated is to be derived from the human good. Hence, all of distributive justice is derived from the human good. I shall refer to such monism as the 'maximal thesis'. It can be seen from the above claims that the term 'monism' covers theories which use only one moral base in order to generate principles of distributive justice. As we shall see in chapter three, the central problem for the monist becomes how we might generate an abstract account of how people should be treated out of a conception of the good.

For the pluralistic internalist, however, a conception of the human good is to be thought of as providing only necessary, but not sufficient conditions for the generation of distributive principles. The pluralist derives an abstract account of how persons should be treated from grounds other than a singular conception of the human good. Pluralistic internalism involves the following argumentative strategy: i) distributive principles should be derived from the conjunction of an account of the human good and an abstract theory of how people should be treated and ii) the abstract theory of how people should be treated is to be derived from grounds other than the human good. This is the 'minimal thesis'. Accordingly, here we have a plurality of first principles, none of which may be conceptually reduced to the other. On one plausible interpretation, John Stuart Mill's ethical system—in which the good is described in non-hedonic utilitarian terms and the 'No-harm Principle' is employed as an answer to the problem of how people should treat each other—is an example of a pluralist theory because it involves the usage of two moral bases, neither of which can be conceptually reduced to the other.

Pluralism, then, involves the employment of more than one normative theoretical base. It is a pluralistic internalism which I defend herein. I combine a neo-Aristotelian conception of the good with the Kantian principle of 'respect for persons as ends', in order to generate distributive principles. (I assume in so doing that neither one of these two components can be conceptually reduced to the other).

The conception of the human good

Thus far I have been talking in rather broad terms of the human good, but as yet I have not specified what I really mean when I speak in this way. The term 'conception of the human good' refers to the classical question concerning the good life for human beings. It refers us to the sort of question which the ancient Greek philosophers, such as Plato, asked concerning how to live the best life. The particular conception of the human good I develop herein will involve the idea that human beings have interests whose realisation is constitutive of human flourishing. I beleive it is sufficiently vague to encompass a wide range of potential good lives that people may wish to lead and hence I suggest is compatible with liberal tolerance.

I have already noted that I shall defend the employment of the human good against externalist critiques, by showing that in all likelihood internalism is the only possible strategy. However, while this strategy may work as a means of justifying the overarching methodology, it does not provide a defence of the *particular* conception of the good which is to be employed. Why should we accept a neo-Aristotelian account of the good in preference to other rival accounts?

However, I do not directly address this challenge. I do not take issue with the question of why neo-Aristotelianism should be preferred to rival conceptions of the good. I do not attack rival moral frameworks. This may at first sight seem a little odd. In philosophy it is generally held to be the case that when defending a particular philosophical position an essential part of the task is addressing its rivals and demonstrating their weaknesses. However, there are a number of reasons for this policy. Firstly, there is the pragmatic point that one cannot deal with all of the potential questions which arise in one single book. The sheer size of the task of generating distributive principles and defending the internalist methodology is such that the additional task of defending the particular moral framework used is beyond the realm of the possible. We must place boundaries around our goals according to what is practically achievable.

Secondly, there are methodological reasons for not directly defending my neo-Aristotelian theory of the human good. The book will be structured—to some extent at least—rather like a hypothetico-deductive thesis. Thus, instead of directly attacking rival moral frameworks, I shall begin with the postulation of a normative framework and then work with it to see what falls out. I do not postulate the conception of the good as an axiomatic truth from which further truths are derived, but rather as a hypothesis from which other answers to standard problems in political philosophy are to be derived. Hence the test of our conception of the good against rival theories will be its fecundity. It is my hope that the book's worth will not be judged according to whether the initial conception of the good can be defended, but rather according to: i) the ***fecundity*** of that moral framework with respect to practical political problems and; ii) the ***coherence*** of the overall argument. While a conception of the good is necessary for a theory of justice, I do not provide apodictic grounds for demonstrating the veracity of my particular conception.

Neo-Aristotelianism

Finally, the question of what it means to call oneself a neo-Aristotelian should be addressed. What does my neo-Aristotelianism consist of? Further, does being a neo-Aristotelian commit one to all of the views of Aristotle?

The project is Aristotelian in two primary senses. Firstly, the value theory from which distributive principles are in part derived, has at its core the Aristotelian notion of well-being. Value is grounded in the idea of various kinds of human potential which might be realised or which might be said to flourish. The good is realised through the transformation of the potential into the actual. Under this conception, value is located in neither psychological states, preferences or reasons for action, but rather in the idea of realising our 'telos'.[30] Secondly, the internalist approach I outline and go some way towards defending is particularly Aristotelian. Aristotle believed that political questions must be answered with reference to questions of the good. It is often said that Aristotle imagined the *Nicomachean Ethics* and the *Politics* as a continuum; that is that the *Politics* was the continuation of the *Nicomachean Ethics*.[31] Aristotle argued in the *Nicomachean Ethics* that ethics was an integral part of the theory of politics; both being concerned with determining the good for humans. While ethics considers the good for humans abstracted from community, politics proper includes the study of civil societies which also exist for the human good in the complete social context.[32]

There are also two conspicuous auxiliary senses in which the project might be thought to have an Aristotelian tone. Firstly, the emphasis upon the social nature of human beings is very Aristotelian. Aristotle considered humans to be 'zoa politika' (literally 'animals of the polis').[33] In this book I assume that human beings are 'social animals', in that our interests are realised in society, through creative cooperative activity. Secondly, the focus on activity itself as being part of the good is particularly Aristotelian. Aristotle continually emphasised the importance of activity as a constitutive component of the good life.

That said there are a number of ways in which the project is *not* Aristotelian. (This list, of course, is only partial.) Firstly, it is not Aristotelian in the sense that Aristotle's broad views on cosmology and biology are not adhered to. Secondly, Aristotle's concrete views on distributive justice, in themselves, are irrelevant to the principles to be generated. (Aristotle was, after all, a meritocrat and believed that equals should receive equal amounts of reward and unequals, unequal amounts).[34] I derive a theory of justice from broadly neo-Aristotelian ethical foundations, not from the actual political works of Aristotle. Thirdly, the project is not characteristically Aristotelian in that it involves a *rule based* approach rather than a *virtue based* one. Pure Aristotelian ethics relies largely upon the attempt to provide a list of virtues and vices which might guide our practice. Aristotle believed that the virtues were central to ethics; eudaimonia, after all, was defined as "activity in accordance with virtue".[35] Of course, this is not to deny the importance of the virtues. Virtues are, after all, an important aspect of human moral life. As John McDowell has noted, there is more to being moral and, indeed, more to morality itself than merely acknowledging conclusions.[36] However, I do not believe that the focus upon rule-based ethics precludes the idea of the virtues; that is, it does not preclude the idea that our generalised ethical judgements should be internalised as ways of life. Finally, my neo-Aristotelianism should not be construed in a communitarian way.[37] I do not argue herein that values can be derived solely from the judgements of community or tradition. This is an important point for much contemporary neo-Aristotelianism is communitarian. Although this is quite a legitimate usage of the term 'neo-Aristotelianism'—indeed, Aristotle himself argues in the *Nicomachean Ethics* that the key to moral virtue is a good upbringing in a good family, and that virtues are of no significance whatsoever to someone who is not already part of that community—nonetheless, it is not a theme in the present work.[38]

The sections and chapters

In defending a neo-Aristotelian internalism which generates broadly egalitarian principles at a general level, the book is divided into three main sections.

In Section I 'Internalism and the Good', I shall focus upon the broad question of what the role of conceptions of the human good should be in distributive theory. I shall argue: (i) that in all likelihood a conception of the human good is necessary for the generation of principles of distributive justice and; (ii) that it is unlikely that it is sufficient. In order to generate principles of justice, a theory of how persons should be treated would also seem to be required. Section I leaves us with the claim that in order to generate distributive principles, we will require both a conception of the human good and an abstract account of how people should be treated. These normative elements shall be provided in Section II.

In Section II, 'The normative elements of distributive justice', the major theoretical concern will be with the elaboration and formulation of our two normative postulates. My first principles will be a neo-Aristotelian theory of the good and the principle of respect for persons as ends.

Finally in Section III, the principles presented in Sections II will be brought together to generate concrete distributive principles. Therein I divide distributive goods into three broad categories and then I apply the principle of equal well-being—which is derived from the conjunction of the account of the good and the principle of respect for persons—to each of these three spheres of goods.

Notes

1. Aristotle, 1969, Bk.V ch.2 [1130b18 - 1131a6]
2. Some readers might find the term 'retributive justice' unsatisfactory. It might seem to lay undue emphasis upon one theory of punishment; namely retributivism. However, for the sake of simplicity, let us continue to use the term to refer to theories concerning appropriate punishment.
3. See Raphael, 1950-51, p.171. It is interesting to note that Thomas Hobbes wished to restrict the question of justice to the keeping of contracts. Hobbes writes that: "The definition of injustice is no other than the not performance of covenant. And whatsoever is not injust, is just.", Hobbes , 1965), Pt.1 Ch.15.
4. One political theorist who would disagree with my assertion of the usefulness of the Aristotelian distinction is Feinberg. He claims that dividing justice into the retributive, distributive and commutative, is an artificial way of imposing unity on the idea of justice. He claims that a more interesting way of understanding justice is to distinguish between comparative justice and non-comparative justice. See Feinberg, 1974. However, analysis of his work would seem to indicate that his distinction is less fecund than the traditional Aristotelian distinction.
5. Rawls, 1972 and Nozick, 1974.
6. We should note that the range of social institutions is wider than people might initially suppose. Here we may quote Rawls who claims that: ".... the legal protection of freedom of thought and liberty of conscience, competitive markets, private property in the means of production and the monogamous family are examples of major social institutions.", Rawls, op. cit., p.7.
7. "Justice is the first virtue of social institutions, as truth is of systems of thought. A theory, however elegant and economical, must be rejected if it is untrue; likewise laws and institutions no matter how efficient and well-arranged must be reformed or abolished if they are unjust.", ibid., p.3.
8. I assume that justice is a reason for action which is distinct from utility. Both however are to be taken into account in our all-things-considered judgements. Other reasons for action may include self defence and economic expansion.
9. Galston, 1980, p.108.
10. See J. Rawls, 1972, p.62. The view that Rawls allows utilitarian considerations into his calculations is highly contentious because of his explicit claim that he constructs his theory of justice in response to various inadequacies of utilitarianism. Rawls might claim that justice is the first virtue, but what counts as justice will vary according to the material conditions. Thus nothing comes before justice as a reason for action. This seems bizarre, however. If this interpretation is correct, then Rawls would seem to be saying that we know that justice is the first virtue before we know what it is.
11. For a useful discussion of this issue see O'Neill, 1985, pp.262-81.
12. Held, 1973, p.12.
13. Rawls, 1972, p.9.
14. ".....in justice as fairness the concept of right is prior to that of the good.", Rawls, 1972, p.31.
15. Nozick, 1974, pp.28-35.
16. Galston, 1980, p.6.
17. However, it should be noted that assertion of the necessity of the good does not commit one to the view that it is impossible to postulate first principles which are non-axiological; indeed one of my first principles is non-axiological. Rather it is merely to claim that at least one of the first principles from which a theory of justice is derived must have axiological content.
18. Peter De Marneffe has distinguished two senses of neutrality toward conceptions of the good: "Neutrality may refer to one of these principles of justice, or it may refer to a principle regulating the justification of principles of justice. Let us refer to the former (neutrality as a first order principle of justice) as *concrete neutrality* and to the latter (neutrality as a second order principle of justification) as *neutrality of grounds*.", De Marneffe, 1990, p.253. It is the thesis of neutrality of grounds which I shall address in chapter one. (We should also note that Adina Schwartz refers to axiological neutrality as 'moral neutrality' in Schwartz, 1972-73, pp.294-307.
19. De Marneffe, *op cit*, p.252. Cf. O'Neill 1987-8, p.84 and Will Kymlicka who writes: "A

distinctive feature of contemporary liberal theory is its emphasis on 'neutrality' - the view that the state should not reward or penalize particular conceptions of the good life, but rather should provide a neutral framework within which different and potentially conflicting conceptions of the good can be pursued.", Kymlicka, 1989, p.883.

20. For a discussion of this belief that one of liberalism's defining elements is an adherence to the thesis of axiological neutrality, see De Marneffe, op. cit..
21. Simon Caney refers to state neutrality as 'justificatory neutrality'. See Caney, 1992, p.41.
22. This idea of the importance of state neutrality is an issue with which Thomas Nagel, in particular, has been concerned. He argues that the State should be neutral between different conceptions of the good life: it should not make policy on the basis that some ways of life are superior to others. Nagel observes a wide variety of conceptions of the good life which reasonable people have advocated and thus concludes that because reasonable people disagree, the State should desist from promoting particular forms of life. See Nagel, 1987, pp.215-40.
23. There are some resonances here with Marx, who asserts that liberal theory is not really neutral, but in facts masks or serves as a screen to conceal the ascendancy of established or aspiring capitalist entrepreneurs within liberal society. See Marx, 1967, pp.216-48.
24. Here I am in close agreement with William Galston who claims that rejection of the use of the good in political theory rests on a caricature of the perfectionist position and the unproved contention that no substantive theory of the human good can be defended. See William Galston, 1980, p.9.
25. See Nussbaum, 1990, p.217.
26. On this issue Jeremy Waldron writes: "....liberalism is also bound up in large part with respect for rationality, with the discipline of self-knowledge and clear-sightedness, and with the celebration of the human capacity to grasp and understand the world", Waldron, 1987, pp.132-33.
27. For useful further discussion of what liberalism consists in see Waldron, 1987, pp.127-50.
28. For Rawls' critique of utilitarianism see Rawls, 1972, pp.22-34. This work has in turn has given rise to the current debate concerning the status of consequentialism.
29. We should note—given the extensive use I make of the of William Galston—that Galston uses these terms differently. Galston discusses monism and pluralism in relation to the competing claims of individuals and collectives. The monist attempts to derive individual right from collective welfare, whereas the pluralist takes individual and collective welfare as being mutually irreducible. See Galston, 1990, p.3.
30. For his critique of hedonism, see Aristotle, 1969, Bk.I ch.4, Bk.II ch.3 and Bk.VII ch.2.
31. Urmson, 1988, p.109. It is worth noting with respect to this point that Aristotle ends the *Nicomachean Ethics* with the words "let us begin".
32. See Aristotle, 1969, Bk.1 ch.1, [1094a25-b4].
33. A certain amount of care must be taken when claiming that this is an essentially Aristotelian idea, because of the various ambiguities in his texts. On the one hand, he claims that we are 'zoa politika' (see Aristotle 1959 [1253a2] and Aristotle 1969 [1169b18]) and yet on the other hand, he argues that the ultimate good is contemplation (Aristotle 1969 Bk.X ch.7). Cf Nagel, 1980, pp.7-14.
34. Alasdair McIntyre argues that Aristotle was in fact a quietist with respect to political activity. "Provided only that there is room for the contemplative elite, the *Nicomachean Ethics* does not provide for a condemnation or an endorsement of any social structure...", McIntyre, 1967, p.99.
35. Aristotle, 1969, Bk.10 Ch.7 [1177a2-22].
36. See McDowell, 1979, pp.351-50 and Scheffler, 1992, pp.11-12.
37. For a useful discussion of the communitarian position see Kymlicka, 1989 and. Buchanan, 1989.
38. Cited Solomon, 1985, p.490.

Section One
Justice and the human good

1 Distributive justice and the human good

The constructivist challenge

My favoured strategy for developing principles of distributive justice is an internalist one. However, such an approach is not without its critics. Many writers have argued that philosophical anthropology has no proper role to play in political theory. Such critics object that internalism is unacceptable for one or more of the following reasons: (i) the employment of accounts of the human good by state authorities has totalitarian consequences; (ii) the adoption of accounts of the human good is subversive of social order; (iii) the epistemological status of accounts of the human good is problematic given that they are based on empirical data. (This list is not in any way intended to be exhaustive). With these concerns in mind, many such critics are drawn towards *externalist* strategies which attempt to derive distributive principles without the employment of accounts of the good; and since the advent of Rawls' *A Theory of Justice*, the most influential of these strategies is a methodological procedure which I shall refer to as *constructivism*. Constructivism, as the term is used herein, denotes any distributive doctrine which attempts to generate principles of distributive justice via reason or rationality and according to which reason is thought of as being independent and separate from the idea of the human good. (Under this rather general definition Rawls' theory is a constructivist one).[1]

Critics of internalism might be inclined to argue that if principles of distributive justice can be generated without reference to the human good, then the internalist strategy should be avoided. *Ex hypothesi*, if theorists such as Rawls can generate distributive theory without recourse to such contentious entities, then it would seem prudent to avoid doing so. The pursuit of an internalist strategy seems to require theoretical justification when conceptions of the good are problematic and non-internalist strategies—namely constructivism—are available. The argument can be outlined schematically in the following manner:

(i) the initial assertion of the problematic nature of the use of accounts of the human good in distributive theory;

(ii) the demonstration of a method of generating substantive distributive principles without the use of the human good (i.e constructivism);

(iii) the argument that given that (ii) can be successfully achieved, then what justification can there be for employing such contentious conceptual entities as accounts of the good.

These three claims constitute what I shall call the 'constructivist challenge' for the internalist. It is this constructivist challenge with which I shall be concerned in this chapter.

The line of response to the constructivist challenge I shall adopt involves casting doubt on the idea that constructivist methodology *does in fact* simultaneously provide both substantive distributive principles and theory which is free from the taint of conceptions of the human good. With this aim in mind, the work of two leading constructivists, Rawls and Kant, will be examined, with a special focus on their constructivist approaches and their explicit renunciations of what I have labelled internalist methodology. Both theorists provide methodological approaches which may be appropriated by those who wish to mount the constructivist challenge. (However of the two theorists more importance will be attached to the critique of Rawls primarily because his works are more directly related to distributive theory). The general line of argumentation against both theorists will involve demonstrating that in order to generate substantive forms of practical reason, these constructivists *smuggle in* accounts of the human good, even though at an explicit level they renounce such conceptions.[2] The aim of the critiques in this chapter will be simply to cast sufficient doubt on the constructivist projects of both Kant and Rawls to enable us to meet the constructivist challenge.

Section A: Kantian constructivism

I begin my response to the constructivist challenge by considering the ethical work of Immanuel Kant. Analysis of Kantian ethics might seem, at first sight, a rather strange place to initiate a discussion of the constructivist challenge to internalist distributive theory, especially when one considers that Kant was not so much concerned with issues of distributive justice as he was with principles of right action. Furthermore, Kant's methodological objections are to what might be termed *moral internalism* (i.e. the belief that moral principles may be derived from accounts of the human good). He makes little explicit reference to internalism in the realm of distributive theory. While it is true that he makes pronouncements on issues of political theory (i.e about the rule of law, property rights etc[3]), Kant does not provide explicit commentary on appropriate distributive methodology. What Kant does provide us with is an ethics of duty: an ethics of duty in which the determinant of the moral acceptability of human actions is a formal test grounded ultimately in reason.

Nevertheless, despite these caveats, I think that there are good reasons to begin my defence of the internalist project at this point. Firstly, Kant's arguments *contra* moral internalism and his constructivist procedure for generating moral maxims can be easily transferred to the distributive sphere. Thus his arguments provide potential ammunition for those who would mount the constructivist challenge. Secondly, I believe that discussion of Kantian ethics sheds light on the constructivist project *in general*; it reveals problems which also plague constructivist accounts of distributive justice. In particular, it throws critical attention on the work of John Rawls. This first section on Kant, then, may be thought of, in part, as a primer for the later section on Rawls.

However, before examining Kantian theory in detail, it is important that the aim of this section not be misinterpreted. I am not concerned here with the provision of an exhaustive explication of Kant's ethical work, but rather with an examination of those aspects of his thought which bear on my internalist project, namely: (i) his critique of internalist moral theory and; (ii) his positive account of ethics in which moral principles are derived from reason.

Kant's antagonism to Aristotelian moral projects

In the *Critique of Practical Reason*, Kant declares that moral principles should not be derived from empirically-grounded beliefs about human nature. Empirically-derived beliefs can furnish no practical laws and cannot be part of a pure philosophy.[4] Hence moral principles derived from accounts of the human good should be rejected. We might extrapolate from this that, according to Kant, principles of distributive justice derived from the human good could also not belong to a *philosophia pura*. Let us consider these claims more closely.

In order to apprehend properly Kant's thinking on this issue, one must recall the distinction which he draws in the *Critique of Pure Reason* between purely rational and empirical concepts and principles. Purely rational concepts and principles are apprehended *a priori*, whereas empirical ones are derived from observation. Kant believed that ideas of the human good are necessarily empirical because they are derived from observation of human behaviour.[5] Hence, for Kant, there exists a clear divide between ideas of reason and ideas of the human good. Reason and the discipline of philosophical anthropology are clearly distinct.

At the heart of the Kantian project is a concern with the kind of motivation which should activate the *will*. He argues that proper moral rules cannot be derived from experience, rather they should be derived from *a priori* principles.[6] Kant believed that the pure will is not directed by empirically-derived *principia*. That which is required of us, i.e. our moral duty, cannot be derived from the supersensuous. Here we can specify at least three separate reasons why Kant might object to the use of the human good in the formulation of moral theory; (i) his belief that empirical knowledge gained via induction is epistemologically problematic; (ii) his belief that ideas of the good are at bottom intrinsically selfish and; (iii) his belief that the will motivated by inclination is not autonomous or free. Let us explore each of these is greater detail.

Firstly, Kant argues that principles derived from experience are notoriously unreliable. This epistemological objection is to be found in the *Metaphysics of Morals*. Kant argues that all apparently *a priori* reasoning about the good in the end comes down to nothing but experience raised by induction to generality; a generality which he believes is so tenuous that everyone must be allowed countless exceptions in order to adapt his choice of a way of life to his particular inclination and his particular susceptibility to satisfaction.[7] Knowledge of what makes us happy ultimately reduces to experience and Kant believes that it would be unwise to seek *a priori* principles from experience.[8] Secondly (and probably more importantly), Kant believes that accounts of the human good are ultimately principles of self-love, and self-love cannot be the proper ground of true morality. He suggests that "when one's happiness is made the determining ground of the will, the result is the direct opposite of the principle of morality."[9] Principles of morality must be based on grounds which are devoid of self-love. Thirdly, Kant argues that the human will, being purely rational, should not be motivated by ideas or principles derived from empirical inclination. According to Kant, any moral theory which attempts to derive the moral law from empirically derived considerations of human nature or the human good is *heteronomous*. Kant labelled the so-called principle of happiness (which dominated ancient Greek moral thinking) the principle of heteronomy. For one's will to be determined by principles of the human good is to permit 'heteronomy of the will'; to act upon such motivation is to act heteronomously. Kant inveighs against the influence of heteronomous theories of morality on our thinking for he believed heteronomy of the will to be the source of all spurious theories of morality.[10]

Kant contrasts heteronomous action with *autonomous* action. A rational person, he argues, is autonomous. The autonomous, truly free, person affirms his freedom by acting upon principles which are neither coerced by others nor determined by information grounded in experience. Moral goodness, or autonomous action, lies in the perfection not of the faculties but of the will.[11] Such a definition of freedom may seem odd to the modern mind, for we inhabit a cultural context in which freedom is typically defined *solely* in terms of freedom from the coercion of either institutions or other persons. Of course, Kant would accept that this is in fact an important part of what it is to be free. However, in addition to freedom from the coercion of others, Kant sees autonomy or freedom as consisting of action which is not guided by principles derived from human interests or desires.[12] Thus in order to be truly free, the will must be guided by motivations which issue from outside of itself; the will must not be determined by external empirical causes.[13]

For these reasons, Kant was antagonistic to ethical projects (such as Aristotelianism) which employ ideas of the human good and which we may refer to as forms of *moral internalism.* In the *Groundwork,* Kant argued that morality and morally good ends cannot be derived from (or based on) philosophical anthropology. Kant regarded the philosophy of *eudaimonism* as the epitome of moral confusion. He believed that deducing the Moral Law from the good was the source of all confusions of philosophers concerning the supreme principles of morals. Philosophers who attempt to do so seek an object of the will in order to make it into a material object and foundation of law. Instead they should look for a law which directly determines the will *a priori* and only then seek an object suitable to it.[14] For Kant, ethical life is comprised of *duties* which we must perform, regardless of (and often in spite of) our inclinations. Duty is simply the requirement that a conditioned will place itself under the governance of good rather than inclination; it is, according to Kant, nothing but the necessity to act out of reverence for the law.[15]

A number of caveats are in order at this point. Whilst Kant believed that empirical inclination should not be employed in the formulation of moral principles, this should not be taken to imply that for Kant self-interest and individual well-being can have no part to play in human action. He thought of self-love as both a natural and progressive force in human affairs. His doctrine is not a Stoic one; on the contrary, Kant believed that self-interest had an important role to play in human affairs.[16] Indeed, Kant even provides advice on the best ways of ensuring satisfaction or pleasure, as the following extensive quote demonstrates.

> If you wish to keep your faculty of senses, you must not begin with very strong sensations because they make us insensitive to subsequent sensations, but rather deny them to yourself and restrain yourself at the very beginning in order to be able gradually to escalate later.[17]

In Kant's moral system, self-interest is recognised as important, but is rendered subject to duty.

However, at first sight, Kant's advocacy of self-interest seems to be at odds with his pronouncements on the role of inclination in moral thinking. Given his disavowal of the human good, how can he assert that self-interest has a legitimate role to play in human affairs? While this may seem problematic, Kant's thinking on this issue becomes clearer when one considers:(i) the distinction which he draws between *prudential* and *moral* reasoning and; (ii) the distinctive role that moral reasoning has to play with regard to the assessment of the maxims of moral reasoning. Let us begin by considering the distinction he draws between different forms of rationality.

Prudential reasoning consists in calculation which is directed towards the satisfaction of individual desire. Prudential rationality concerns itself with the most rational and efficient means for the achievement of an individual's pre-given ends. Kant defines prudence as the skill of a man in influencing others in order to use them for his own ends.[18] However, reason also has a moral component. Moral reasoning for Kant is reasoning determined by *a priori* considerations, rather than inclination. It is reasoning untainted by empirical concerns. This form of reasoning does not coordinate our desires and inclinations but rather directs us toward universal law. Furthermore, the relationship of moral reasoning to prudential reasoning is that of the *formal* to the *material.* Moral reasoning involves the formal assessment of the *maxims* of prudential reason: ethics does not provide laws for human actions, but only for the maxims of action.[19] According to Kant, laws proceed from the will, while maxims proceed from choice.[20] Hence it is not that moral thinking replaces prudential reasoning, rather moral reasoning involves assessment of the maxims of prudential reasoning. Moral reasoning is a formal test of the moral legitimacy of maxims of prudential reason.

For Kant, then, self-interest has a role to play in the formation of prudential maxims. However, in his schema self-interest does not have a role to play in the moral principles with which we assess those prudential maxims. So long as it is confined to practical decisions and is not employed in the moral theory which assess the moral status of self-interested actions, self-interest is an appropriate element in human decision-making. *Virtue* consists therefore not in the absolute renunciation of self-interest, but in the assessment of one's maxims of action by principles which are not contaminated by empirical inclination.

In Kantian ethics, then: (i) our duties are derived from principles which issue from non-empirical grounds and; (ii) those actions whose maxims which do not conform to the supreme principles of morals must be constrained. Of course, there is here a tension between duty and inclination. Indeed, Kant admits that there may be many instances where actions motivated by inclination may coincide with that which duty requires. There may be occasions where that which makes us happy is also that which is required of us by duty; or alternatively, we may decide, via the legacy of experience, that it will probably be to our advantage in the long run to obey the commands of morality rather than to transgress against them. Observing the latter phenomenon, Kant draws a distinction between those actions *performed according to duty* and those *performed from duty.*[21] He argues that actions performed merely according to duty have a *legality*, but not a *morality.*[22] Whilst he acknowledges that it is indeed a very beautiful thing to do good because of love and a sympathetic good will, this is not the genuine moral maxim of our conduct.[23] Kant unequivocally condemns any tendency to mix or confuse the radically different incentives of happiness and duty. We cannot give a warning too strongly or too often, he claims, against relying on alien empirical inducements to help motivate us to act rightly. Kant believes that deliberately introducing non-moral prudential motives to support dutifulness contaminates a person's intentions, making his or her will impure.[24] The virtuous person acts upon moral principles determined solely by duty.

Kant's position here might be usefully contrasted with that of Aristotle, for whom acting morally typically did not frustrate, but rather actualised, a person's fulfilment; that is, Aristotle believed there to be an isomorphic relationship between good persons, right and pleasure.[25] Kant, on the other hand, was convinced that heteronomous moral theories, grounded in empirical considerations of the human good were not ethical theories at all, but rather were, at best, theories of rational prudence.

Kant, then, provides an explicit methodological critique of not only Aristotelianism, but also of *moral internalism in general.* According to Kant, although philosophical anthropology has a role to play in prudential reasoning, it should have no place in moral thinking. However, here again we should issue a note of caution. Whilst Kant explicitly condemns philosophical anthropology in the *Groundwork*, in his later works he is far more circumspect. In particular, in the *Metaphysics of Morals*, Kant appears to modify his earlier views and admit the necessity of accounts of human nature and the human good. In this later work he writes:

> But just as there must be principles in a metaphysics of nature for applying those highest universal principles of a nature in general to objects of experience, a metaphysics of morals cannot dispense with principles of application, and we shall often have to take as our object the particular nature of men, which is known only by experience in order to show in it what can be inferred from universal moral principles. But this will in no way detract from the purity of these principles or

cast doubt on their *a priori* source. This is to say, in effect, that a metaphysics of morals cannot be based upon an anthropology but can still be applied to it.[26]

It is possible to interpret this as a retreat on Kant's part from pure constructivism and an admission that the derivation of moral principles requires more than that which is supplied by *a priori* reasoning. On the other hand, his comments might also be interpreted simply as the claim that although the *formal* principles of morality can be derived *solely* from *a priori* reasoning, their application requires examination of empirical issues, such as the nature of the human good.

The ambiguity in the Kantian corpus leaves two questions unanswered: (i) whether there is a significant shift in Kant's position between the *Metaphysics of Morals* and *the Groundwork* such that he abandons his anti-internalism and; (ii) if such a theoretical shift exists, which account should be taken as the best interpretation of Kant's considered views. Fortunately, while these are complex issues, they need not be addressed here. The task in this chapter is simply to cast doubt on the constructivist strategy and hence repel the constructivist challengers; it is not my aim to resolve all the important topics in Kantian scholarship. If Kant does abandon his anti-internalist convictions and admits the necessity of the human good in moral reasoning, then this is simply more grist to the internalist mill. Hence, in this chapter I shall focus my attention on the strong anti-internalist interpretation (which is most readily discerned in the *Groundwork*) for the very reason this is the position which provides those who wish to mount the constructivist challenge with the most ammunition.

Kant's rational foundationalism

If Kant believed that philosophical anthropology has no legitimate place in moral theory, as I have suggested above, then how might moral principles be generated? If one eschews internalist methodology, what is to be the source of ethical obligation? In this section Kant's *positive* account of ethics I shall briefly consider Kant's constructivist methodology in which the moral law is derived from the analysis of *reason*.

According to Kant, the proper foundation of morality is to be found in reason and in the conformity of the will to universal law. For Kant, pure reason, unadulterated by empirical consideration, is the appropriate ground of ethics. He argues that the only reverence to which we are bound is reverence to universal law as such.[27] Whilst Kant acknowledges that human beings are sensual dependent beings, he stresses our capacity for rationality.[28] It is this rational element which should be the foundation of our will; reason should be the determining ground of our moral thinking. To conform to the moral law, maxims of action must be judged in a disinterested rational fashion. Kant argues that human beings only assert their freedom or autonomy through the use of reason. It is through reason that we express the law of our being as free agents and in acting autonomously that we prove ourselves as beings determined only by laws of our own making. For Kant, then, virtue signifies a moral strength of the will.[29] Virtue of the will involves the rational being acting only in accord with its own ideas of law; that is, it involves action which is determined neither by our heteronomous desire or inclination nor by the laws of others.[30] Kant was convinced that no command issuing from an external source could be unconditionally binding on the will. Autonomy, therefore, involves the observance of self-legislating principles of action; that is, of principles which are in accord with reason.

A pertinent question to ask at this juncture is "What exactly does Kant intend by the term 'reason'?". How does he define the 'rational'? Surprisingly, Kant defines the essence of reason as being the Aristotelian law of non-contradiction; the law of non-contradiction being the one essential condition for the very existence of reason.[31] Kant employs this law in his analysis of maxims of action. Just as rationality involves *inter alia* ensuring that one does not fall into contradiction, similarly in order for maxims of action to be rational they must also avoid contradiction when presented as universal laws. In order for our maxims of action to conform to the moral law, their universalisation must not involve the willing of a contradiction.[32] Those actions which must not be performed are those which violate the law of non-contradiction when universalised. (In fact, Kant thought that maxims governing immoral acts generate contradictions when universalised). Thus, when used by pure practical reason, the principle of non-contradiction does not remain a mere logical norm; instead it becomes the measure of our willingness to respect our own autonomy and rationality and that of every other person. We can only will or intend that which is *possible* or *consistent* for us to will as a universal law. Such *rational foundationalism* is expressed in his first and primary formulation of the Categorical Imperative, the *law of universalisability*:

> Act only according to that maxim whereby you can at the same time will that it should become a universal law.[33]

For Kant this is the Moral Law. In essence it is the idea that in order for a rational agent to be rational, she must act upon maxims that she would agree to no matter what position she was in. The Categorical Imperative demands of an individual agent that she examine the maxims of her actions and ask herself whether she would want it to apply, regardless of whether it was applied to herself or to others. If the answer to this question is "No", then the law of non-contradiction is contravened. If one would not want the maxim of an action universalised, then the performance of that action cannot be a categorically binding imperative. The Categorical Imperative, then, provides a *formal test* of maxims of action, which enables us to evaluate the moral status of the maxims motivating particular actions.

In order to understand more fully how the Categorical Imperative functions, imagine a maxim of action which stated that burglary was permissible. Would you agree to that maxim no matter what position you were in or who you were? If there are conceivable conditions under which you would disapprove of the maxim, e.g. if you were burgled, then the maxim of action is morally impermissible. We can see that for Kant the principle of non-contradiction, when applied to pure practical reason, is not simply a law of logic, but becomes the foundation of the Moral Law. Kant contends that the law of universalisability is the principle that all truly rational agents would agree to. A rational agent—in order to be a rational agent—must act according to the dictates of this ideal of universalisability. The law of autonomy is a purely rational norm and holds universally for all rational agents. The virtuous or good will then wills universal principles and according to Kant the only thing that is truly good is a good will. A good will is good not because of what it accomplishes or effects, nor because of its suitability to attain some proposed end; it is good only through its willing.[34] Further, it is only a good will that can be considered good without qualification.[35] Kant argues that it is impossible to conceive of anything at all which can be thought of as good without qualification except for a good will. This chain of reasoning is the basis of Kant's constructivist moral theory in which an attempt is made to generate forms of practical reason from rationalist grounds.

An interesting aspect of Kant's theory is his claim that the law of universalisability is the source of all other moral principles. In the *Groundwork* he declares that all moral principles can be derived from the first formulation of the Categorical Imperative. Thus he derives the second and third formulations of the Categorical Imperative from the law of universalisability. Although morality is unitary, it does admit of various formulations. The second formulation reads as follows:

> Act in such a way that you treat humanity, whether in your own person or in the person of another, always at the same time as an end and never simply as a means.[36]

This formulation of the Categorical Imperative requires that we regard ourselves and every other person as having a dignity, and which provides the ground for self-esteem and self-respect. The Third Formulation is stated in the following manner:

> ...all maxims proceeding from his own legislation ought to harmonize with a possible kingdom of ends as a kingdom of nature.[37]

According to Kant, the first formulation contains the others within itself; ultimately all correct moral principles flow from the first formulation.[38] For Kant, the three ways of representing the principle of morality are, at bottom, only so many statements of one and the same law.[39] Thus Kant holds that all correct moral principles flow from the first formulation which ultimately is derived from reason itself.

Kant and the constructivist challenge

Let us now consider Kant's rational foundationalism and its connections to the constructivist challenge. The central problem which the Kantian system poses for the internalist is its putative capacity to generate *substantive* normative principles without recourse to the employment of a conception of the good. This is the use to which the anti-internalist may wish to put Kant's doctrine.

However, in relation to the constructivist challenge an important question which should be asked concerns the extent to which Kant himself actually believes his system is capable of performing the tricks which those who would mount the constructivist challenge may require of it. Does Kant actually believe that he generates substantive normative principles without reference to an account of the human good? On one interpretation, the Kantian system is simply a formal test for the maxims of action which requires an account of the human good in order to generate concrete moral pronouncements. According to this weaker interpretation, the Kantian system must be applied to accounts of the good (as well as other empirical data) in order to generate substantive moral claims. On this view, there is a distinction to be had between the *purely rational* on the one hand and *the rational* as filled out by considerations of human nature and the human good on the other. Alternatively, according to a separate interpretation, Kantian ethics may be said to involve an attempt to provide the grounds for the formulation of substantive moral rules without reference to accounts of the good. I shall refer to this stronger thesis as *pure constructivism.* According to the pure constructivist interpretation of Kant, reason is intended to provide *sufficient* grounds for the generation of ethical duties.

There is ample evidence to support both interpretations of Kant's work. Both may be thought of as plausible representations of his position. On numerous occasions, Kant seemingly disavows the employment of accounts of the good in the generation of concrete forms of practical reason. For instance, in *The Critique of Practical Reason* he suggests that the "action which is objectively practical according to this law and excludes inclination for its determining grounds is called duty".[40] Yet, on the other hand, in the *Metaphysics of Morals* he argues that the determination of the moral status of actions requires philosophical anthropology.[41] There he appears to distinguish (in a manner compatible with the internalist project advocated herein) between the purely rational and the rational as filled out by considerations of the human good. This latter interpretation is championed by various philosophers who assert that it is wrong-headed to ask of the Categorical Imperative that it generate practical imperatives, without the use of conceptions of the good. Such philosophers have claimed that those who criticise Kant's bloodlessness are attacking a straw person. Marcus George Singer, for instance, argued that the Categorical Imperative is meant to be applied to heteronomous detail. He argues in *Generalization in Ethics* that it is wrong to assume that the Categorical Imperative is supposed to apply in a vacuum, or, in other words, it is not to be applied to anything with the possible exception of itself.[42] Singer claims that this is not Kant's intention. The original maxim of the action provides the content which the universalisability principle is applied to and without which one cannot generate contradiction. Another moral philosopher, C.D. Broad argues that the Categorical Imperative is not a set of rules of conduct, but rather a test for such rules.[43] Just as it is not the business of logic to provide arguments, but to provide tests for arguments, so too the business of ethics is to provide tests for rules of conduct. Broad argues that the nature of the Categorical Imperative is analogous to that of a rule of a syllogism, rather than a premise from which any conclusion can be drawn.

However, with regard to the constructivist challenge to internalism, it is only the pure constructivist interpretation of Kant which is of any concern. The weaker thesis presents no problems for the internalist. According to this view (at least as stated) the good has a role to play in the application of the formal test of the maxims of action, even though it has no role to play in the formation of this test. The internalist need have no quarrel with this interpretation, for philosophical anthropology has a home, so to speak, here. It is only the pure constructivist interpretation which represents a threat for the internalist because it purports to generate substantive moral maxims without recourse to an account of the good. Given that it is this stronger interpretation which presents problems, it is this pure constructivist interpretation of the Kantian text with which I shall concern myself. (We need not enter into debates over which interpretation should be thought of as representing Kant's considered position). In dealing with this stronger interpretation in the following sections I shall: (i) provide a formal argument against the idea that pure reason could generate substantive normative judgements and; (ii) provide an analysis of the *duties* which Kant actually presents and attempt to demonstrate that these duties could not have been arrived at without reference to an account (or accounts) of the human good.

The paradox of willing the willing of nothing

Let us firstly consider a formal reason why the pure constructivist interpretation of Kant should not be thought to provide an alternative to internalism. The focus here will be primarily on the *Groundwork* because it is in this work that Kant presents his doctrine most clearly as a form of pure constructivism.

The First Formulation of the Categorical Imperative commands that we act only on those maxims which we can will as universal law. However, if it is possible to will a contradiction in any maxim, i.e. if we can make an exception of ourselves, then we should not act upon that maxim. On the pure-constructivist interpretation of Kant this process of generating contradictions can be *formally generated* without reference to any material facts about human nature. However, I think that a conception of the good derived from empirical claims about human nature is, in fact, a necessary condition for the generation of the contradictions to which Kant appeals.

Let us consider, given Kant's emphasis upon acting only on non-contradictable maxims, what a maxim actually is. In the Kantian system there are two kinds of maxims: the Hypothetical and the Categorical. Hypothetical maxims can be defined as follows:

> To achieve ends E, use means M.

Here all actions are defined as the pursuit of ends by given means. Categorical Imperatives, on the other hand, are defined simply as:

> Do X or Refrain from X.

For Kant, it is the Categorical Imperatives which are of primary significance for moral theory. Central to Kant's theory is the claim that if the maxim of an action willed generates a contradiction when universalised, then that action should not be performed. If I would want to make an exception of myself with regard to a maxim proposed by myself as an ethical law, then that maxim cannot be a Categorical Imperative. For instance, the rule that it is permissible for persons to be killed could not be a Categorical Imperative because I cannot rationally make an exception of myself with regard to this rule. However, any contradiction that is generated, cannot be generated between the maxim of an action (such as the command 'Do X') and the universal application of such a command. It is impossible to derive contradictions from any maxim (such as "One should kill people") and its universal application without empirical presuppositions about human life, such as the putative empirical fact that people cannot rationally will their own deaths, i.e., that it is impossible from a purely formal conception of a maxim to derive a contradiction without empirical presuppositions about human life.

Let me illustrate this claim by considering what can be adduced about the good that reason aims at, without the inclusion of considerations of the human good. What might the good, which reason or the will aims at, be? What are the ends toward which rational means are directed? Kant believes that the only thing that is good is a good will. When Kant asks himself what the Good might be, he answers "the Good Will"; that is, that will which determines its actions by reason. However, if a Good Will is to determine its actions by reason alone, it must will certain ends for there to be action at all.

What then are the ends which the Good Will wills? The end which it wills is the Good and involves the determination of action by reason or Good Will. Thus the Good that the Good Will wills is a Good Will. Kant is thus caught in what might be called, somewhat pretentiously, the 'Paradox of Willing the Willing of Nothing'. To illustrate this point, let us consider the pre-philosophical version of the Categorical Imperative, the Christian Golden Rule (although it must be noted that Kant was at pains in the *Groundwork* to distinguish the Categorical Imperative from the Golden Rule). Of this rule the question can be asked, "How is it possible to act according to its dictates without a conception of individual good?". How can you do unto others as you would have them do unto you, without a conception of what you would have them do unto you? While the idea of a thoroughly rational agent is the idea of an agent who acts on reason alone, reason alone cannot provide reasons for action.

The idea that Kant's system is formal and arid has come to be known in some philosophical circles as the 'Hegelian Objection'.[44] Hegel argued in his early works that the Kantian Categorical Imperative could not generate forms of practical reason and reiterated the point in the *Philosophy of Right* and *The Phenomenology*. It was a criticism which Hegel never tired of directing at Kant.[45] It is also an objection many other philosophers since Hegel have made, including Fichte, John Stuart Mill and Henry Sidgwick.[46] We should not imagine, however, that Kant was entirely oblivious to the sorts of objections which might be brought against his moral system. There is good evidence that Kant was perfectly aware of the perceived limitations of his moral schema and *a propos* such concerns we may cite Kant's response in *Theory and Practice* to Garve's charge of formalism, as vindication of this claim.[47]

Kantian duties and the human good

In the preceding section I suggested that pure Kantian reason cannot generate adequate normative theory without recourse to an account of the human good. However, seemingly in contradistinction to my claim, Kant does in fact pass judgement on a wide range of concrete moral issues including murder, suicide, drug-taking and masturbation. The existence of such pronouncements may seem to represent a refutation of the claim that philosophical anthropology is required for the generation of substantive forms of practical reason. In this section I intend to examine various concrete pronouncements which Kant presents in the *Groundwork* in the form of duties with the aim of demonstrating that Kant is only able to pass judgement on such practical issues because he smuggles into his constructivist theory, *ad hoc* conceptions of the good. (We will concentrate on the duties outlined in the *Groundwork* because it is in this text that his work can be least ambiguously labelled a form of pure constructivism). It will be argued that his practical normative philosophy is not derived purely from the Categorical Imperative, but rather is partially deduced from empirical observations of human nature and the human good, that is, it is not a pure *a priori* derivation of the law of universalisability.

In the second section of the *Groundwork*, entitled 'Transition from a Popular Moral Philosophy to a Metaphysics of Morals', Kant outlines four duties which flow from the Categorical Imperative. He argues that the Categorical Imperative forbids any rational agent to: i) commit suicide; ii) borrow money which he knows he cannot repay, even if he is in desperate need; iii) neglect to develop talents which he or she may possess; iv) neglect to help those in need. Kant discusses these duties with the aim of demonstrating how his rationalistic ethical system might generate forms of practical reason.

Kant claims in the *Groundwork* that we are forbidden to commit suicide. He arrives at this conclusion by analysing the maxim of action which lies behind the act of suicide. Kant believes that the maxim of the person who commits suicide is essentially:

> ....from self love I make as my principle to shorten my life when its continued duration threatens more evil than it promises satisfaction.[48]

He argues that such a maxim could not become a universal law without the willing of a contradiction: he contends that a contradiction resides in a system of nature whose essential law would destroy life, by means of the same motivation that acts towards the goal of stimulating life's continuation. According to Kant, destroying one's ability to be an end-in-oneself for prudential reasons clearly constitutes an attack on proper self-respect. Kant believes that suicide could not become a universal law of nature without threatening the very existence of the system of nature out of which such laws arise.

Kant argues that his second duty, the duty to only borrow money when one can repay it, is also derived from the Categorical Imperative. He asserts that if one universalised such deceitful borrowings, then the institution of promise keeping would be completely undermined, ceasing to have any meaning:

> ....no one would believe what was promised him, but would merely laugh at all such utterances as being vain pretences.[49]

Thirdly, Kant considers the failure to develop one's talents. Again he claims that such action could never be part of a universal system of nature. According to Kant, a system of nature in which people all resolve to devote their lives to "idleness, indulgence, propagation" could not be a universal system of nature. As rational agents we necessarily will that our faculties be developed.[50] Finally, Kant argues that the Categorical Imperative requires all rational agents to perform the 'duty of beneficence': we must help others primarily because there may be times when we ourselves may require sympathy and benevolence. Thus we cannot will it a universal law that the world be devoid of these virtues, without lapsing into contradiction.

Having listed these duties, Kant makes a further distinction. He suggests that while the duties relating to suicide and borrowing are *perfect* duties, the latter two duties—those of beneficence and self-development—are *imperfect* duties.[51] The perfect duties (also called at various times 'rigorous', 'strict' or 'narrow') are perfect because any action which violates them is morally wrong. The maxim of a perfect duty, when conceived of as a universal law, can be assessed without examination of empirical considerations. A perfect duty, then, admits of "no exception in favour of inclination".[52] The imperfect duties, on the other hand, are not absolutely obligatory. An imperfect duty allows a certain latitude for free choice in the observance of moral law; it allows for discretion in the formulation of principles of action.

Whilst not pretending to be able to second-guess Kant's inner psychological processes, I think that we can say with a reasonable amount of certainty that part of his motivation for casting some duties as imperfect is his belief that we cannot describe exactly how a person should behave for the reasons that different actions can fit equally well under the same positive maxim or policy.[53] For example, the imperfect duty of beneficence requires me to have the general end of assisting deserving charities, but it does not tell me exactly which charity to assist nor how much I should donate. In this sense, an imperfect duty permits a degree of freedom or discretion in how it is to be satisfied. Perfect duties require one either to omit or to perform specific kinds of actions. One is simply prohibited from stealing or killing or failing to pay one's debts. Kant is also motivated to cast some duties as imperfect because of his belief that imperfect duties may be limited by other imperfect duties. For example, we may limit the extent to which we exhibit obligatory beneficence towards others by the obligation to love our parents. A third reason is that these wide or imperfect duties require us to take into account *empirical* facts about the various situations in which we find ourselves, and exactly how an individual should do that is a matter of judgement.

Since the publication of the *Groundwork*, there have been many arguments mounted with the expressed aim of demonstrating the necessity of *empirical* data if one is to generate the duties listed above; arguments of the kind made by Hegel and many philosophers since. However, my aim here is simply to cast doubt on the idea that without reference to an account of the human good that reason alone could generate substantive forms of practical reason. Let us reconsider Kant's categorical duties with this aim in mind.

The first duty specified in the *Groundwork* is the duty not to commit suicide. Kant argues that the maxim of the person who commits suicide could not serve as a universal law because it involves a contradiction between the faculty of self-love and our own self-preservation. The maxim of the person who commits suicide is "from self-love I decide to take my own life". Kant argues that there is a contradiction in a system of nature whose law would destroy life by the means of the same feeling which is directed toward the furtherance of life. However, implicit within this argument is the teleological assumption that human beings have the faculty of self-love in order to serve the purpose of self-preservation. This notion is neither derived from reason nor is it intrinsic to the idea of self-love, rather what it represents is the *surreptitious* incorporation of normative views about what the human good consists of.

The claim that Kant smuggles in axiological assumptions about human nature finds support from an examination of the third of the duties outlined in the *Groundwork*, namely, the duty to develop one's talents. Kant argues that failing to develop one's talents could not be part of a universal law of nature because as rational beings each of us wills that all of one's faculties should be developed. In this case we have, beyond doubt, clear evidence of philosophical anthropology. Kant takes it to be self-evident that human beings should develop their talents; and implicit within this assumption is the idea that self-development is a good. The central intuition here seems to be that we have talents so that we might use them.[54]

Such seemingly *ad hoc* insertions of the good are problematic if one intends to defend the pure constructivist thesis that Kant's works may be used to generate substantive normative judgements without reference to an account of the good.[55] Of course, the employment of accounts of the human good is not problematic if one adopts the weaker interpretation of Kant's system. The criticisms advanced in this and the previous section have little force against the weaker interpretation. However, equally the weaker interpretation provides little succour for the constructivist challenge.

In summary, then, the choice would seem to be between an arid formal rationalism which can yield no conclusions relevant to practical reason and an axiologicallydependent ethical system which yields practical imperatives. Hence, we may conclude that the internalist need not fear that the constructivist challenge will be fortified through the use of the works of Kant.

Section B: John Rawls' constructivist theory of social justice

Having discussed Kant's constructivist moral theory, I want to look now at the work of John Rawls who employs constructivist methodology in the generation of principles of distributive justice.[56] There are some substantive differences between the two. While Kant relies upon the notions of universality and non-contradiction to generate moral theory, Rawls attempts to generate substantive normative principles from the consensual agreement of rational contracting agents. Rawls asks us to imagine what principles of justice hypothetical contractors in an *original position* under a *veil of ignorance*, would assent to and claims that the principles they would agree under such conditions are the principles which should be adopted by social institutions and arrangements. (These terms of art will be explained as the chapter unfolds).

However, although Rawls differs from Kant in a number of significant respects, like Kant, his work potentially provides ammunition for those who would mount the constructivist challenge because his principles of distributive justice are ostensibly derived from sources other than the human good. Further, at various points he provides explicit condemnation of internalist methodology. The aim of this section shall be to examine Rawls' constructivist methodology—and in particular his claim to derive the right prior to the good—with the aim of demonstrating that Rawls does not actually generate substantive principles of justice without reference to some idea of the human good.

However, my task is somewhat complicated by the highly ambiguous nature of Rawls' work; particularly his pronouncements about the role of the human good in his theory. This problem has been amplified by the frequent shifts in position since the publication of *A Theory of Justice*. In order to deal with this ambiguity, I shall focus primarily upon *A Theory of Justice* because this is his clearest and most unambiguously constructivist work. However, equally, the later works cannot be ignored. Where shifts have occurred they will be noted and special attention will be given to his recent pronouncements on his so-called 'thin theory of the good'. In discussing the later works of Rawls, I will follow Kukathas and Pettit by dividing these works into two main periods.[57]

Nevertheless, regardless of the difficulties cited above, I believe that Rawls' doctrine can be sufficiently 'pinned down' to cast doubt on his capacity to generate distributive principles without the human good. If anything his frequent shifts should be seen as more reason to doubt that the constructivist challenge will gain much from the works of Rawls.

Rawls and the human good

John Rawls' project is probably best understood in the light of the relative ascendancy of utilitarianism in Anglo-American philosophy for the greater part of the twentieth century. Rawls believes many aspects of utilitarian theory to be problematic. He condemns utilitarianism *inter alia* for its attempt to derive the just from the human good. However, his foundational criticisms do not apply solely to utilitarianism, but to any theory which attempts to ground principles of distributive justice in a conception of the good. Rawls, like Kant before him, is particularly antagonistic to normative principles being derived from conceptions of the human good and would therefore presumably be fundamentally opposed to the internalist project.[58]

Rawls takes utilitarianism to be essentially a teleological ethical theory. It is teleological because the good is defined independently of the right and then the right is defined as that which maximises the good.[59] This means that those institutions and acts are right which out of the available alternatives produce the most good, or at least as much good as any of the other alternatives.[60] Rawls contrasts utilitarianism's teleological ethical schema with his own deontological system which he refers to as 'justice as fairness'.[61] In justice as fairness the right is prior to the good[62]; hence before we attempt to describe the good, we must firstly define the right.[63] Thus, for Rawls: i) the good is neither ultimate nor intrinsic[64] and; ii) principles of justice, like those of government, should be neutral towards the question of the good life.[65] Rawls advocates the adoption of a deontological theory of axiological neutrality.[66] Rawls' account is deontological because it asserts that "something is good only if it fits into ways of life consistent with the principles of right already on hand".[67] His methodological distaste for internalism in *A Theory of Justice* is driven primarily by his account of human nature in which our essence is defined primarily in terms of rational agency. He acknowledges that in this he is adopting Royce's thought that a person may be regarded as a human life lived according to a plan.[68] Rawls is not so much concerned with the incorporation of empirical detail into normative theory, nor with the fact that there exists a wide variety of competing and conflicting accounts of the good, as he is with the State respecting the potential of persons to be rational agents. Identifying persons with *particular conceptions* of the good restricts that potential.

This idea that it is important that provision be made merely for a conception of the good life—rather than for any actual concrete formulation of the good life—is central to Rawls' system. He believes that the State must not coerce people nor offer incentives in the way of distributive shares in order to promote human activities of intrinsic value.[69] According to Rawls, human beings are rational agents capable of revising their ends and, to some extent at least, of controlling and adjusting even their individual desires. Teleological theories such as utilitarianism, which give priority to the good identify people with their *actual* desires and interests and thus do not respect their capacity to transform their own goals and interests.

> Persons do not take their wants and desires as determined by happenings beyond their control. We are not so to speak assailed by them, as we are perhaps by disease and illness.[70]

It is our capacity to revise our ends which leads to the wide variety of accounts of the human good. Rawls notes that the "human good is heterogenous because the aims of the self are heterogenous".[71] Thus, for Rawls to say that justice as fairness gives priority to the concept of right is to say that one "does not take men's propensities and inclinations as given, whatever they are, and then seek the best way to fulfil them."[72] Rawls believes that we should not base our political theory on accounts of the human good grounded in limited conceptions of the human agent; principles of justice should not attempt to determine what an individual's good should be.[73] Rawls concludes that any ethical theory which defines right conduct in terms of the maximisation of some particular good is morally unacceptable.

In his later works, Rawls' concerns about accounts of the human good shift from their potential to quash our capacity to be rational self-choosers to a concern with firstly the idea that implementation of accounts of the good by the State requires *repressive* and coercive State action and secondly the belief that the imposition of one single view of the good life will bring about social instability.

Rawlsian rational foundationalism

Instead of adopting an internalist approach, Rawls attempts to generate distributive principles from rationalistic foundations. One of Rawls' most important contributions to political theory has been his attempt to forge principles of social justice out of the 'original position'; from a situation in which those determining the principles of justice follow rational procedures which coincide with the demands of justice.[74] It is the methodology which Rawls outlines in *A Theory of Justice* which provides ammunition for the constructivist critique of internalism. In this brief section I shall consider why Rawls might legitimately be thought of as a constructivist and how his work can be employed by those mounting the constructivist challenge.

Let us think a little more about the original position. The original position is a hypothetical set of circumstances in which contracting agents, who are neither aware of what position they will occupy in society nor what conceptions of the good they will hold, deliberate upon the basic design of the principles of justice which are to govern the social institutions and arrangements of a society in which they are to live.[75] According to Rawls, the justice of social institutions in the real world depends upon their conformity to the principles which are generated in the original position. In order to determine those principles, we must firstly ask what principles agents in such an original position would agree to. Only under a veil of ignorance in the original position can genuine principles of justice be formulated because in such conditions contracting agents do not know firstly what position they will occupy in society nor what conception of the good they might have. This latter condition is just as important as the first, for if a contractor knows in the original position that she likes playing tennis, then she might opt for principles of distribution which favour tennis players. The aim of the veil of ignorance is to:

> ....rule out those principles that it would be rational to propose for acceptance, however little the chance of success, only if one knew certain things that are irrelevant from the standpoint of justice.[76]

Thus the veil of ignorance is a procedural mechanism for avoiding the problem of principles of justice merely consisting of rationalised self-interest. Principles of social justice are to be generated from the decisions of rational agents *qua* rational agents. It is this element of his thinking that leads us to label him a constructivist.

In order to say more about how agents in a hypothetical original position would, in fact, behave and thus determine the kinds of principles they would generate, Rawls employs his *maximin rule*, which he derives from various game-theory studies concerning rules of choice under conditions of uncertainty.[77] The maximin rule advises that alternatives be ranked according to their worst possible outcomes: we should adopt the alternative, the worst outcome of which is superior to the worst outcomes of the others.[78] (We should note that in Rawls' later works he drops this reliance upon the maximin rule as the means of determining how his hypothetical contractors would choose in the original position, instead relying upon the idea of the *reasonable*—more of which later).

Rawls argues that agents in the original position would choose the following two principles: i) the equal basic liberty principle and; ii) the difference principle. According to the equal basic liberty principle, each person is to have an equal right to the most extensive basic liberty compatible with a similar liberty for others.[79] Rawls' second principle, the difference principle, states that social and economic inequalities are to be arranged so that they are firstly to the greatest benefit of the least advantaged and secondly attached to offices and positions open to all under conditions of fair equality of opportunity.[80] These two principles—which Rawls claims are the principles to which rational agents in a veil of ignorance would give assent—are lexically ordered. This means that all of the conditions of the first principle must be satisfied before the second can be considered. Rawls argues that these two principles should be thought of as the correct principles for ensuring the justice of social institutions and arrangements for the very reason that they are generated from procedures which coincide with the demands of justice. They are just because they are grounded in the consensual agreements of *rational* agents. When persons act on the principles adopted in the original position, their actions do not depend upon natural or social contingencies.[81]

Here Rawls echoes Kant in arguing that the only binding normative principles are those which are generated by autonomous rational agents. The choice is open to us not to adopt the point of view of the original position; nevertheless our decision to adopt such a viewpoint "expresses our nature as free and equal rational persons".[82] Rawls is well aware of his Kantian heritage. In *A Theory of Justice* he notes that: "The original position may be viewed, then, as a procedural interpretation of Kant's conception of autonomy and the Categorical Imperative."[83] Furthermore, using other Kantian categories Rawls suggests that "we think of the original position as the point of view from which our noumenal selves see the world."[84] Rawls also implies that the Difference Principle is equivalent to the Kantian principle of respect for persons.[85]

However, while Rawls' Kantianism becomes more pronounced in the body of work produced immediately after *A Theory of Justice*, the Kantian component of *A Theory of Justice* should not be overstated. Firstly, the choice of principles of justice is made by self-interested contractors who choose, employing motivations grounded in sensuous inclination, rather than discern via *a priori* reason, the principles in question. Rawlsian contractors do not act autonomously in the Kantian sense because they are motivated by inclination rather than the moral law. (In this sense they are Hobbesian rather than Kantian agents).[86] Secondly, Rawls incorporates heteronomous empirical detail into his theory. Observation of this led Martha Nussbaum to refer to Rawls as an 'empirical Kantian'.[87] Thirdly, Rawls readily admits the necessity of an account of the good in distributive theory, albeit a 'thin' account (I shall say more about this in the next section). Nonetheless, Rawls' work can be thought to contain two key neo-Kantian elements: i) his explicit antagonism to normative principles being derived from the good and; ii) his constructivism or rational foundationalism. While both claims involve contentious interpretations of Rawls' work, and one might want to argue that it should be interpreted differently (especially in light of recent developments), any attempt to mount the constructivist challenge using Rawls' work would in all likelihood be grounded in an interpretation in which these two claims are given some prominence.

The thin theory of the good

Given Rawls' explicit rational foundationalism, how does he deal with the 'Paradox of Willing the Willing of Nothing'? I argued in an earlier section that this paradox was the central problem for Kantian moral theory—given of course that one interprets Kant as being a pure constructivist. I argued that if his work is interpreted as excluding considerations of philosophical anthropology then Kant cannot generate substantive normative principles. By implication, this paradox should affect any form of constructivism. Given that Rawls is a constructivist, how then does he generate substantive normative principles?

The answer to this is quite simple. The Paradox of Willing the Willing of Nothing does not trouble Rawls for the reason that he eschews what we might call pure constructivism. He does not claim that all of the distributively just can be grounded in reason.[88] Rawls believes that neither value nor justice can be grounded purely in reason; rather he acknowledges the need for a conception of the human good. While the 'right' is prior to the 'good', in order for the principles of right to be established it is necessary to rely on some notions of the human good because assumptions about the parties' motives in the original position are required. Since these assumptions must not jeopardise the priority of the right over the good, the theory of the good used in arguing for the principles of justice is "restricted to the bare essentials". This scaled down account is Rawls' so-called 'thin theory' of the human good.[89]

We may surmise that one of the motivating factors behind Rawls' provision of this so-called thin theory of the good is a recognition of the necessity for constructivist theory to deal with what I have termed the Paradox of Willing the Willing of Nothing.[90] He argues—before introducing his so-called Aristotelian principle—that although the notion of deliberative rationality and the principles of rational choice rely upon concepts of considerable complexity, we still cannot derive from the definition of rational plans alone what kinds of ends these plans are likely to encourage.[91] Without his thin account of the good, his rational contractors do not have enough information to generate principles of justice. Let us turn our attention to this thin theory of the good.

In explicating his thin theory of the good, Rawls contrasts it with a *thick* or *full* theory of the good.[92] The thick theory and the thin theory of the good have different roles to play in the generation of distributive principles. Whilst a thin theory is involved in the generation of principles of justice, once we have determined the proper principles, then a full theory of the good may be brought to bear upon these principles.[93] According to Rawls, this is consistent with the priority of the right over the good. Rawls' thin theory of the good consists of a stripped down version of human goods, and includes only those goods which are good no matter what ends reason pursues. These are the 'primary' goods. The primary goods comprise liberties, opportunities, income and wealth and bases of self respect. They are conceived as the universally desirable goods which societies' social structures directly control.[94] Rawls asks us to assume that the chief primary goods at the disposal of society are rights and liberties, powers and opportunities, income and wealth and self-respect. These are the *social* primary goods. He also lists a number of *natural* primary goods, namely "health and vigour, intelligence and imagination". These are natural because although their possession is influenced by the basic structure, they are not so directly under its control.[95]

The thin theory, then, has a pivotal role to play in Rawls' theory. In the original position all persons accept the thin theory of the good. Rawls notes three other places where the thin theory has a role to play in his theory. He claims that the thin theory of the good: i) helps define the least favoured members of society which the difference principle is to apply to; ii) specifies the index of well-being and the 'expectations of representative men' and; iii) has a role to play in the argument for his two principles of justice.[96]

At this point one might be tempted to ask why anyone should accept Rawls' claim that his thin account of the good is not open to criticisms of privileging particular forms of life. How is the use of the thin theory of the good consistent with the right being prior to the good? Given that the State is to implement his principles of justice, how is the use of a thin theory of the good in the generation of these principles consistent with the idea that the State should not promote activities merely because they are of intrinsic value?

Rawls' response is that the primary goods are things that every rational man is presumed to want. This is the central claim of his doctrine of 'goodness as rationality'. Primary goods are the goods required for the successful execution of a rational plan of life.[97] In order for agents to conceive of such a rational plan, no matter what form it takes, there are certain goods which he or she must have. Rawls believes that "it is rational to want these goods whatever else is wanted, since they are in general necessary for the framing and execution of a rational plan of life."[98] Primary goods are things that every rational man is presumed to want.[99] They are useful no matter what else rational agents desire, for they are essential in enabling people to choose their own conception of the good life. They are universal means.

In *A Theory of Justice* Rawls seemingly grounds his primary social goods in reason, so to speak. Underpinning this idea that the primary goods should be thought of as the index of well-being would seem to be his conception of persons as rational choosers of ends.[100] Thus Rawls employs a conception of persons, which he says is adapted from Josiah Royce's thought that "a person may be regarded as a human life lived according to a plan".[101] Whilst Rawls acknowledges the necessity of some conception of the good, he believes that by employing a thin theory of the good, which all rational persons would agree to and which is compatible with all possible rational plans of life, he has avoided the problem of favouring particular ways of life. In *A Theory of Justice* Rawls claims that preference for primary goods does not commit one to claims about the moral acceptability of particular conceptions of the good. Hence he assumes that there is a *congruence* between justice as fairness and goodness as rationality.[102]

Before outlining my objections to the thin theory of the good, various modifications that Rawls has made to the doctrine since the publication of *A Theory of Justice* should be noted. Following Kukathas and Pettit, these changes will be divided into two broad periods: the first, from 1971-82, is characterised by an exploration of the Kantian elements of his theory and a restriction of its range; and the second, from 1982 onwards, is characterised by a move away from the Kantian interpretation toward a concern for how we should define a *liberal* political culture. I make no pretence that the account provided here is exhaustive or definitive of the theoretical shifts Rawls has made since *A Theory of Justice*, rather I shall focus on those moves of direct significance to the constructivist challenge and, in particular, those which concern the thin theory of the good.

In the first period a number of important moves are made. Firstly, Rawls explores and expands upon the Kantian element of his theory. While many commentators have drawn attention to the Kantian elements of *A Theory of Justice*, nevertheless, at that stage, it was relatively minor part of Rawls' explicit project. In this first period from 1971-82, Rawls explores the notion of autonomy. For Rawls a well-ordered society is one which is peopled by autonomous citizens. While 'justice as fairness' is not an entirely Kantian doctrine, Rawls leaves us in no doubt that his theory "sufficiently resembles Kant's in enough respects so that it is far closer to his view than to the other traditional moral conceptions that are appropriate for use as benchmarks of comparison."[103] The important point here is that the content of a conception of justice is determined not by some account of human nature, but by a conception of the person that is more or less Kantian.

Secondly, Rawls restricts the *range* of the thin theory of the good to Western democratic societies, such as the United States. He moves away from a concern with ideals of universality and acknowledges that the notion of autonomy is, in fact, culturally dependent. Rawls relinquishes his commitment to the view that the primary goods are the goods that *all* rational persons are presumed to want, and instead argues that they are simply those goods presumed to be desired by persons in democratic cultures. In his *Dewey Lectures* Rawls explicitly acknowledges that his concern is not to supply a universal standard of justice, but simply to discover those moral principles which might serve his own society with its particular concerns. He aims to discover a conception of justice which would command allegiance because it is expressive of our moral personhood. He settles on a conception that is most reasonable for persons in such societies. Rawls writes:

> An immediate consequence of taking our inquiry as focussed on the apparent conflict between freedom and equality in a democratic society is that we are not trying to find a conception of justice suitable for all societies regardless of the particular social or historical circumstances. We want to settle a fundamental disagreement over the just form of basic institutions within a democratic society under modern circumstances.[104]

Autonomy is not a value revered by all societies.

In this work his distinction between the *rational* and the *reasonable* comes to the fore. Rawls characterises the context within which rational choice takes place as 'the reasonable', and it is supplied by one's own society. In the original position, the rational is interpreted in terms of persons' desires to realise and to exercise the moral powers and to advance their conception of the good, but it is always constrained by the reasonable. At the heart of the reasonable lies the notion of the fair terms of cooperation which all rational choosers in the society accept. Rawls emphatically maintains that he does not derive his conclusions from an *abstract* account of rationality. (We should also note that here Rawls drops his earlier reliance upon decision theory to characterise the motives of the agents in the original position).

Two important facets of Rawls' work in this period are as follows: (i) the development of the theory of the original position as the framework of reasonableness which constrains and ultimately yields the substantive content of rational contemplation and; (ii) the eschewal of a framework of reasonableness cast as a universal one, but rather it is developed with his particular society in mind. In this modified view, the original position becomes a doctrine which seems to draw out the principles of justice appropriate for a society which implicitly holds to a model of the person and the well-ordered society grounded in the Kantian idea of autonomy.

In the second period from approximately 1982 onwards, the relevant shifts in Rawls' position concern; (i) his assertion that justice as fairness involves a *political* but not a *metaphysical* conception of the good and; (ii) his movement away from a Kantian interpretation of his theory. Rawls moves from the so-called Kantian interpretation for fear that it be misconstrued as a comprehensive doctrine of the good or indeed that it involves such a conception. This is part of a changed perception on Rawls' part of what the proper grounds of liberalism might be.

The crucial distinction which Rawls makes in this later period of work is between a political and a metaphysical conception of the good.[105] The difference between a political conception of justice, which only incorporates a political account of the good, and a metaphysical conception is largely one of scope. A comprehensive conception involves an account of what is of value in human life and ideals of personal virtue and character which are to govern all parts of one's life and not just the political. A fully comprehensive doctrine covers all values and virtues within a well articulated scheme of thought.[106] On the other hand, a partially comprehensive (or political) doctrine is one which comprises some, but not all, non-political values and virtues in a loosely constituted scheme. A political doctrine is one which is compatible with a variety of comprehensive moral doctrines. According to Rawls, there are three distinguishing features of a political conception of justice. Firstly, it is a moral conception worked out for a specific subject, namely the basic structure of a constitutional regime. Secondly, accepting a political conception does not require accepting any particular religious, philosophical or moral doctrine: "the political conception presents itself as a reasonable conception for the basic structure alone".[107] Thirdly, the political conception of justice is formulated not in terms of any comprehensive doctrine, but rather in terms of certain fundamental intuitive ideas viewed as latent or implicit in the public political culture of a democratic society.[108]

Rawls insists that we should avoid any epistemological claims which draw on a comprehensive moral view. What he desires is a public philosophy which does not incorporate or amount to any comprehensive doctrine and which can be the fair basis of a stable political community. On this view, justice as fairness should not be thought of as a conception of justice that is necessarily true, but rather as one that can serve as a basis of informed and willing political agreement between citizens viewed as free and equal persons.[109]

Rawls' attempt to avoid comprehensive moral doctrine because he believes: (i) that modern democratic societies are characterised by a pluralism of views about comprehensive moral, religious and metaphysical issues and; (ii) that this pluralism is permanent. In an article entitled 'The Domain of the Political and Overlapping Consensus' he argues that only the oppressive use of state power can maintain a continuing common affirmation of one comprehensive religious, philosophical or moral doctrine.[110] Rawls argues that in the absence of such state coercion there will be no tendency for persons' ideals to converge toward anyone comprehensive world-view. It is this fact of continuing pluralism which lies behind Rawls' insistence that we adopt a political conception of justice that can be the object of an *overlapping consensus.*

Justice as fairness, according to Rawls, provides such a political conception; it represents a common idea of justice acceptable to the major diverse standpoints and hence it can be the grounds of a stable political order. (Implicit within Rawls' thinking here is the notion that justice as fairness presupposes no particular controversial metaphysics of the self). In this later period, Rawls asserts that political philosophy should be free of controversial moral doctrines in order that it might provide a shared public basis for the justification of political and social institutions which will help to ensure social stability from one generation to the next.[111] A practical aim of political philosophy should be the achievement of stable political unity.

It is the fear of invoking a comprehensive doctrine of justice—and in so doing undermining political liberalism—which is the primary motivation for Rawls' renunciation of the Kantian interpretation. In the later period of work, Rawls argues that the liberalisms of Kant and Mill—and indeed possibly a good many other forms of liberalism—rest in part on ideals and values that are not generally shared in a democratic society.[112] For example, Kant and Mill focus on the notions of autonomy and individuality respectively and these represent comprehensive ideas which are not widely accepted in democratic society. He argues that such ideals are problematic because they undermine the possibility of a workable tolerant society.

> Philosophy as the search for truth about an independent metaphysical and moral order cannot....provide a workable and shared basis for a political conception of justice in a democratic society.[113]

Rawls believes that liberalism grounded in a comprehensive moral doctrine cannot provide a sound basis for a liberal society. Thus Rawls abandons the defence of liberalism as a comprehensive world-view in favour of what he terms 'political liberalism', a liberalism which is not dependent upon any particular comprehensive moral ideal such as autonomy. Political liberalism remains a form of liberalism nevertheless in that it stresses the importance of toleration and demands that social policy be governed by principles which are not comprehensive, i.e. which do not in themselves presuppose that some particular way of life is preferable to any others. The concern here is with what is most feasible, i.e. with ensuring that social policy encourages social stability. Hence the contractarian device of the original position is reinterpreted in this later work as a solution to the problem of how we might discover the proper grounds of a stable tolerant democratic society.[114]

The thin theory is not so thin!

Whilst Rawls argues that the conception of the good he uses in generating his principles of justice is a thin one, I believe that closer analysis reveals that it is not as thin as he would have us believe or at least it is thick enough for us to rebuff the constructivist challenge.

I shall begin by considering what it is that is valuable about being a rational agent. The reader will recall that Rawls' stated justification for the admission of the primary goods into his schema in *A Theory of Justice* was that these are goods which any person would want in order to pursue a rational plan of life. However, there are other possible conceptions of the good which do not involve a rational plan of life. Thomas Nagel makes this very point, when he objects that Rawls' primary goods are not equally useful whatever one's plan of life.[115] They reflect a certain conception of the human good, in which following a rational plan is a necessary condition of the good life. The primary goods invoke a conception of the good which privileges rationality and in which rationality involves the successful execution of a life plan.[116] Such conceptions cannot be drawn solely from the dictates of reason.

Furthermore, not only is the underlying rationale for the thin account of the good partial, the *particular* Rawlsian primary goods are not neutral among life plans; they are not, as Rawls would have us believe, universal means. William Galston notes that Rawls offers only the most casual support for his contention that his primary goods are *universal* means, and it is easy to discover counter-examples.

> If it is rational to want to go to heaven, and if Jesus' claim about the relation between wealth and the attainment of heaven is true, then there is at least one important plan of life that wealth impedes rather than furthers.[117]

Indeed, we might well question not only whether wealth is a universal means, but whether any of the other primary goods are neutral among life plans. Self-respect and self-worth are not part of all possible accounts of the good life. For instance, according to the Rule of St. Benedict, the highest spiritual stage consists of truly believing that one is the 'worst of all men'.[118] Such examples demonstrate quite clearly that Rawls' so-called thin theory is not neutral between particular conceptions of the good. We do not need to investigate the nether regions of the logically possible to find other examples of conceptions of the good life which run counter to his thin account.

Some critics have argued that Rawls' thin theory of the good is neutral in the relevant sense, i.e., that Rawls has identified the primary values that any reasonable person would accept as the basis of moral claims.[119] However, this line of response smuggles in assumptions about the kinds of values which a rational person would have. Why should we accept this notion of what constitutes the good life? It does not seem intuitively obvious, to the author at least, that in the great scheme of things the faithful Benedictine monk is any less rational *ceteris paribus* than the person who aims to augment her self-esteem.

Rawls' modifications of his theory in his Kantian period might well be interpreted as an acknowledgment of the point that the notion of rationality underpinning the thin theory cannot be thought of as universally applicable. In 'Kantian Constructivism in Moral Theory' he argues that the theory of justice which he has elaborated is only directly valid within a democratic society under modern circumstances.[120] In other words, the persuasiveness of his argument extends only so far as the deep normative structures of Western consciousness.[121] However, this modification on Rawls' part would seem to undermine his prior claim that the thin theory of the good is non-axiological. It appears to be an admission that its employment involves the invocation of an account of the good—the goods required for a rational plan of life may vary from culture to culture. Yet it is the putative universality of the primary goods in the pursuance of the rational which was originally provided as reason for their being thought of as axiologically-neutral. Thus this modification would seem to undermine the aforesaid congruity between justice as fairness and goodness as rationality.

In highlighting the *axiological* components of Rawls' work, we should also address the modifications of his second period, which involve the claim that the theory of the good presented in Rawls' system is "political but not metaphysical". Rawls claims that this move avoids the kinds of problems normally associated with accounts of the good in political theory. While we may require a theory of the good, so long as the theory is political and not metaphysical, then no serious problems should arise from its use. I have a number of objections to this distinction between the political and the metaphysical. Firstly, I am sceptical about whether such a distinction can plausibly be drawn. Is there really a sensible distinction to be had between a political and a metaphysical conception of justice? Do not claims about the nature of political value also incorporate more comprehensive values? Secondly, even if we admit the possibility of there being purely political conceptions of the good, we might well question the extent to which this political conception is compatible with a variety of comprehensive world-views. While a political conception may not privilege any particular comprehensive doctrine that does not mean that it is compatible with all such views. As Amy Gutmann notes, it is one thing to claim that liberalism does not presuppose a single metaphysical view of the individual, but quite another to claim that it is compatible with all such views.[122] Furthermore, there will *necessarily* be occasions when the State must exert its own comprehensive account of the good. For instance, in circumstances where some person or persons decide that the realisation of their political goals requires force, then the State must at the very least enforce its own views about the value of social stability. Rawls acknowledges the force of this pragmatic objection, conceding that "whenever someone insists, for example, that certain questions are so fundamental that to ensure their being rightly settled justifies civil strife," we may have to assert certain aspects of our own comprehensive doctrine.[123] It would seem then, at least on cursory inspection, that Rawls' later works provide little cause for optimism on the part of those intending to mount the constructivist challenge.

Some further normative elements in *A Theory of Justice*

The thrust of this part of the chapter *contra* Rawls has been that his thin theory imports significant claims about the nature of the human good life. However, further examination of *A Theory of Justice* reveals that it is not just in relation to the primary goods that one might detect non-neutral conceptions of the human good; other elements of the presented doctrine might also be said to be at least implicitly axiological. For instance, if we consider the Hobbesian aspect of the original position in which the contracting parties, who are to determine the principles of justice, are cast as self-interested rational agents, then we find that Rawls incorporates into his theory elements of want regarding naturalism, i.e. the theory that the good involves want or desire satisfaction. The parties in the original position are motivated in the main by their desires.[124] The assumption that this is how rational agents *would* act seems to be some kind of endorsement of the want-regarding view. However, in making this point, we should exercise some caution. Brian Barry argues in his *Liberal Theory of Justice* that Rawls has introduced the primary goods into his theory because otherwise the parties behind the veil of ignorance would have to formulate these principles in terms of want satisfaction. Barry claims that Rawls is in an awkward dilemma; on the one hand, he does not like the implication of the want regarding view.[125] Yet, on the other hand, by denying actors information about themselves in the original position, this seems to lead inexorably toward the formulation of principles in want-regarding terms.[126] Thus, even with respect to the *motives* of the agents in the original position, Rawls smuggles in *de facto* accounts of the human good.

In considering Rawls' attitude toward the human good, we should make mention of his 'Aristotelian Principle'. Rawls believes, all other things being equal, that human beings enjoy the exercise of their realised capacities (which includes both innate and trained ability), and this enjoyment increases the more the capacity is realised, or the greater its complexity.

> The intuitive idea here is that human beings take more pleasure in doing something as they become more proficient at it, and of two activities they do equally well, they prefer the one calling on a larger repertoire of more intricate and subtle discrimination.[127]

This means that if a person can play both checkers and chess equally well, they will prefer playing chess. Rawls introduces the Aristotelian Principle because of the impossibility of deducing from the definition of rational plans alone what sorts of ends those plans are likely to encourage. It appears that Rawls' theory of social justice contains Aristotelian moral components, in addition to the want-regarding naturalist ones.[128]

Whilst Rawls proclaims the priority of the right over the good, in order to perform the necessary task of transforming his constructivist account into a practically applicable theory of justice, he employs a conception of the good. Although Rawls claims to be neutral toward conceptions of the good, close analysis reveals that his work contains a particular account of the good which privileges rationality. Rawls thus fails to determine the right prior to the good, that is, he fails to demonstrate that there is no incongruity between justice as fairness and goodness as rationality. This is just as we might have expected, for it seems unlikely that the right could be determined prior to the good.

Summary

In this chapter, in defending internalism against the constructivist challenge, I have firstly provided an objection in the form of the paradox of willing the willing of nothing which I believe applies to all forms of constructivism and secondly, I have examined the constructivist writings of Kant and Rawls and shown that in fact these would-be constructivists actually make use of accounts of the human good, despite protestations to the contrary. (These arguments are consistent with the more contentious general claim that a conception of the human good is necessary for the generation of concrete forms of practical reason). These two moves are sufficient I believe for the constructivist challenge to be countered.

It should, of course, be acknowledged that I have not as yet demonstrated the impossibility of constructivist social theory, nor have I dealt with the charge that the implementation of internalist theory leads to totalitarianism, social instability and intolerance. All that I have provided are arguments against the work of Rawls and Kant and these of course represent only two possible forms of constructivism. Arguments *contra* these philosophers do not, in themselves, provide knock-down evidence that constructivist methodology should be abandoned, nor do they allay fears that internalist social policy has dire social consequences.

However, we should not let this concern us unduly for the following reasons. Firstly, Rawls and Kant provide two of the most sophisticated constructivist projects. If their programs fail to deliver concrete normative theory which is not reliant upon the human good, then one must be sceptical about the possibility of other less sophisticated constructivists succeeding. Secondly, The Paradox of Willing the Willing of Nothing—which involves a critique of the constructivist strategy—provides further cause for being sceptical about the possibility of generating coherent constructivist distributive theory which does not rely upon accounts of the human good. Finally, if we employ what Martha Nussbaum calls a 'thick, vague' account of the good, I believe that many of the concerns which have been voiced about internalism may be avoided.[129] A thick vague account of the good is compatible with a tolerant society. The first two claims shift the onus of proof onto the constructivist to provide a theoretical framework which does not surreptitiously smuggle in accounts of the good, while the third claim holds out the hope that conceptions of the good might not be as problematic as previously thought. It is my hope that the concept of the human good developed in chapter four is sufficiently broad and vague to enable us to side-step at least most of the objections raised against internalism.

Notes

1. As shall become apparent the notion of reason is far more precisely defined in the works of the two philosophers to be examined in this chapter; Rawls and Kant.
2. The term 'practical reason' refers to reason or reflective thought which concerns the issues of voluntary decisions and actions. It will be assumed throughout the length of this chapter that the ability to generate forms of practical reason is a touchstone of theoretical adequacy for normative projects.

3. For instance, see Kant, 1991, [245-247].
4. Kant, 1989, [64], p.66. Cf. Reich, 1939, pp.446-63.
5. Kant, 1991, [215], p.43.
6. "The morally good...is something which by its object is supersensuous; nothing corresponding to it can be found in sensuous intuition...", Kant, 1989. [69], p.71.
7. Kant, 1991, [216], pp.43-44.
8. Ibid., [215], p.45.
9. Kant, 1989, [35], p.36.
10. Kant believes that the assumption of the good prior to the moral law produces heteronomy and rules out the moral principle concerned. See Kant, 1981, [441], p.45.
11. See Kant, 1963, [266], 26.
12. "Freedom and self-legislation of the will are both autonomy and are hence reciprocal concepts.", Kant 1981, [450], p.52.
13. "For we know freedom ....only as a *negative* property in us, namely that of not being necessitated to act through any *sensible* determining grounds.", Kant, 1991, [226], p.52.
14. Kant, 1981, [441], p.45. Cf. Silber, 1959, p.85.
15. Kant, 1981, [400], p.13.
16. Kant, 1970; reprinted 1977, p.45
17. Kant, 1978, p.53
18. Kant, 1981, [416n], p.26.
19. Kant, 1991, [388], p.193.
20. Ibid., [226], p.52.
21. Kant, 1989, [81], p.84.
22. Ibid., [71], p.74. Cf. *The Metaphysics of Morals* where he writes: "The mere conformity or non-conformity of an action with law, irrespective of the incentive to it, is called a *legality*; but that conformity in which the idea of duty arising from the law is also the incentive to the action is called its morality.", Kant, 1989, [219], p.46.
23. Kant, 1991, [40], p.203.
24. "....when we assume any object, under the name of good, as the determining ground of the will prior to the moral law, and then derive the supreme practical principle from it, this always produces heteronomy and rules out the moral principle.", Kant, 1989, [109], p.113.
25. See for instance, Aristotle, 1969, Bk.1 ch.6 [1096b23-25]; Bk.1 ch.8 [1099a11-22]; Bk.6 ch.12 [1144a1-3] and; Bk.7 ch.13 [1153b7-18].
26. Kant, 1991 , [217], p.44.
27. Ibid., [468], p.259.
28. "For since he is a creature, and consequently is always dependent with respect to what he needs for complete satisfaction with his condition, he can never be wholly free from desires and inclinations which, because they rest on physical causes, do not of themselves agree with the moral law, which has an entirely different source...", Kant, 1989, [84], p.86.
29. "It is only the strength of one's resolution, in the first case, that is properly called *virtue*.", Kant, 1991, [390], p.194.
30. "Virtue is, therefore, the moral strength of a *man's* will in fulfilling his *duty*, a moral *constraint* through his own law giving reason in so far as this constitutes itself as authority *executing* law.", ibid., [405], p.206.
31. Kant,1956, A151/B190. Cf. Kant, 1989, [120], p.124
32. Kant obviously intends 'reason' to be a non-empirical concept in the same way that he argues that a cause is non-empirical.
33. Kant, 1981, [421], p.30.
34. Ibid., [394], p.7.
35. Ibid., [393], p.7.
36. Ibid., [436], pp.41-42
37. Ibid., [436], pp.41-42.
38. There are in fact a number of interesting issues concerning the relationship between the various formulations of the Categorical Imperative, but which lie outside of the scope of this chapter; the most interesting of these being the question of whether the other two formulations do follow

necessarily from the first. See Norman, 1983, pp.100-105 and Sullivan,1989, p.194.

39. Kant, 1981, [436], p.41. Cf. Reich, 1939, p.452.
40. Kant, 1989, [80], p.83.
41. Kant, 1991, [217].
42. Singer, 1961, p.251.
43. Broad, 1959, pp.122-23.
44. See Riley, 1983, p.194 f.n.183.
45. For useful discussions of Hegel's criticisms of Kant see Wood, 1990, pp.154-173 and Solomon, 1985, p.569.
46. For a discussion of the various critiques of Kant see Wood, 1990, pp.154-172.
47. Kant, 1970, repr. 1977, pp.65-68.
48. Kant, 1981, [422], p.30.
49. Ibid., [422], p.31.
50. Kant repeats this argument: "Man has a duty to himself to cultivate his natural powers (powers of spirit, mind and body), as means to all sorts of possible ends. Man owes it to himself (as a rational being) not to leave idle and, as it were, rusting away the natural predispositions and capacities that his reason can some day use.", Kant, 1991, [444], p.239.
51. Kant, 1981, [421n12], p.30.
52. Ibid., [421n12], p.30.
53. Kant, 1991, [389-90].
54. This line of argumentation is similar, in some senses, to that of the German philosopher Gottlob August Tittel and the British philosopher J.S. Mill who both attempt to portray Kant as a covert consequentialist. See Wood, op. cit., pp.155-59.
55. As John Silber notes in relation to Kant's 'Aristotelian' notion of our duty to perfect our natural talents: "....the very same theory of perfection was rejected again by Kant...on the grounds that it was based upon the determination of a material object of volition prior to the moral law and consequently was incapable of relating itself to the will as duty.", Silber, 1962-63, p.190.
56. Kant did however have a theory of justice. Kant believed that the idea of moral community must underlie the structure of the just political state. For a discussion of this see Riley, 1983.
57. Kukathas and Pettit, 1990, p.120. Also useful on Rawls' later work are the following; Galston, 1989; Hampton, 1989 and; Baier, 1989.
58. For a discussion of the distinction between the 'right' and the 'good' in Anglo-American ethics, see Feinberg, 1974, p.309.
59. Rawls claims that the structure of an ethical theory is largely determined by how it defines and connects the two basic notions: the right and the good. See Rawls, 1972, p.24.
60. Ibid., p.24.
61. Adina Schwartz claims that justice as fairness is more of a teleological theory than Rawls would like to admit. See Schwartz, 1972-73, p.294.
62. Rawls, 1972, p.31.
63. Interestingly, Rawls claims that the priority of the right is a central feature of Kant's moral philosophy, ibid., p.31n.
64. Ibid., p.31.
65. Ibid., p.69.
66. By 'axiological neutrality' I mean the claim that distributive principles *should* be derived from sources other than the good.
67. Rawls, 1972, p.396.
68. Ibid., p.408.
69. Ibid., p.329.
70. Rawls, 1975, pp.94-99.
71. Rawls, 1972, p.554.
72. Ibid., p.31.
73. It is worth noting that Rawls also finds utilitarianism's possible 'radical inegalitarianism' a source of concern. This objection to utilitarianism, which may be called the 'Objection from Distributive Justice', will be dealt with in chapter two.
74. Another important constructivist is Bruce Ackerman. Ackerman uses the idea of neutral dialogue

as a means of generating distributive principles. See Ackerman, 1980.

75. Rawls does not claim that such a situation ever existed: it is merely hypothetical. See Rawls, 1972, pp.21-22.
76. Ibid., p.18.
77. Ibid, p.152. Rawls cites the following works as being the sources of his work on game theory: Baumol, 1965 and Luce and Raiffa, 1957.
78. Rawls, 1972, pp.150-161.
79. Ibid., p.60.
80. Ibid., p.83.
81. Ibid., p.252.
82. Wolff, 1977, pp.112-15.
83. Rawls, 1972, p.256.
84. Ibid., p.255.
85. Rawls writes: "To regard persons as ends in themselves in the basic design of society is to agree to forgo those gains which do not contribute to their representative expectations. By contrast to regard persons as means is to be prepared to impose upon them lower prospects of life for the sake of the higher expectations of others. Thus, we see that the difference principle, which at first appears rather extreme, has a reasonable interpretation.", ibid., p.180.
86. Similar claims concerning the non-Kantian aspects of Rawls theory have also been made by Sutton, 1979 and Johnson, 1977.
87. Nussbaum, 1990, pp.242-43.
88. Rawls, 1972, pp.395-399.
89. Ibid., p.396.
90. As Stephen Darwall notes when examining Rawls's Kantian foundations: ".....it is difficult to see how the universal law formulation of the Categorical Imperative can be used to ground duties to perform particular actions in particular circumstances without reference to an account of the Good for rational agents conceived as such.", Darwall, 1980, p.325.
91. Rawls, 1972, p.424.
92. Ibid., p.396.
93. This is in fact analogous to Singer's defence of Kantian ethical theory, in which it is claimed that the formal Categorical Imperative is to be brought to bear on empirical details concerning such things as the human good. See Singer, 1961, p.251.
94. Rawls, 1972, p.62.
95. Woolcock, 1984, p.238.
96. Rawls, 1972, p.396.
97. Ibid., p.395.
98. Ibid., p.433.
99. Ibid., p.92.
100. As Stephen Darwall argues: "Primary goods are of value to the parties not just because they will enable them to advance their aim, whatever they happen to be, but also from the standpoint of the parties flourishing as rational choosers of ends. Liberties, opportunities and wealth assure the scope rationally to criticise pursuits in a meaningful way.", Darwall, 1980, p.325.
101. Rawls, 1972, p.408.
102. Ibid., pp.398-99.
103. Rawls, 1980 p.517.
104. Ibid., p.518.
105. Rawls, 1988, p.252.
106. Ibid., p.253.
107. Ibid., p.252.
108. Ibid., p.252.
109. Rawls, 1985, p.230.
110. Rawls, 1989, p.35.
111. Rawls, 1987, p.1.
112. Rawls writes of the liberalisms of Kant and Mill that they are: "....general in that they apply to a wide range of subjects and comprehensive in that they include conceptions of what is of value in

human life, ideals of personal virtue and character that are to inform our thought and conduct as a whole. Here we have in mind Kant's ideal of autonomy and his connecting it with other values of the Enlightenment, and Mill's ideal of individuality and his connecting it with values of modernity." Rawls, ibid., p.6.

113. Rawls, 1985, p.230.
114. See Rawls, 1987, pp.1-25. Cf. Hampton, 1989, p.794.
115. See Nagel, 1975, p.7.
116. It is this conception of humans as 'autonomous' that is one of the main factors which separates Rawls' rationalism from the pure want-regarding naturalism of the Humean tradition, of which David Gauthier is the most recent exponent. See Gauthier, 1986.
117. Galston, 1980, p.114.
118. See de Vogue, 1983.
119. De Marneffe, 1990, pp.252-74. Cf. Doppelt, 1989, pp.815-51.
120. Rawls, 1980, p.518.
121. Cf. White, 1988, p.22.
122. Gutmann, 1985, p.319.
123. Rawls, 1987, p.14
124. "...I suppose with utilitarianism that the good is defined as the satisfaction of rational desire.", Rawls, 1972, p.30.
125. According to Barry, Rawls wishes for example: " ...to say that the desire of someone to practice his religion freely should have priority over the desire of another man to stop him, even if the second man's desire is more intense than the first, or if those who want to worship are outnumbered by those who want to suppress and each person has the same intensity of desire for what he wants.", Barry, 1973, p.22.
126. Ibid., p.22.
127. Rawls, 1972, p.426.
128. Ibid., p.424.
129. Nussbaum, 1990, p.217.

2 Distributive justice and the necessity of sacrifice

Sacrifice and internalism

In this chapter I shall consider a second Rawlsian argument which bears on my internalist methodology. This Rawlsian argument concerns the putative connection between consequentialist social theory grounded in conceptions of the individual human good and various undesirable conclusions which contravene our intuitions about justice. For the purposes of simplicity let us assume that this Rawlsian argument against utilitarianism concerns utilitarianism's consequentialism, not its employment of a conception of the good. Thus it is of relevance to my central thesis because the conception of the good I shall use is broadly consequentialist; accordingly it is of relevance as a critique of my particular internalism, not internalism *per se*. Rawls' attack is focussed upon utilitarianism, arguing, as he does, that this doctrine is morally unacceptable because:

i) it sanctions the possibility of social institutions sacrificing persons' interests, rights and lives (the Objection from Sacrifice) and;

ii) it is insensitive to the shape of distributive outcomes (the Objection from Distributive Justice).

For Rawls, the cause of these repugnant phenomena is to be found in the application of maximising consequentialist moral reasoning to problems of social justice. While appropriate when applied to the realm of prudential reasoning, i.e the individual's pursuit of his or her own good, consequentialist ethical theory is inappropriate, according to Rawls, when applied to issues of social justice. Rawls attempts to formulate his theory of justice in the light of these perceived inadequacies.[1]

However, because his objections concern utilitarianism's maximising tendencies, his criticisms actually pertain to all forms of consequentialism. Given that the internalist methodology of this dissertation involves the application of a consequentialist account of the human good to the question of distributive justice, we can see that Rawls' criticisms must be addressed. In this chapter I shall also consider Nozick's criticisms of utilitarianism which, unlike those of Rawls, focus directly on the relationship between conceptions of the good and sacrifice. As such Nozick provides an externalist critique of utilitarianism which also must be addressed.

In meeting the challenge laid down by Nozick and Rawls, then I shall argue:

i) that the social practice of distributive justice necessarily requires sacrifice (that is, sacrifice is a constitutive component of distributive justice);

ii) that the sacrifice that any particular distributive theory permits is determined either tacitly or explicitly by the theorist's conception of the human good;

iii) employing a conception of the human good which is characterised by hierarchically ordered categories of interests, it is possible to maximise across persons without sacrificing whole persons and to be 'distributively sensitive'.

It is my hope that such arguments will provide the grounds for an adequate defence of the use of consequentialism in distributive theory. Furthermore, given that Nozick's criticisms are criticisms of internalism *per se*, rejection of his position will provide further argumentation in support of the internalist project.

Consequentialism

Given that it is utilitarianism's maximising consequentialism which Rawls finds problematic, let us begin by clarifying to what the term 'consequentialism' refers. It is probably easiest to initiate discussion of this matter by contrasting consequentialism with deontology. For the deontologist, there are some actions which one should never undertake (such as killing, lying or breaking promises) regardless of their consequences. Such an approach to moral issues can be found in the works of philosophers such as Kant and W.D. Ross, as well as being a central plank of many religions. On the other hand, according to the consequentialist whether any action should be undertaken depends upon its consequences. The right action is the one directed toward the production of the best overall balance of good over bad, subject to the definition of some fundamental value. Thus no action or social policy is necessarily ruled out until one examines the consequences.

The source of the difference between these two approaches can be found in their contrasting ethical foundations. Deontic theorists locate the rightness or wrongness of an action in the action itself: for instance, it is the very act of killing in itself which is wrong. Consequentialist theories, on the other hand, locate value in the consequences of action; that is, in states of affairs causally connected to various actions. Here we may follow Bernard Williams who takes the central idea of consequentialism to be that the only kinds of things which have value in themselves are states of affairs and that anything else which has value, has value because it conduces to some intrinsically valuable state of affairs.[2]

> A distinctive mark of consequentialism might rather be this, that it regards the value of actions as always consequential (or as we may more generally say, derivative) and not intrinsic. The value of actions would then lie in their causal properties of producing valuable states of affairs.....[3]

Williams contrasts consequentialism with views which ascribe moral significance to actions in themselves.[4]

In short, then, we may ascribe the following characteristics to consequentialism: i) value is located in states of affairs; ii) the value of actions lies in their causal properties of producing valuable states of affairs; iii) actions therefore are not valuable in an intrinsic sense, but rather are only valuable derivatively.

There are other salient features of consequentialist theories. Given that the right action is the one which brings about valuable states of affairs, it would seem to follow that the greater amount of valuable states of affairs that an action produces, then the more valuable it is. As Williams notes, the right action is that which out of the actions available to the agent brings about or represents the highest degree of whatever it is the system regards as intrinsically valuable – and in the central case, utilitarianism, this of course is happiness.[5] Accordingly, consequentialism is a *maximising* doctrine. We may say, given the relationship outlined above between value and consequential states of affairs, that maximising is a *constitutive* property of consequentialism. Moreover, consequentialism's maximising properties do not only extend to the moral decisions of individuals; in both moral questions and issues of social policy, consequentialism is a maximising doctrine.[6] According to the consequentialist, society is rightly ordered when its major institutions are arranged so as to maximise certain valuable states of affairs.

Maximising and sacrifice: the Rawlsian critique of consequentialism

Thus far, then, I have argued that a conceptual relation holds between consequentialism's location of value and its maximising tendencies, and accordingly we may conclude that if particular accounts of the human good are consequentialist, then, they too must be maximising.[7] Let us now examine some criticisms of consequentialism.[8]

It is probably best to begin our discussion by considering some toy examples to illustrate the problems which arise when one employs the utilitarian calculus to determine social theory.[9]

Example 1: The majority of the people in a democratic country come to realise that they are thoroughly sick of household chores; the performance of such chores wastes their precious time and is the cause of much domestic conflict. Thus, it is democratically decided to enslave all of the aboriginal inhabitants of that country, who constitute only a tiny minority of the population and assign to them the household tasks of the rest of the population. This act is seen to increase the sum total of happiness.[10]

Example 2: A local council decides to build a highway over an Indian burial ground, in the belief that the highway will shorten the time most people spend on the road each day and thus make the majority of citizens happier.

Example 3: A doctor on the verge of discovering a cure to a disease which kills millions of people has run out of bodies on which to experiment. He thus buys corpses from the Mafia, in full knowledge of the fact that the Mafia has killed these people in order to supply him with the necessary experimental material.

Each of these cases involves actions which many persons would intuitively find morally repugnant. They involve violations which are generated because of the usage of the utilitarian calculus. The first example contravenes our belief that it is wrong to enslave people; the second, the belief that Indian sacred sites should be respected; and the third, the belief that all human beings have a right to life. These three examples involve sacrificing social policy which social institutions may assent to when following the utilitarian calculus. They are sacrificing in the sense that they lead to the loss of some person's interests in order to improve the lot of the members of society as a whole. In the first a minority people are enslaved, in the second basic rights of persons are sacrificed, while in the third the lives of whole persons are sacrificed for the greatest good of the greatest number. It seems that these problems might arise for the utilitarian—regardless of whether one characterises the maximisation of utility as the greatest sum total of utility or as the greatest number of people receiving the benefits of utility[11]—so long as one characterises justice as derivative of efficiency.[12]

Employing the utilitarian calculus for social decision-making may also make it possible to justify massive inequalities of wealth, so long as these inequalities give rise to the greatest amount of total utility. Rawls claims that utilitarianism gives no direct weight to considerations of justice or fairness in the distribution of goods. Such a possibility has led to what I will call the 'Objection from distributive justice' according to which utilitarianism is a morally repugnant doctrine because it is insensitive to the actual shape of distributive outcomes.[13]

It is just these sorts of cases to which Rawls addresses his criticisms of utilitarianism. In attempting to locate the theoretical cause of utilitarianism's counter-intuitive conclusions, Rawls begins by noting that according to utilitarianism, a society is properly arranged when its institutions maximise the net balance of satisfaction – the correct distribution being that which yields maximum fulfilment.[14] Rawls then points to utilitarianism's ambivalence toward the ways in which satisfactions are distributed amongst individuals. He argues that the striking feature of the utilitarian view of justice is that it does not matter, except indirectly, how this sum of satisfaction is distributed.[15] Provided that net aggregate satisfaction is maximised, utilitarianism is indifferent as to how various satisfactions and dissatisfactions are to be distributed. So, if overall satisfaction will be maximised under an arrangement in which goods and resources are channelled to people whose circumstances are already comfortable, while other people are allowed to languish in abject poverty, then that arrangement is precisely the one that the utilitarian will endorse. Alternatively, if the total happiness will be minimally increased by denying freedom to a few, then, again that is what utilitarianism will recommend. The utilitarian calculus may even require one to perform the 'horrible act', such as killing innocent persons. Utilitarianism requires people to do whatever will, in a given situation, produce the best overall outcome; and as Thomas Nagel emphasises in 'War and Massacre'[16], this may mean doing something quite horrible.

Rawls believes the conceptual mechanism which generates these sacrificing outcomes is the extension of permissible cases of sacrifice from individuals to whole societies. He argues that whilst it is permissible for individuals to sacrifice *across their own lives,* i.e. across single lives, sacrifice should not be allowed to go beyond these boundaries.[17] Rawls points out that utilitarianism involves the application of the same process of reasoning across the whole of society.[18] It attempts to sum satisfactions and desires across individuals as if they were the satisfactions and desires of an individual at different times of their life.[19] (This criticism of utilitarianism presumably would apply to any form of consequentialist social policy, because it involves the application of what is an acceptable individual moral theory at the level of social policy).

According to Rawls then, such a process of reasoning is morally unacceptable because it leads ultimately to the unjust sacrifice of human interests and human lives. Rawls' view here is predicated upon the moral intuition that justice must involve all people; that is, it assumes what we may call 'moral equality'.[20] (This claim, of course, is Kantian in inspiration, even though Kant himself never drew egalitarian conclusions from the condition of treating each individual as an end in himself).[21] Rawls claims that for the utilitarian there is no reason in principle why the losses of some should not be compensated by the greater gains of others, or alternatively, why the violation of a minority may not be made morally permissible by the good it causes for the majority.[22] (This point is reminiscent of our earlier example of the enslaved aborigines.)

Thus, according to Rawls, utilitarianism is ultimately said to founder because it fails to recognise the *separateness of persons* in its normative calculations.

> This view of social cooperation is the consequence of extending to society the principle of choice for one man, and then, to make this extension work, conflating all persons into one through the imaginative acts of the impartial sympathetic spectator. Utilitarianism does not take seriously the distinction between persons.[23]

The failure to respect the separateness of persons is problematic because of the sacrifice and distributive insensitivity it engenders.[24]

Partially in response to the perceived failures of utilitarianism[25], Rawls formulates his theory of 'justice as fairness' in which the 'right' is given priority over the 'good'.[26]

Rawls thus advocates an externalist strategy in which principles of distributive justice are derived from the right, rather than the good. This theory he categorises as non-teleological, rather than as characterising the rightness of institutions and acts independently of their consequences.[27]

We may also discern this concern with utilitarianism's sacrificing tendencies reflected in the manner in which Rawls formulates the difference principle. This principle, which states that inequalities are only permissible if they make the worst-off better off, protects the welfare of those whom implementation of the utilitarian calculus may possibly harm.

Another theorist who finds utilitarianism (and consequentialism more generally) problematic is Robert Nozick. In *Anarchy, State and Utopia*, after arguing in accordance with Rawls that utilitarianism has a counter-intuitive willingness to sacrifice across lives, Nozick uses the concept of 'rights' to make sense of where utilitarianism goes wrong. He claims that utilitarians fail to take rights and their non-violation into account, instead leaving them a derivative status. He believes that many of the counter-intuitive examples used to discredit utilitarianism, such as punishing an innocent man to save a neighbourhood from a vengeful rampage, can be understood as arising from a failure to recognise rights.[28] For Nozick, the greatest good for the greatest number inevitably leads to the sacrifice of persons' rights to liberty and property.

Nozick claims that the origin of such sacrificing behaviour is to be found in the failure of utilitarianism to treat persons as ends. With this in mind he attempts to develop a non-consequentialist theory which reflects the Kantian Principle that people are not merely means, but ends in their own right and thus may not be sacrificed or used for the achievement of ends which are not their own.[29] For Nozick, it is the failure to treat people as ends which leads maximising consequentialism to sacrifice.

Nozick connects this failure to treat persons as ends not simply to consequentialism, but to conceptions of the human good. He thus sees sacrifice as a *necessary* condition of any teleological theory of justice, such as utilitarianism, which grounds social justice in conceptions of the human good. Nozick's work here constitutes a direct attack upon internalism.

However, lest my claim be misunderstood, we should note that Nozick's non-consequentialist strategy, unlike that of Rawls, is not based on the denial of the good in moral calculation, but rather on the claim that in the generation of distributive principles, the good must have *side-constraints* placed upon it. These side constraints impose non-consequentialist limits upon the good. Instead of incorporating rights into the desired end-state, Nozick advocates placing them as side-constraints upon the required action. Thus the rights of other people determine the constraints upon any of a person's actions.[30] This means in effect that a goal directed approach with constraints added would generate an imperative of the following form: "...among those acts available to you that don't violate constraint C, act so as to maximize goal G."[31] Here the rights of others would constrain a person's goal-directed behaviour. It is from these side constraints that principles of distributive justice are to be derived. Nozick contrasts this approach with the consequentialist view of right, in which an attempt is made to build the side constraint C into the goal. A side-constraints approach forbids the violation of moral rights, when persons are in pursuit of their goals; whereas an approach which advocates the minimisation of the violation of such rights enables persons to violate these moral constraints in order to lessen the total violation of such rights in the society as a whole.[32]

We can see from Nozick's discussion that he believes the problem is not just consequentialist conceptions of the good, but conceptions of the good *per se*. Nozick believes that principles of distributive justice should be derived from such side-constraints and that the human good should have no place in the generation of such principles. Nozick presents what is essentially an externalist strategy in which distributive rules are derived from non-axiological principles; in which distributive principles are derived from deontic side constraints.[33]

From the foregoing discussion, it would seem then that any consequentialist social theory requires some justification. Rawls and Nozick both desire to generate social theory which respects the separateness of persons and both attempt to generate distributive principles from sources other than conceptions of the human good. With Nozick and Rawls, we have examples of the two major sources of opposition to the internalist approach and two alternative strategies; firstly, a rights based view, which generates principles of justice from certain rights (which he characterises as deontic side constraints upon action); and secondly a neo-Kantian theory, which on the interpretation given above, attempts to generate principles of justice from the decisions of rational agents.[34] Rawls' opposition to internalism has already been dealt with, and Nozick's will be briefly examined as this chapter proceeds. I shall argue that both theorists actually employ conceptions of the good in formulating principles of distributive justice and, moreover, that this is *necessarily* the case because the good is a necessary condition of any theory of distributive justice.[35]

Commensurability and sacrifice

It would seem then that consequentialism's location of value in overall states of affairs and its accompanying maximising strategy brings with it a failure to recognise the separateness of persons and thus gives rise to sacrifice. It is this issue of sacrifice which I shall consider in this next section. Is it possible to avoid sacrifice in the context of issues of distributive justice or is sacrifice a necessary condition of the practice of distributive justice?

If the practice of distributing benefits and burdens is examined closely, it becomes apparent that this practice operates within the context of an important empirical constraint; namely, the fact of scarcity. This is a constraint which any theory which attempts to formulate principles to determine just distributions must take into consideration.

Scarcity

The practice of distributive justice is intimately connected to constraints imposed by the empirical fact of scarcity. By 'scarcity' I mean that state of affairs in which the world is such that it is impossible for all of the human interests which distributive goods realise to flourish. Such scarcity may be the product of human interference or alternatively the result of natural processes. Scarcity may be usefully contrasted with abundance. Abundance refers to states of affairs in which sufficient resources exist for the flourishing of all of the human interests which distributive goods might possibly realise. We may also distinguish between two kinds of scarcity: namely *moderate scarcity* and *hard scarcity*.[36] In conditions of moderate scarcity it is possible to distribute goods universally. However, it is characteristic of hard scarcity that resources cannot be distributed universally. In conditions of hard scarcity supplies of goods reach such low levels that if they were to be distributed universally, they would no longer be the goods that they are. If we consider the case in which there are only two kidney machines in a remote village and fifty people who wish to use that resource, then we would be confronted with a case of hard scarcity. Conditions of hard scarcity give rise to distributive issues, just as conditions of moderate scarcity do.

The ideas of abundance and scarcity have had a central role to play in much philosophical discussion of distribution. For instance, Hume, in considering the relation between justice and the quantity of goods available for distribution in *An Enquiry Concerning the Principle of Morals*, invites us to compare three different situations. If goods were so abundant that everyone could satisfy all claims and desires without exhausting the available supply, no questions of justice would arise, and thus no rules about distribution would be required. If goods were so scarce that some persons must perish and all be wretched, then the strict laws of justice would be suspended. Thus justice, according to Hume, corresponds to conditions of moderate scarcity, in which claims and desires exceed available resources, but in which no individual need be deprived of existence or the bare necessities of life.[37] Similarly, Rawls excludes conditions of hard scarcity from distributive justice. He distinguishes between scarcity, sufficiency and luxury and notes that it is moderate scarcity with which distributive justice is concerned.[38]

In the writings of Marx we may also discern a concern with the relation between conditions of supply and the issue of distributive justice. On some plausible readings of Marx, it is belief in the possibility of abundance that led him to reject the issues of distributive justice.[39] Marx believed that the development of the means of production by the capitalist mode of production would eventually lead to the elimination of scarcity and the realisation of a condition of *universal bounty*.[40] Marx held little hope for the resolution of conflict over the distribution of resources in conditions of scarcity. He thus ignored issues of distributive justice, believing that the problem would be eliminated by the development of society's productive forces. Many people would now argue that such a view is untenable because of their belief that the earth's ecology cannot sustain the kind of industrial development that universal bounty would require.[41] However, those environmental issues notwithstanding, Marx's concerns provide a clue to what the problem of distributive justice consists of. His work refers us to the intimate connection between scarcity and problems of distributive justice.[42] If conditions of scarcity obtain then the problem of distributive justice arises.[43]

At this point it might be tempting to make the claim (as Hume in fact does), that scarcity is a *necessary* condition of the practice of determining how benefits and burdens should be allocated, i.e. that the existence of scarcity is necessary for issues of distributive justice to arise. On this view, while the existence or non-existence of scarcity would be an empirical question, which could only be answered by empirical observation, the idea that scarcity is required for the existence of the practice of determining the justice of various distributions would be a conceptual truth. While the practice of distribution does not require scarcity, the practice of distributive justice would be said to require it. This theory concerning the relation between scarcity and the problem of justice would explain many phenomena such as the fact that often in periods of economic expansion questions of distributive justice are muted.

However, it is difficult to defend this claim that scarcity is *constitutive* of distributive justice, for the simple reason that it implies that in conditions of abundance there would no longer be any disputes about the distribution of social resources. Consider the following counter-examples.[44] Firstly, it is possible in conditions of abundance that people would not know that abundance had been achieved, and thus they would fight over distributive goods. Thus, due to the ignorance of the agents in question, debates about appropriate patterns of distribution would still arise. Secondly, even if material abundance were to be achieved, it is quite possible that people would fight over non-material positional goods which confer status and power. William Galston notes in *Justice and the Human Good* that Hume's tendency to restrict the *scope* of justice to material goods enabled him to imagine that abundance is at least a logical possibility and thus that the bounty of nature could make the problem of justice disappear. Galston argues that this overlooks the existence of goods which are not subject to natural increase, "competition for which *in principle* produces a shortage". Here he is thinking of positions of authority, political power and all *positional* goods.[45] A Humean might reply that the elimination of disputes over material goods would mean that coercive political organisation would no longer be needed and thus positional goods would also be eliminated in conditions of abundance.[46] But political disputes also arise in relation to the question of what the ends of collective activity should be. Non-material positional goods will therefore continue to exist. Similarly the Marxian emphasis upon material abundance, overlooks the fact that there are non-material goods with which principles of distributive justice must deal. Finally, we might wonder whether in situations of extreme necessity justice as a whole is suspended or only the rules that usually obtain.[47]

Given these difficulties, we must be content with simply claiming that material scarcity is a *sufficient*, rather than a necessary condition, for questions of distributive justice to arise. However, what can be said more confidently is that where there is competition for goods, there will be a problem of allocation, and scarcity is one such situation which gives rise to competition for goods. Moreover, given the empirical fact of scarcity it will follow that the problem of determining the distribution of benefits and burdens will arise.

This argument which aims to establish the intimate connection between scarcity and problems of distributive justice can be outlined schematically in the following manner:

1. Where there is competition for goods, there will be a problem of allocation.
2. Scarcity is one way in which competition may be engendered.
3. It is an empirical fact that we are currently in conditions of scarcity.
4. Thus, the problem of distributive justice necessarily arises in the current conditions.

This, of course, is not to say that the problem of distributive justice could not arise in other circumstances. The argument simply demonstrates the intimate connection between distributive justice and scarcity, which is such that where there is scarcity, there will be problems of distributive justice. Theories of distributive justice must take this connection into account.

Commensurability and scarcity

Let us now consider what might be involved in the formulation and implementation of principles of distributive justice (which jointly we may refer to as the '*practice of distributive justice*'). Amongst other things, the practice of distributive justice necessarily requires that the principles formulated be *commensurable*. (By 'commensurable' I simply mean the capacity to be standardly applied across relevant groups of people.) The practice of distributive justice involves *inter alia* the formulation and application of allocative principles across whole groups of people, using standards which are to apply to all relevant persons. In effect, it is a practice which requires that decisions be made *across* persons, regardless of the fact that not all such interests can be satisfied. If this fact of *commensurability* is considered in the light of the constraint of scarcity, it seems inevitable that we reach the conclusion that this practice of distributive justice necessarily requires sacrifice in terms of loss for some members of the society concerned. (Here the term 'sacrifice' is used to designate *potential loss* rather than the voluntary relinquishing of goods) When conditions of scarcity obtain then the practice of distributive justice necessarily requires sacrifice in the sense outlined above. Let us consider this connection between conditions of scarcity and sacrifice in more detail.

The existence of conditions of scarcity ensures that not all potential interests social resources could realise are in fact realised. However, principles of distributive justice provide distributive agencies with guidance in the allocation of goods. Using commensurable standards they provide means of assessing various competing claims on social resources and in so doing direct distributive agencies towards the satisfaction of some interests in preference to others. Thus, while bringing about the satisfaction of some interests, the practice of distributive justice inevitably results in the sacrifice of other interests which social resources could have been used to realise. For instance, if conditions of scarcity obtain, and the choice must be made between the allocation of social resources to gifted children or to the disabled, then whichever group is chosen will receive those goods at the expense of the other group. The group which is denied resources will, in a certain sense, be sacrificed. So long as there is scarcity, the allocation of social resources toward the realisation of specific interests will necessarily sacrifice other interests which would have been realised by these resources. Given the fact of scarcity, sacrifice is a necessary condition of the practice of distributive justice.[48] Of course, this does not mean that the implementation of principles of distributive justice necessarily requires any *particular* sacrifice (such as the killing of the weak for scientific experimentation), however it does require sacrifice of some kind.

Let us outline this argument about the relationship between the practice of distributive justice and sacrifice schematically.

1. The practice of distributive justice, i.e. the formulation and implementation of principles of distributive justice, occurs under conditions of scarcity.
2. Scarcity ensures that not all interests which social resources could potentially realise, can be realised.
3. The practice of distributive justice involves the formulation and application of *commensurate* principles of allocation *across* social groups; these social groups possessing sets of interests, not all of which can be satisfied.
4. These commensurate principles: (i) contain rules about which sets of interests should be satisfied; (ii) when implemented guide distributive agencies in choosing which sets of interests (out of the complete set) are to be satisfied.
5. Hence, by parity of reasoning, these commensurable principles also guide distributive agencies in choosing which interests are *not* to be satisfied.
6. Those interests which are not satisfied may be said to be 'sacrificed' in favour of other interests.
7. Thus, the practice of distributive justice necessarily involves sacrifice.

My argument that the allocation of distributive resources necessarily involves sacrifice rests on what might be called a *modal* account of sacrifice.[49] By 'sacrifice', I mean the failure to satisfy any *possible* claims on distributive resources. It is thus a modal account because sacrifice is not defined in terms of legitimate claims on distributive resources, but rather in terms of *possible* claims. Applying this modal account to the issue of distributive justice is to say that any distributive principle implemented will involve the sacrifice of some possible claim on distributive resources.

In short then the argument here is that: (i) principles of distributive justice contain certain rules concerning which interests should be satisfied; (ii) the application of principles of distributive justice involves the satisfaction of particular interests and hence; (iii) the practice of distributive justice necessarily involves sacrifice (at least in a modal sense). In order to illustrate this argument about the nature of the relationship between sacrifice and distributive theories let us consider an actual distributive principle, Rawls' difference principle which we mentioned in passing in the previous chapter.

As outlined in *A Theory of Justice*, the difference principle states that "social and economic inequalities are to be arranged so that they are both a) to the greatest advantage of the least advantaged and b) attached to offices and positions open to all under conditions of fair equality of opportunity".[50] While acknowledging the necessity of some social and economic inequalities, the difference principle directs distributive agencies towards ensuring that these inequalities are arranged so as to further the welfare of the worst-off. What is of importance here for Rawls is that the level of welfare of the worst-off be maximised.

With this in mind let us return to the example provided earlier of a conflict over whether resources should be allocated to the disabled or to the gifted (the arguments here are not Rawls' of course, but rather a hypothetical extrapolation of Rawls' principle, given certain empirical circumstances). Let us suppose that the disabled are to count as the least-advantaged and also that empirical conditions are such that in this case the worst-off will be best off if resources are diverted from the more advantaged (the gifted) to the least-advantaged. Having decided that Rawls is correct and hence that his principles of justice are truly just, the distributive agency, confronted with a dilemma over how to distribute resources, implements the difference principle. This particular distributive agency, assessing the empirical conditions, decides that resources must be allocated to the disabled rather than to the gifted. Hence social resources are directed towards the provision of wheelchairs, rather than towards programs for further encouraging the gifted. In this case, there are possible interests of the gifted which could have been realised had resources not been directed towards the disabled. Thus, we may say that, in the sense outlined earlier, the implementation of the difference principle sacrifices potential interests of the gifted. Equally, if resources had been directed towards the gifted, it might be said that implementation of the difference principle sacrifices potential interests of the disabled. Either way the difference principle, when implemented, necessarily sacrifices some potential interests which could have been realised by social resources.

In summary then, given the existence of conditions of scarcity, the implementation of principles of distributive justice necessarily involves sacrifice because: (i) there will be some possible interests not realised, which could have been realised had not social resources been directed elsewhere; (ii) it is the distributive principles themselves which direct distributive agencies in not realising these particular interests. Sacrifice then is a necessary condition of the practice of distributive justice.

What then are we to make of this claim that given certain empirical facts about the world, sacrifice is a necessary condition of systems of distribution? Does it make a nonsense of the 'Rawlsian' critique of utilitarianism outlined earlier? If all theories of distributive justice necessarily involve sacrifice, then what is the point of accusing utilitarianism of permitting unacceptable sacrifice? Does this mean that we should disregard the various critiques of utilitarianism, in relation to distributive theory?

I think that there is sense to be found in the Rawlsian critique of utilitarianism: the thesis merely needs to be more carefully stated. What critics of utilitarianism oppose is not sacrifice *per se*, for it is practically impossible to do so, but rather they are opposed to *specific kinds* of sacrifice. For instance they are opposed, amongst other things, to the sacrifice of whole human lives, for the greater good of the greatest number. Yet, while most of these critics are opposed to the sorts of sacrifices which are standardly thrown at utilitarians, beyond these standard cases there is no real consensus over what sorts of sacrifices are acceptable. If we take Nozick as an example, we discover that he finds the sacrifice of a person's property morally abhorrent,[51] while Rawls is quite willing to sacrifice some property rights if such sacrifice is required to make the worst off best off. Thus, there is a large degree of variance over which kinds of sacrifice are acceptable.

You might of course argue that I am misrepresenting Rawls' views. If we cast our minds back to the discussion of Rawls' objections to utilitarianism, we will recall that Rawls made two claims about the doctrine:

i) utilitarianism is not a respecter of the separateness of persons and;

ii) utilitarianism is prepared to sacrifice persons.

One might not be convinced of the moral repugnance of i) and be tempted to question what is wrong with failing to respect the separateness of persons; the reply to which would be that i) is problematic simply because it leads to ii).

Indeed, it is this very concern with respecting the separateness of persons that in part leads Rawls to construct the original position in the way that he does. The aim of the original position is to derive principles of justice which respect the separateness of persons and thus do not sacrifice people. Have I thus not misrepresented Rawls by arguing that his theory, like all theories of distributive justice, must inevitably lead to the sacrifice of persons?

There is some truth in such criticism. It does seem to be quite plausible to argue that in the original position persons are not sacrificed and the separateness of persons is respected. However, the original position is *not* itself a distributive principle. It is not a principle which Rawls believes should govern the distribution of benefits and burdens. It is merely a hypothetical position from which principles of justice can be derived. In fact, close examination of the difference principle reveals that it cannot respect the separateness of persons because it involves *commensurating* across persons. At the level of the original position his theory involves recognition of the separateness of persons, but it does not respect their separateness at the distributive level. Thus, the difference principle involves sacrifice, in that the interests of the well-off will be sacrificed for the worst-off, so long as such sacrifice enables the worst-off to be better off.

Some readers might also object that my argument works only because the word 'sacrifice' is used equivocally; that is to say that defining sacrifice in modal terms involves a significant shift in meaning from its ordinary language usage as well as its usage in the Rawlsian critique of utilitarianism. According to this objection, we should not talk about 'sacrifice' in modal terms, because the word properly applies to specific claims about the illegitimate treatment of persons. To sacrifice a person or their interests in some manner should be thought of as a way of treating them illegitimately.

However, let us firstly consider the ordinary language usages of the term. If we do so, we discover a wide variety of uses which cannot be unified under any one particular theory of legitimate treatment. Furthermore, examination of ordinary language also reveals no intimate connection between the ideas of sacrifice and legitimate treatment. It is possible to imagine cases where we would consider that some person is being sacrificed without believing it to be an illegitimate form of treatment. Finally, if we consider Rawls' usage of the term, we find that although he discusses *particular* cases of sacrifice (which presumably are to be thought of as illegitimate forms of treatment according to some moral standpoint), Rawls uses these example to make a connection between utilitarianism's maximising tendencies and sacrifice in general.[52] Thus, use of a modal account is appropriate because Rawls' critique involves the idea of sacrifice in general and the modal account is the best way of accounting for sacrifice in general.

Sacrifice and the human good

Thus far, I have argued that rather than being opposed to sacrifice *per se*, critics of utilitarianism who focus on sacrifice are antagonistic to specific forms of sacrifice. This, in effect, is a consequence of the fact that, given the empirical fact of scarcity, sacrifice is a necessary condition of the practice of distributive justice. Furthermore, as I noted in previous sections, there is no real consensus amongst the various opponents of utilitarianism as to which forms of sacrifice are acceptable. How then, given these facts, do they choose between forms of sacrifice? What criteria are to be used (or are, as a matter of fact, employed) for determining whether or not a form of sacrifice is acceptable?

Closer inspection reveals that what is required to choose between forms of sacrifice is a conception of *priority* or *urgency*, which orders the various possible sacrifices in a list from the most acceptable to the least acceptable. However, we can say more than this. This ordering of priority is not just a random process; but reflects the theorist's explicit or tacit conception of the human good. Regardless of whether or not a person has an explicit theory of the good capable of being expressed propositionally, the ordering of these sacrifices reflects at the very least a *tacit* theory what it is that makes human lives good.

Examination of Nozick's rights-based deontic theory is illustrative of the claim that the sacrifice chosen reflects the theorist's conception of human nature. Nozick asserts that his principles of distributive justice are derived from deontic side constraints, rather than the good, these side-constraints being grounded in the Kantian principle of Respect for Persons. From this principle he derives the conclusion that all persons are self-owners[53], and it is from this conception of self-ownership that he grounds his attack upon Rawlsian redistribution (and indeed upon redistribution by governments more generally). Nozick argues that no one has a right to something whose realisation requires certain uses of things and activities that other people have rights and entitlements over.[54] Nozick is not concerned about whether redistribution would be used to save another's life or contribute to their freedom. For Nozick, it does not matter that some other approach better serves peoples' material interests or their autonomy.[55] He believes that redistribution is incompatible with recognising persons as self-owners.[56]

Clearly, Nozick tacitly endorses the right of all persons to self-ownership and this is incompatible with the idea of a necessary right of all persons to a share of the goods and services that a society produces. In order to understand this claim, it is necessary to understand the conception of persons that Nozick is using. Nozick believes that self-ownership not only involves the individual's body, but also ownership over external resources; self-ownership yields absolute property rights. This is his central claim about what matters morally about human beings.

Nozick's theory, then, involves a view of the human good which determines the shape of his so-called side-constraints upon the good. The existence of this conception is at odds with the externalist claim that his principles are derived from side-constraints upon the good, rather than from the good itself.[57] The side-constraints which he actually chooses reflect his tacit conception of the human good, for the reason that there is an infinite variety of possible, competing side-constraints from which one could choose. That Nozick chooses the particular side-constraints he does, demonstrates that these side-constraints constitute a *de facto* theory of the human good. Whilst it might appear at first sight that Nozick successfully generates externalist principles of distributive justice, when implemented as distributive policy his theory will necessarily contain criteria for choosing between various human interests and thus encoded within the theory must be an implicit principle of priority in relation to the human good. Again, this is no accident. In formulating his principles of justice, Nozick uses a tacit conception of persons which, when implemented, enables these principles to distinguish between competing claims for distributive goods.

The most obvious conclusion to draw from this discussion is that given that sacrifice is a necessary condition of distributive justice (assuming scarcity) and given that the sacrifice which any particular theory prohibits or permits is determined by its conception of human nature, then, it seems to follow that under such circumstances, a theory of human nature is a necessary condition of the practice of generating principles of distributive justice. This again provides further vindication of the internalist thesis.

An internalist solution

Where does all this argumentation lead us? Does it deliver us to the abyss of what we might call 'distributive scepticism', i.e. the view that we cannot form genuine theories of distributive justice. Given that sacrifice of some sort is a necessary condition of the practice of distributive justice, does this mean that we must accept the justice of the enslavement of our group of aborigines for the good of the whole, or the killing of the weak and the elderly for experimentation which may save thousands of lives? Do we have grounds for asserting which forms of sacrifice are just and which are unjust?

In order to determine where we should go from here, I think it is important to begin with what has already been ascertained. Firstly, I have argued that any plausible theory of distributive justice must ultimately be an internalist one. Given that sacrifice is constitutive of distributive justice under conditions of scarcity, and that the sacrifice which any theory permits or disavows is dependent upon a theory of human nature, then the practice of implementing principles of distributive justice relies upon a theory of the good.

Secondly, if the conception of the good is consequentialist—and there is some good evidence that all conceptions of the good are consequentialist—then, it would seem that the conception of the good is a maximising notion. *Ipso facto,* this is neither implausible nor problematic.[58]

However, it is precisely with respect to this issue of maximising that it is thought that utilitarianism's problems arise. Indeed it seems that it is the aggregative nature of the utilitarian calculus that leads to the counter-intuitive conclusions spoken of earlier. We must ask whether it is possible to maximise across persons without the sacrifice of human lives. While the implementation of all theories of distributive justice necessarily involves sacrifice, can we provide a model based on conceptions of the good which avoids specific kinds of sacrifice? Can we provide an internalist approach that does not involve the sacrifice of whole persons and in which issues of distributive shares are not mere derivative issues?

In attempting to solve this dilemma, let us begin with the 'Objection from Distributive Justice'; that is, with the claim that consequentialist social policy is insensitive to the actual shape of distributions. The first general point to be made here in defending consequentialism is that utilitarianism is only one form of consequentialism. There are other possible versions. All that is required of a theory for it to be characterised as consequentialist is that its conception of the right demands that action be directed toward the production in terms of the human good of the best overall state of affairs.[59] Utilitarianism is a specific form of the doctrine which ranks overall states of affairs from best to worst, according to the *total satisfactions* they contain. Thus, utilitarian calculations of total utility are not the only means of demonstrating concern with overall states of affairs. Secondly, it would be wrong to equate the consequentialist's concern with maximisation with concern for total satisfactions. Consequentialists may wish to maximise valuable overall states of affairs, but the valuable states may not be the greatest good of the greatest number. Thus, it might be possible to claim that the Objection from Distributive Justice only applies to utilitarian consequentialism, rather than consequentialism *per se*.

However, this response, as it stands, represents only a promissory note. How should an alternative conception of consequentialism, which ranks states of affairs from best to worst, and yet which is *distributively sensitive,* be formulated? What is required of a consequentialist theory for it to avoid the Objection from Distributive Justice?

I think that T.M. Scanlon provides the theoretical contours of such a form of consequentialism in an article entitled 'Preference and Urgency'.[60] Scanlon argues that any plausible theory of distributive justice must involve objective criteria. (This connects with our earlier point about the role of commensurability in distributive justice.) Scanlon argues that any distributive theory must have some objective standard of interest, need or urgency, distinct from mere subjective preference. Despite the apparent attractiveness of distributive subjectivism—i.e. the doctrine that distributive outcomes should be determined by subjective preferences—Scanlon argues that the criteria which we *actually* employ in making decisions are objective.[61] In support of this he argues that the strength of a stranger's claim on us for resources in the fulfilment of some interest depends on what that interest is and need not be proportional to the importance he attaches to it. For instance, the fact that Person A would be willing to forego a decent diet in order to build a monument to his god, does not mean that his claim on Person B for aid in his project has the same strength as a claim on resources for food.[62] Some claims have greater urgency than others. However, this does not mean that Scanlon denies the relevance of subjective preference altogether. Scanlon notes that the standard of objectivity—which he claims that distributive theory requires—still involves the possibility of a wide range of morally relevant interests which will vary from person to person.[63]

Secondly, Scanlon claims that the maximising system must involve a theory of human nature which includes an intra-personal scale of urgency or priority: that is, these objective interests, which are constitutive of the required theory of the good, must be hierarchically ordered.[64] We have already noted the necessity of a theory of the human good in choosing acceptable forms of sacrifice. In order to formulate distributively sensitive principles, we must have a theory of human nature which includes a scale of priority ordering interests from the most distributively urgent to the least.[65]

These two claims of Scanlon's provide the grounds for a possible distributive strategy which (i) employs consequentialist conceptions of the human good and is therefore maximising and yet (ii) is sensitive to distributive arrangements. The usage of an objective criterion of human well-being, which is ranked in terms of a system of priority, enables us to formulate a consequentialist theory which is distributively sensitive. (Similar points have been made elsewhere by Thomas Nagel and Samuel Scheffler.)[66] In a sense, the wrong villain has been identified. It is not consequentialism *per se* which is problematic, but rather utilitarian consequentialism which focuses exclusively on total utility as the determinant of the best state of affairs.

Following on from Scanlon's work, Samuel Scheffler has pointed out that at least two important variants of this distributively sensitive consequentialism may be distinguished. The first—which he calls 'Pluralistic Lexical Consequentialism'—identifies the best state of affairs from among a set, as the one that moves as many people as high up as possible in the hierarchy of well-being. It uses a *lexical* principle for ranking overall states of affairs. If forced to choose between two states of affairs, the preferable state is the one which maximises the position of the worst off. If the two states of affairs are identical in this respect, the better state of affairs is the one which minimises the number of people in the worst-off group.[67] If the two states of affairs are identical in both of these respects, then the better state of affairs is the one that maximises the position of the next worst-off group.[68] This theory is consequentialist because of its concern with bringing about the best state of affairs; lexical because states of affairs are to be brought about in order of significance.

The second way of characterising the view—which Scheffler dubs 'distributive consequentialism'—also involves ranking of states of affairs in terms of improving the lot of the worst-off, however, it does not adhere to strict lexical ordering; rather it incorporates a more flexible distributive principle, according to which the lower a person's level of relative well-being is, the greater weight that is given to benefiting that person.[69] Thus, the claims of those who are worst-off often take priority over the claims of those who are better off, regardless of whether allocating goods to the better off would bring about greater total utility . As Scheffler notes that "although this view gives *much greater weight* to benefiting those who are worst-off, it does not give *absolute priority* to doing so".[70] Scheffler prefers this second variant of consequentialism, because of its greater flexibility. Although the lexical form is simpler and easier to use, he believes that it sacrifices plausibility because of its rigidity in order to gain this simplicity.[71] However, despite their differences these two variants of consequentialism avoid the Objection from Distributive Justice because, unlike utilitarian consequentialism, their overall ranking of states of affairs is directly affected by the ways in which benefits and burdens are distributed within these states of affairs.[72] We should also note that the net effect of employing a system of priority or urgency in sacrificing across interests across lives will be in many respects similar to that of Rawls' difference principle.

We might also apply Scanlon's approach to the Objection from Sacrifice, employing a consequentialist theory characterised by a hierarchically ordered conception of well-being to mark off less acceptable sacrifices from more acceptable ones. With such a hierarchically ordered division of the human good, it is possible to sacrifice *across persons across interests*. We not only sacrifice across persons—which is a necessary component of the practice of distributive justice—but, additionally, with a hierarchically ordered conception of persons, we sacrifice across their interests. In practical terms this means that the individual with the more urgent claim has priority in distributions.

Giving resources to the starving beggar, rather than to myself for a sauna, would count as an example of sacrificing across persons across interests. Some of my interests are sacrificed for the interests of another which are perceived to be more urgent. The urgency accorded particular claims on distributive resources will be determined by the nature of the interests which will be satisfied by those resources.

Thus, it is possible to rule out sacrifices which sacrifice people's lives, or which give rise to dubious distributive outcomes, by the employment of an appropriate hierarchically ordered conception of the human good. This, of course, does not privilege any particular conception of the good, it merely requires that it be one that is structured in such a way that it ensures that whole human lives are not sacrificed.

However, we should not overstate the strength of this approach. There will still be cases in which sacrifice of whole human lives occurs. There will be cases where one is forced to choose between various interests, each of which is as urgent as the others. For example, we may be forced—because of a scarcity of food—to choose between feeding two starving people. Alternatively, there may well be circumstances in which there is still not enough food to feed everybody even if all the resources are taken off the rich. Thus, there is a limit to the range of cases which the policy of maximising across persons across interests can solve. However, the cases that it cannot deal with are marginal and extreme.

This strategy will enables us—in the majority of cases at least—to maximise across persons without sacrificing whole persons. It allows consequentialist conceptions of the human good to be employed when generating principles of distributive justice, without such usage necessarily leading to unacceptable sacrifice.

Summary

In this chapter, in dealing with objections to the employment of consequentialist conceptions of the good, in the generation of distributive principles, I have argued that:

i) the Objection from Sacrifice is misleading because it glosses over the fact that given conditions of scarcity, all distributive theories when implemented lead to some sacrifice;

ii) in fact, what critics of utilitarianism are objecting to is not sacrifice *per se*, but rather specific kinds of sacrifice;

iii) using a hierarchically ordered conception of the good, in which various component elements are ordered in terms of their distributive priority, it is possible for a consequentialist to prohibit certain kinds of sacrifice, just as the deontic theorist does;

iv) this strategy, which involves sacrificing across persons across interests, enables the consequentialist to avoid criticisms of consequentialism's tendency to countenance unacceptable forms of sacrifice in the majority of cases;

v) using such a hierarchically ordered conception of the good, it is possible to formulate a version of consequentialism which avoids the Objection from Distributive Justice in the majority of cases.

Thus although I take the objections to utilitarianism seriously, it does not lead me to abandon consequentialism altogether – rather it merely leads to the employment of a hierarchically ordered conception of the good when generating principles of distributive justice. We do not need to abandon consequentialism in order to avoid repugnant sacrifices and distributive insensitivity.

Finally, the foregoing arguments, concerning the role that a conception of the human good has to play in determining the specific sacrifices which a theorist endorses or condemns, provide a critique of Nozick's externalism. Nozick implicitly uses a conception of the good by the sacrifices which he excludes and those which he condones. Thus, the above arguments also function as a further defence of internalism.

Notes

1. Since the publication of Rawls' work, a large number of social theorists have addressed this problem; while some have tried to resuscitate utilitarianism, others such as Nozick, Dworkin and Foot have forged deontic theories of justice, which reject utilitarianism because of its tendency to sacrifice persons. For a discussion of their respective views see Scheffler, 1988.
2. Williams, 1988, p.20.
3. Ibid., p.21.
4. However, it should be noted that the definition provided above does not necessarily describe all possible forms of consequentialism. I think that it is possible to formulate a version of consequentialism which locates value not only derivatively in the consequential states of affairs of specific actions, but also in specific actions which are characterised as states of affairs. This we may call 'indirect consequentialism' and it may be contrasted with 'direct consequentialism', which locates value solely in consequential states of affairs. For the indirect consequentialist the value of an action is not just derivative of its consequences, but may also be intrinsic. However, for the purposes of this chapter I shall be content merely to examine what Williams call direct consequentialism; that is the version in which actions are only derivatively valuable. Thus, whenever the term 'consequentialism' is employed, it should be assumed that it is direct consequentialism to which reference is being made.
5. Williams, op. cit., p.23.
6. As Rawls notes of the dominant consequentialist doctrine, utilitarianism: " The main idea is that society is rightly ordered, and therefore just, when its major institutions are arranged so as to achieve the greatest net balance of satisfaction summed over all the individuals belonging to it." Rawls, 1972, p.22.
7. We should be careful not to conflate the ideas of conceptions of the good and consequentialism. While typically conceptions of the good are consequentialist, it is possible to imagine non-consequentialist accounts of the human good.
8. In recent years, the debate between consequentialism and deontology has been undertaken using the terms 'agent-neutral reasons' and 'agent-relative reasons'. Following Samuel Scheffler, deontological systems have been redescribed as 'agent-relative' and consequentialism as 'agent-neutral'. Thus consequentialist reasons are agent-neutral and deontological reasons agent-relative. However, for the purposes of a dissertation in political philosophy, I think that the terms 'consequentialism' and 'deontology' are sufficient. Scheffler's redescription is part of a general attempt to solve problems in moral philosophy, particularly the objection that utilitarianism demands too much of individuals and thus destroys their integrity. See Scheffler 1982 and Nagel, 1986 for a discussion of this conceptual schema. Initially Scheffler distinguished between 'agent-centred' and 'agent-neutral' moral theories. However, in his later work 'agent-centred' has become 'agent-relative'.
9. Traditionally, a number of objections have been raised against consequentialism. Firstly, some philosophers have questioned its legitimacy because of what they see as the limited capacity of human beings to have control over the consequences of their actions (see Norcross, 1990). Secondly, some critics have argued that consequentialism is an excessively demanding normative doctrine. It seems to demand that an individual neglect or abandon their own pursuits, whenever that individual could produce even slightly more good in some other way. Many theorists have found this aspect of consequentialism disturbing. Bernard Williams, for example, suggests (op. cit.) that the demands of consequentialism are so extreme as to undermine the integrity of the individual agent. These criticisms are, in fact, criticisms of consequentialism as moral theory. However, this is a work in political rather than moral theory and as such Williams' concerns stand outside its purview.
10. See Rawls, 1958.

11. For useful discussions of the difference between these two different interpretations of utility-maximisation, see Kymlicka, 1990, p.47; Griffin, 1986, pp.151-54; and Rescher, 1966, pp.25-8.
12. Rawls writes of utilitarianism: "The conception of justice as derivative from efficiency implies that judging the justice of a practice is always, in principle at least, a matter of weighing up advantages and disadvantages, each having an intrinsic value or disvalue as the satisfaction of interests, irrespective of whether or not these interests necessarily involve acquiescence in principles which could not be mutually acknowledged. Utilitarianism cannot account for the fact that slavery is always unjust, nor for the fact that it would be recognised as irrelevant in defeating the accusation of injustice for one person to say to another.... that nevertheless it allowed of the greatest satisfaction of desire." Rawls, 1958, p.188.
13. Samuel Scheffler notes: "Given any two outcomes with different totals of aggregate satisfaction .... utilitarianism will always say that the outcome with the higher total is better, even if satisfaction is distributed very unequally in that outcome and much more equally in the other, and even if the difference in total satisfaction between the two outcomes is small.", Scheffler, 1988, p.6.
14. Rawls, 1972, p.24.
15. Ibid., p.26.
16. Nagel, 1988, pp.51-73.
17. "For consider: each man in realising his own interests is certainly free to balance his own losses against his own gains. We may impose a sacrifice on ourselves now for the sake of a greater advantage later." Rawls, 1972, p.23.
18. "Just as the well-being of a person is constructed from the series of satisfactions which are experienced at different moments in time and which constitute the life of the individual, so the well being of society is to be constructed from the fulfilment of the systems of desires of the many individuals who belong to it.", Rawls, ibid., p.23.
19. Galston notes similarities between Rawls' critique of utilitarianism and Aristotle's critique of Plato's *Republic*. He notes that both are critical of what he calls 'hyperorganicism'. See Galston, 1980, pp.2-3.
20. For a discussion of moral equality in political philosophy, see Kymlicka, 1990, p.4.
21. See Nagel, 1991, pp.66-67.
22. Rawls, 1972, p.26.
23. Ibid., p.27.
24. Here the claim is predicated upon a belief in the importance of moral equality.
25. For criticisms of Rawls' approach see Kymlicka, 1988, pp.173-90.
26. For further discussion of how Rawls generates principles of distributive justice see chapter one 'Distributive Justice and the Human Good'.
27. Rawls, 1972, p.30. Later, Rawls goes on to say that theories must have some connection to consequences; arguing that all ethical doctrines worth our attention take consequences into account in judging rightness and that one which did not would simply be irrational.
28. Nozick, 1974, p.29.
29. Ibid., p.30.
30. Ibid., p.29.
31. Ibid., p.29.
32. Ibid., p.29.
33. Thomas Nagel notes in relation to Nozick's right-based theory: "....a theory based exclusively in rights leaves out too much that is morally relevant, even if the interests it includes are among the most basic. A moral view that gives no weight to the value of overall outcomes cannot be correct." Nagel, 1979, p.123.
34. Thomas Pogge (1989), attempts to show that while Nozick is a deontologist, Rawls is actually a consequentialist.
35. It is worth noting at this point that although Rawls and Nozick are both critical of utilitarianism, they advocate vastly different political theories. While Rawls objects to the needless sacrifice of lives which would occur if the state did not intervene in certain circumstances and the injustice of certain unequal distributions, Nozick objects to welfare state intervention because he believes such action may sacrifice some persons' rights to property. This difference between Rawls and Nozick

will take on greater significance later in the chapter when we examine the role that the human good has to play in one's notion of illegitimate sacrifice.

36. Nicholas Rescher (1966, pp.87-112) provides a typology of four types of supply conditions that influence principles of justice. There are four levels, he argues: *superabundance*, in which the problem of justice disappears; *abundance*, in which the total available for distribution exceeds the totality of valid claims and inequalities are justified if they are to everyone's advantage; *sufficiency*, in which the available total roughly equals valid claims and distribution must be determined by them alone; and *scarcity*, in which the available total falls short of valid claims and highly disproportionate distributions may be judged optimal. Cf. Galston, 1980, p.119.
37. Hume, 1975, pp.15-18. Cf. Galston, 1980, pp.116-17.
38. "Finally, there is the condition of moderate scarcity understood to cover a wide range of situations. Natural and other resources are not so abundant that schemes of cooperation become superfluous, nor are conditions so harsh that fruitful ventures must inevitably break down.", Rawls, 1972, p.127.
39. "Marx was emphatic about the need for abundance, for he thought that scarcity made conflict unresolvable. The highest development of the productive forces, 'is an absolutely, necessary practical premise [of communism] because without it *want* is merely made general, and with *destitution* the struggle for necessities and all the old filthy business would necessarily be reproduced. It was perhaps because he was pessimistic about the social effect of scarcity that he became so optimistic about the possibility of abundance.", Kymlicka, 1990, p.166.
40. On this issue of Marx's views on scarcity and distributive justice, see Lukes, 1985, pp.63-66; Buchanan, 1982, pp.165-69; Kymlicka, 1989a, pp.114-122; and Nove, 1983, pp.15-20.
41. For a discussion of the question of whether the achievement of universal bounty would require substantial destruction of the environment, see Balbus, 1982 and Gorz, 1980.
42. Economists make a similar point about the relation between scarcity and problems of allocation. However, they tend to think that scarcity arises because of the insatiable nature of human wants and desires. See Lipsey, 1989, p.39; and Jackson and McConnell, 1988, p.17.
43. Waldron argues that the institution of private property is in fact a response to the problem of scarcity. See Waldron, 1986, pp.478-79.
44. David Gauthier makes a similar point about the relationship between conditions of scarcity and justice. See Gauthier, 1986, pp.333-36.
45. Galston, 1980, p.116.
46. See ibid., p.117.
47. It might also be argued that human beings are constructed in such a way that abundance is an incoherent notion. If it is in the nature of people always to want more, then abundance would be incoherent.
48. This claim about the necessity of sacrifice in the *implementation* of distributive principles should not be confused with the 'Problem of Dirty Hands', which concerns the idea that the vocation of politics somehow rightly requires its practitioners to violate important moral standards. While it is true that the practice of distributive justice requires the sacrifice of some possible interests, it is difficult to ascertain whether this actually contravenes everyday morality, given the fact that sacrifice is an important part of everyday morality. On the problem of dirty hands see Walzer, 1973.
49. The term 'modal' usually refers to the structure of possibility. In logic it refers to the logic of necessity and possibility. A modal statement is one in which something is said to be necessarily or possibly the case.
50. Rawls, 1972, p.83.
51. A subsidiary point to make about Nozick is that acquisition may, in fact, make some people become resources for others.
52. See Rawls, 1972, pp.22-23.
53. Kymlicka, 1990, p.103.
54. Nozick, 1974, p.238.
55. Kymlicka, op. cit., p.114.
56. This seems rather odd. As Kymlicka notes: "....the claim that we own ourselves does not yet say anything about owning external resources. And the claim that we have rights to a fair share of

society's resources does not seem to preclude the possibility that we own ourselves", ibid., p.105.

57. I am, of course, not asserting that Nozick actually explicitly advocates externalism; his claims about his principles of distributive justice being derived from side constraints, rather than a conception of the good is an externalist one.
58. As Nagel notes it seems that no plausible theory can avoid the relevance of numbers altogether. See Nagel, 1979, p.125.
59. "Different consequentialist theories, of course, incorporate different principles for ranking overall states of affairs, and hence embody different conceptions of what it is best to have happen in the world.", Scheffler, 1982, p.123.
60. Scanlon, 1975, pp.655-69.
61. Ibid., p.658.
62. Ibid., pp.659-60.
63. Ibid., p.658.
64. Ibid., p.660.
65. A similar claim about the importance of a system of significance is made by Charles Taylor. See Taylor, 1979, p.183.
66. See Scheffler, 1982, p.35.
67. Of course we should not fetishise mathematical exactitude. For egalitarian purposes, it is of no consequence if the quantities are not exactly equal, just as it does not matter in relation to fairness if one child is given ninety seven marbles, one ninety three and another ninety five.
68. Scheffler, 1982, pp.26-7.
69. Ibid., p.31.
70. Ibid., p.31.
71. Ibid., p.31.
72. Ibid., pp.29-30.

3 The human good, others and justice

Is a theory of the good sufficient to generate distributive principles?

In chapters one and two I argued that it is unlikely that principles of distributive justice can be generated without reference to a conception of the human good. In all likelihood, a conception of the good is a necessary condition for the distributively just. However, this is still rather imprecise. Not only have I failed to specify what conception of the good it is which should be employed, I have as yet not indicated in what sense a conception of the good is necessary. Is it necessary and sufficient or is it merely necessary but not sufficient? This question is important, for the way in which we characterise the relationship between conceptions of the good and distributive principles, will determine the very kind of internalism formulated.

One way of characterising the role of the good in distributive theory is to say that all of justice can be derived from one normative base. I shall call this approach the *maximal thesis*. This maximal thesis is normatively monist. Implicit within this monistic methodology is the assumption that a conception of the good supplies both necessary and sufficient conditions for the generation of distributive principles. On the maximal thesis, no normative foundational grounds other than the human good are required to generate principles of distributive justice.[1]

The maximal project may at first sight appear rather quixotic. A theory of the individual human good by itself appears to provide only information on what the good life consists in, not fully blown rules concerning how the State should distribute resources to its citizens. *Prima facie* any single theory of the good would appear to be compatible with a wide variety of distributive principles. What is, in fact, required to bridge the gap between the good and the distributively just is an abstract account of how the State should act towards its citizens. Given the apparent necessity of such an account, one may well wonder how the foundational monist expects to realise the maximal project satisfactorily.

However, the maximal thesis is not as implausible as one might initially think. The monist believes that we can derive an abstract account of how the State should treat its citizens from an appropriate account of the human good. Hence, while an abstract account of how people should be treated by the State is required to bridge the gap from the good to the just, according to the monist this abstract account can be derived from the good itself and thus we can derive all of the just from the good. How this might be possible will become more apparent as concrete examples of this monist strategy are explored.

The maximal thesis then requires: (i) the provision of an abstract account of how the

State should treat its citizens and; (ii) the derivation of this account from an account of the human good. In order for the human good to perform this function, the State's ethical obligations must be thought of as analogous to the moral obligations of individuals to other persons. Given that fact, the central question for the maximal theorist becomes "Why should I be moral?". Much of this chapter, then, will be devoted to considering some strategies for deriving individual ethical obligation from the human good.

One may well wonder, however, why we should be delving into the realm of moral philosophy in the context of discussion of the just distribution of benefits and burdens. Why should we be concerned with the obligations of individual persons to others, when it is the justice of social institutions and arrangements with which we are actually concerned? Indeed, if we consider a number of contemporary theories of distributive justice, we discover that the problem of others is not an issue with which such theories overly concern themselves. For instance, Rawls' account of justice does not require an answer to this question in order to kick-start justice, as it were (although it should be noted that he presupposes that his hypothetical contractors have a sense of justice[2]). Why, then, is it of concern for the maximal distributive theorist? The answer to this question seems to be that once one begins distributive theorising with a conception of the human good, and one attempts to derive the whole of justice from such a conception (as the proponent of the maximal thesis does), then one is inevitably drawn to the issue of what one's proper relations with others should be. There seems, therefore, to be some basic connection between monistic internalism and the problem of why it is that we should act morally towards other persons.

Monism, of course, is not the only procedural mechanism on offer. Internalism can also be developed along pluralistic lines. This is the *minimal thesis*. The minimal thesis is foundationally pluralist because more than one normative foundation is employed in the generation of distributive theory.[3] This minimal doctrine involves the following assumptions: i) that the normative foundations to be employed are conceptually irreducible and; ii) that a conception of the good is necessary, but not sufficient for the generation of principles of distributive justice. According to advocates of the minimal thesis, conceptions of the human good require further supplementation—presumably from deontic sources—if it is to provide grounds for social theory.

It should also be noted *en passant* that both the maximal and minimal theses will require further supplementation from non-normative sources. There will be empirical material, such as information about human populations, the availability of distributive resources, the special requirements of the good in question, the level of social development, and so on, all of which must be supplied before full-blooded distributive theory can be generated.

The question which I shall address in this chapter concerns precisely the species of internalism to be adopted. Of course, in terms of theoretical simplicity, the maximal thesis would be preferable because of its use of only one normative theoretical foundation.[4] However, it is quite possible that it gains simplicity at the expense of being implausible. In this chapter I shall consider both of these internalist strategies with the aim of determining which is the more appropriate for the task of generating principles of distributive justice.

Glaucon's challenge

In a central passage of *The Republic* in which Glaucon and Socrates argue about the role of morality in the 'good life', Socrates takes up Glaucon's challenge to demonstrate that the traditional good and virtuous life is one which we have reason to follow since it is the happiest and most fulfilling.[5] In this passage, Socrates defends the claim that the just life—in which concern is shown for others—is in fact better than the unjust life.

For Socrates, being just is not merely a matter of obligation, nor is it (as many might argue) merely a qualificatory requirement for entry in a mutual insurance policy in which people bother about others in order to insure that they are also treated well – rather it is an *intrinsic* good. According to Socrates, concern for others is good, regardless of its external consequences.

Glaucon objects to Socrates' thesis, believing justice merely to be an instrumental good. He contends that Socrates needs to demonstrate that the life of the perfectly good person is better for that agent than the life of the perfectly unjust person. With the aim of demonstrate that justice is not an intrinsic good, Glaucon recounts the story of The Ring of Gyges. This mythical tale concerns a ring found by the shepherd Gyges. The ring has magical powers which are such that they enable the wearer to become invisible; with it a person may do whatever he likes without fear of being discovered. He may act immorally toward others without incurring external penalties; he may rob, destroy and murder without fear of being caught or punished. Given this immunity from both punishment and community disapproval, what reasons can be given as to why the ring-bearer should not take full advantage of his invisible condition? Why should he not rape, murder or steal?

Glaucon sharpens the issue by asking us to imagine that Gyges has the reputation of being a just and worthy member of the community, even though unbeknownst to his fellow citizens he uses the ring to murder and steal, while another member of the community, who is in fact perfectly just, has the reputation of being unjust and is blamed for the sins of Gyges. This second person is despised and shunned by the community at large. Glaucon then asks Socrates to prove that, despite his treatment by the community, the just person in this case is better off than Gyges. I shall call this puzzle 'Glaucon's Challenge'. It is the challenge to demonstrate that the benefits of just action are not merely the consequential benefits of community approval, but rather are of intrinsic value.[6] It is, in effect, another way of asking the age old question, which philosophers from Plato onwards have struggled with, namely, "Why should I be moral?".

Glaucon's discussion of the story of the Ring of Gyges is instructive because it dramatises the differences between two major variants of the maximal thesis. In the one corner, we have Socrates who attempts to show that by treating other persons as ends-in-themselves—regardless of consequential benefit—a person lives a better life. For Socrates, there exists an *internal* relation between the good life and moral action. He believes that acting morally is intrinsically valuable. In the other corner, we have Glaucon who defends the thesis that treating others well is only of consequential benefit and believes that if such consequential benefit disappears, then there can be no reason for treating others well. Here the relationship between the good life and the life of moral action is an *external* one. Glaucon believes that morality is merely an instrumental good. His approach to morality is but one example of what I shall call '*mutual advantage theory*'; that is, theory according to which we should treat each other well in order to secure consequential benefits. Nevertheless, despite the obvious differences between the approaches of Glaucon and Socrates, in both cases the attempt is made to derive an account of how persons should be treated from a conception of the good.[7]

Mutual advantage theory

A little earlier I made mention of mutual advantage theory. Let us say a little more about what it consists in. Put crudely, it is the view that morality is *nothing but* a system of advantage, such that it is to the benefit of every person involved if all accept and act upon moral norms, even though acting on this system of principles requires that some persons will on occasions be forced to perform disadvantageous acts.[8] Mutual advantage theorists claim that reasons for acting morally towards other persons can be provided by a proper examination of self-interest. Most simply described, mutual advantage theory endorses Glaucon's account of morality. It is a thesis which, broadly stated, can be ascribed to a wide number of philosophers, including Thomas Hobbes, Kurt Baier and David Gauthier.

According to mutual advantage theorists, morality should be thought of as a set of principles by which groups of persons agree to abide because of the mutually beneficial consequences of such agreement. Baier, for instance, argues that being moral involves following rules designed to overrule self-interest whenever it is in the interest or advantage of everyone alike that every person should set aside his interest.[9] This advantage primarily concerns the kind of social context which persons inhabit. Acceptance of moral norms by groups of people allows those people who abide by them to inhabit a more beneficial social context than would be the case if people acted purely prudentially. Morality, according to this doctrine, is a mere means for the realisation of advantage. Kurt Baier argues that the "very *raison d'etre* of a morality is to yield reasons which overrule the reasons of self-interest in those cases where everyone's following self-interest would be harmful to everyone".[10] From such an account of morality, the mutual advantage theorist furnishes reasons why we should act morally. Persons should act morally towards others because such action is of benefit to everyone including ourselves, even if this at times involves performing what, on the face of it, appear to be disadvantageous acts. According to the mutual advantage theorist, persons should act morally because of the beneficial external consequences of such action.[11] The human good of each individual will be advanced by adopting conventions of morality. The adoption of these conventions of just action, or of conventions which prevent unjust action, generates a beneficial context within which agents can operate. For example, the adoption of a convention against injury to others can be thought of as being mutually advantageous; with such a convention in force individuals would not have to waste resources defending their personal safety. For the mutual advantage theorist, it does not matter that our concern for one another is purely instrumental: they believe that the net effect of such instrumental reasoning will be the same as if everyone treated each other justly with the intrinsic value of such just action in mind. The mutual advantage theorist typically takes there to be no reason to try to solve the puzzle of why it is that we should be concerned with others in terms of duty and obligation when it can be resolved simply with reference to personal advantage.[12] For the mutual advantage theorists there exists a connection between morality and advantage such that the answer to the problem of why we should be moral is to be found in a proper analysis of personal advantage.[13] The outcome of persons acting with personal advantage in mind will be, for all intents and purposes, the same as if they acted upon reasons based on notions of duty or obligation.

Mutual advantage theory provides what might be called a 'contractarian' account of morality and justice.[14] Justice and morality are ultimately thought of as consequences of groups of individual persons bargaining so as to achieve the best possible conditions for themselves. Individuals consent to covenants of moral action with other persons whom they deem it advantageous to do so; it is not that people agree to act morally because of the intrinsic value of such action in itself. Thus, for any individual agent morality's binding character is derived solely from the contractual bindingness of her agreement to act well towards other persons with whom she considers it advantageous.

At first sight, mutual advantage theory may appear to be rather appealing, for if morality can be justified with reference to personal advantage, why bother with duty, obligation and genuine concern for the well-being of others? However, on closer inspection a number of problems emerge. To make this apparent, let us begin by reconsidering the central intuition of mutual advantage theory. The main claim of such theory is that each person should act morally (in this minimal sense), towards others because of the benefits it will bring him or her. *Ex hypothesi*, the net effect of such action will be the production of a society in which people treat each other exactly the same as they would if they were all treating each other as 'ends in themselves',

However, I think that our ordinary sense of morality is not adequately captured by the mutual advantage account according to which morality should be understood simply as a system of advantage. Let us consider, the relationship between a healthy person and a child afflicted with Down's Syndrome. The Down's Syndrome child can do the healthy person no harm nor provide any substantial benefit of his own volition and it is of no advantage to help that child if we think of advantage in terms of external benefits. What is to stop the healthy person letting the Down's Syndrome child starve to death or to stop the healthy person teasing or torturing him? In many societies, social conventions and taboos would stop such behaviour; however, these conventions are grounded in the assumption that the rightness or wrongness of an action is determined by the nature of the act itself, not its instrumental consequences. Mutual advantage theorists cannot employ these arguments because such arguments are grounded in a moral ontology to which they do not ascribe. It would seem, then, that the mutual advantage theorist can provide us with no reason as to why it would be wrong to let Down's Syndrome children starve and be tortured and it would seem that the adoption of this normative system could lead to the creation of a society in which people regularly tortured the disabled.

Similar kinds of counter-intuitive examples can be generated with respect to the treatment of a variety of groups in society who are incapable of providing benefits for others. For example, the terminally ill, the elderly, the physically handicapped and even children (though it is less clearly the case with this last class), are all groups of people towards whom it is possible *ceteris paribus* to act unjustly without fear of retribution or loss of consequential benefits. Mutual advantage theory, as it stands, cannot tell us what is wrong with such acts of cruelty, and it is for this very reason that the theory should be rejected. As Brian Barry notes, there is something odd about theories which allow such treatment of human beings because it is normally regarded as a paradigm of injustice to kill some innocent person simply because that person is in the way of your getting something you want, or alternatively to take what you want from someone under the threat of death. To claim that such murder is rendered just by the inability of the victims to organise an effective resistance would surely be a hollow mockery of the idea of justice. Barry contends that justice is normally thought of not as ceasing to be relevant in conditions of extreme inequality in power, but rather as being especially relevant to such conditions.[15]

The source of these difficulties is to be found in the account of morality upon which mutual advantage theory rests. By defining morality in terms of advantage and in terms of a contract between persons who will mutually benefit from it, the possibility is left open that those outside the system of advantage will be excluded from the class of proper objects of ethical concern. Mutual advantage theory thus fails to capture adequately what we mean by the term 'morality'.[16] Indeed David Gauthier concedes this point in the introduction to *Morals By Agreement* when he acknowledges that only beings whose physical and mental capacities are either roughly equal or mutually complementary can expect to find cooperation beneficial to all.[17] Nonetheless, Gauthier believes that the economic expansion characteristic of the modern era means that the group outside this sphere of mutual benefit will be very small, and will only include the mentally and physically retarded and similarly weak groups.[18] According to Gauthier, the fact that modern industrial capitalism requires co-operation from people means that coercive relationships will be kept to a minimum.[19]

In response to this last claim we might firstly question the factual correctness of his claim that economic expansion has enabled all able-bodied and mentally competent persons to regard one another as contributing partners to a joint enterprise. Is it really the case in modern capitalist societies that all participants have incentives to treat each other morally? Secondly, even if his rather contentious claim is true, his account still leaves out the mentally and physically defective and thus fails to capture what is commonly meant by morality. Therefore, his contractarian account does not capture what the term 'morality' properly refers to. While it is true that morality may be advantageous in certain instances, it does not follow from this fact that defining morality in terms of advantage adequately characterises what the term means. What mutual advantage theorists, such as Gauthier and Baier, mean by 'morality' should more properly be referred to as enlightened self-interest. Presumably, such theorists believe that what has previously passed for morality is for various reasons unavailable.

I take it that the foregoing discussion illustrates my claim that a society organised according to principles of mutual advantage would not be identical with a society which treated people as ends in themselves. Moreover, it is because some people, such as the disabled, slip the net of instrumental concern—and thus may in fact be treated badly—which leads us to reject mutual advantage theory. Any theory which provides grounds for the justification of the torture and neglect of those who lack the means to defend themselves, can hardly be accorded the privilege of being considered to be an adequate theory of justice.

One way in which mutual advantage theory might be modified so as to avoid such moral transgressions would be by employing the idea of moral behaviour as habits of action. The argument here would begin with the assumption that it is instrumentally preferable for contracting agents to internalise the moral treatment of others as habits of actions. Such habituation is preferable because persons will naturally and automatically act benevolently towards their fellow contractors out of sheer force of habit. Thus the benefits of moral action already outlined will be maximised. The next step in the argument is to claim that once a person adopts these benevolent habits of action, benevolence will flow over into that person's interactions with non-contractors; that is, persons with whom one gains no advantage from acting morally towards. Finally, we might argue that this indiscriminate moral action does not constitute a problematic waste from the point of view of maximising individual benefit. Even though one gains no actual advantage from benevolence enacted toward non-contractors, on the whole it is more advantageous for one to adopt benevolent behaviour as a habit, than it is not to do so. Instrumental advantage is thus said to be best served by indiscriminate moral behaviour.[20]

Let us further illustrate the claim by re-examining our earlier example of the Down's Syndrome child. Imagine that a group of persons (of which our Down's Syndrome child is a member) decides to develop benevolent habits of action. They believe it to be instrumentally advantageous for all members of the group to act benevolently towards one another automatically. However, one consequence of this decision is that they come to act benevolently towards our Down's Syndrome child. They refrain from torturing him and become concerned with his welfare. Now the claim of this modified version of mutual advantage theory would be that this group of persons will be *better off* than a comparable group which decide to avoid the adoption of such habits for the very reason that the benefits of automatic benevolence outweigh the wasted acts of benevolence enacted toward non-contractors, such as our Down's Syndrome child. Thus *ex hypothesi*, mutual advantage theory, appropriately modified is capable of providing reasons as to why one might act benevolently toward the weak and incapable.

Interestingly, here one may discern some resonances *mutatis mutandis* with arguments to be found in the works of both Aquinas and Kant concerning the reasons why we should not be cruel to animals, even though animals are not proper objects of moral concern. (Although it should be noted that both believe that acting morally toward human beings is more than just a matter of instrumental advantage). Aquinas, for example, claimed that although human beings have no obligations towards animals because God has granted us dominion over all animals, nonetheless it is important that we treat animals well so as to ensure that we act well towards people. Acting cruelly towards animals is wrong because of the effect it might have on the way we treat humans.[21] In a similar vein, in his *Lectures on Ethics* Kant contends that one should avoid harming animals because of the injury that one does to oneself in acting cruelly rather than because they are proper objects of moral concern. Kant believes that the man who kicks a dog injures the humanity in himself.[22]

However, this modified account of mutual advantage theory seems no more likely to succeed than the original version because of its reliance on the dubious claim that people require indiscriminate habits of action in order to benefit from benevolence internalised as habits of action. It seems quite possible that people could habituate themselves to acting benevolently towards specific groups of people and not towards others. Indeed the empirical evidence here would seem to suggest that this is how human beings have acted, as a matter of fact, for much of human history. We need only to think of various systems of discriminatory behaviour, such as, for instance, the caste system of India, to find cases of persons not needing to universalise their benevolent behaviour in order to ensure that they act benevolently towards those whom they consider to be of importance. Instrumental benefit does not seem to require that we adopt indiscriminate conventions of benevolent action. It would appear, then, that this modified account goes no way toward saving mutual advantage theory.

To recap then, although it is true that morality and advantage sometimes coincide, defining morality solely in terms of advantage does not provide an adequate account of what morality is. Mutual advantage theory therefore fails to answer the question of why it is that we should be moral, because it is in fact responding to a separate problem; namely, "Why should I be enlightenedly self-interested?". One of the consequences of this is that it fails to provide rules of treatment applicable to all human beings. Transferred to the realm of distributive theory, this would mean that many persons, such as the weak and disabled, would be outside the domain of justice. Given the difficulties encountered, I turn now to some putative monistic ways of generating obligation to treat others as *ends*.

The general features of a monist argument for the intrinsic value of acting morally

Let us begin our examination of theory which posits an *intrinsic connection* between the human good and moral action by reconsidering what Socrates had to say about justice and morality.

I noted earlier that Socrates refuses to admit the legitimacy of the opposition between personal benefit and conventional justice. For Socrates, justice is an intrinsic good, whereas for Glaucon it is an instrumental one.[23] Thus, for Glaucon, the relationship between justice and happiness is that of means and ends; justice is not desirable in itself, but it secures happiness as a consequence because it ensures that other people will act benevolently toward oneself. For Socrates, on the other hand, the just life is, *by its very nature*, the best life.

However, Socrates' justification, on first reading at least, appears rather weak. In Book VIII of *The Republic* he says of Glauconian virtue that the person who acts justly, as an external means to his own self interest, is there said to be ruled by desire rather than reason.[24] Obviously, great emphasis is placed on living the fully human life of reason and it is for this reason that the best life is the just life. However, stated in this way it seems nothing more than bald assertion. In order to understand more fully Plato's line of thinking here, it is useful to consider his account of mental health.[25]

In The *Republic* Plato provides a tripartite account of the soul which he uses to analyse mental health. The soul is to be thought of as having three parts; reason, spiritedness and appetite. (Elsewhere, in *The Phaedrus*, he talks metaphorically of reason as a charioteer in charge of the two horses, spiritedness and appetite). Good mental health arises when the soul is ruled by reason; alternatively, bad mental health arises when the soul is not governed by the rational part of the soul.

Socrates then proceeds to draw an analogy between the soul and the State. Just like the soul, the State has three parts. Moreover, for Plato both the soul and the State are to be thought of as organisms, as complexes of parts with characteristic functions. These quasi-physiological notions of both an organism and function or characteristic activity are the primary grounds for the claim that the just state and the just person are organisms in which all elements are functioning as they are intended to. Kenny notes of Socrates' view that justice in state and soul is what health is in body, namely the right functioning of the elements of the organism.[26] In *The Republic* Socrates argues that the just state is one in which the rational element of society, namely the philosopher-kings, are in control. So too with the soul of the just man. Plato identifies justice as the soul being ruled by reason. Injustice in persons is a falling-out of the elements of the soul.[27] Reason, thus, is to rule the soul, educated temper is to be its ally, and both are to rule the insatiable appetites and prevent them going beyond the proper bounds. Injustice, for Plato, is akin to civil strife amongst the elements. The unjust man is one whose soul's elements are not properly ordered. Injustice may be thought of, as it were, as a form of disease – as a form of mental illness; the occurrence of injustice means that the natural order of the soul has been subverted.[28]

The object of Socrates' *elenchus* is achieved when Glaucon agrees that since virtue is the health of the soul, it would be absurd to ask whether it is more profitable to live justly or unjustly. All of the wealth and power in the world cannot make life worth living when the bodily constitution is going to rack and ruin.[29] William Galston notes that the Platonic answer to Glaucon's challenge turns on the meaning of *advantage*: "The *Republic* culminates in the contention that the human good consists in the right ordering of the individual soul, with reason ruling, spiritedness a submissive ally, appetitiveness a chastened slave." But, Galston says, we learn, justice is precisely this ordering. In choosing justice we in fact choose the greatest advantage for ourselves and hence the problem of motivation disappears.[30] Plato thus uses this tripartite theory of the soul to prove the superiority of the just person's happiness. This is his means of countering the Glauconian challenge.

However, such an account of justice's benefits is of limited use in our attempt to meet Glaucon's challenge. Firstly, in order to accept it one must accept Plato's rather dubious account of mental health. To the modern mind, his psychological theory may appear rather quaint (although to give Plato his due, one may well be driven to ask whether modern theories of mind are as capable of describing the phenomenological experience of mental life as adequately as Plato can). Secondly, one must remember that Plato's hyperorganicism, i.e. his belief that society has moral significance over and above the interests or concerns of individuals, means that his account of what it is to be just or moral differs from the sort of conception generally in usage today. Indeed, Karl Popper goes as far as to suggest that Plato uses the term 'just' as a synonym for that which is in the interest of the best state.[31]

Here we should exercise some caution. While the Popperian critique of Plato, which focuses on Plato's putative hostility toward the individual, is in many respects correct, we should also note that in the *Phaedo* we find Socrates talking of the after-life as a place where he will enjoy the company of wise and good men.[32] Here there is no talk of social structures, so presumably Plato's hyperorganicism does not extend to the spiritual realm. Nevertheless, it is still the case that for Plato to be just or moral in the material world means to know one's place in the schema of society and to act accordingly. This makes his theory irrelevant to the project at hand, for what we are looking for is a reason for persons, who matter in their own right, to act morally toward other persons. Plato does not furnish us with any such reasons.

My discussion, thus far, has not taken us any closer to an answer to why we should be moral. What we seem to need is an outline of some of the general features of an argument which is capable of answering Glaucon's challenge; one which assumes that persons are separate and not mere components of some supra-human entity, such as the state. In the rest of this section, I shall provide such an outline.

A social conception of the self

In order for it to be possible to claim that a life of just action, in which others are treated as ends, is the best possible life, we need to demonstrate that humans are in some relevant sense social animals. Imagine, for example, a hermit who lives on a desert island and by virtue of never interacting with other people, never treats any one justly; (and it must also be the case that he never treats anyone unjustly).[33] For it to be possible for us legitimately to claim that the just life is the best possible life, we need to show that the hermit's life is not preferable to the life of just social interaction. Thus a necessary condition of a monistic internalist political theory is that people be conceived of as being essentially *social beings*.

Although a social conception of human self-realisation is a necessary condition for a monistic account of internalism, it is not a sufficient condition. It is plausible of course that some person might be tempted to argue that because we are social beings that therefore we should treat others as ends. However, I think this is a spurious line of thought. The fact that we are social animals does not furnish us with any reason for treating others as ends. We can of course claim (1) the good life requires society; the truth of which is contingent upon facts about the way that human beings are actually constituted. However, while the good life requires society it cannot just be *any* society. For example, it seems difficult to defend the idea that a slave owned by a brutal master would be living a better life than his master.

Thus we must alter our claim about the relationship between society and the individual's good life: (2) the good life requires the good society. However, making the point in this way enables us to see why merely asserting a social conception of human self-realisation is not sufficient for us to show that the just life is the best life possible. For (2) is a claim which Machiavelli would presumably be content to endorse. From the mere fact that the good life requires a good society, it does not follow as a matter of logic that for any individual that (3) the good society is a just society. From the point of view of Machiavelli's Prince it may be that an unjust society, in which he is in the position to treat all of the citizens as means to his ends, would be the best possible society and lead to the best possible life for himself. Thus more than a social conception of the self is required.

An internal telos

Earlier I noted that Plato's argument rested on the assumption that there was an *internal* relationship between the location of value and the just act. This then is a second necessary condition of any argument which aims to establish that the best possible life is the just life. Human beings' self-realisation must involve an internal connection between just action and individual benefit: the benefit must be in the action itself, not an external consequence of it. It is this condition which rules out the Machiavellian claim that the good society is an unjust one. *Pace* Machiavelli and his ilk, for whom others are merely means to one's individual ends, it is claimed by theorists such as Plato that one only properly gains benefits from others when one performs just acts and it is in the performing of the act that one gains benefit. The just action must be valuable regardless of its consequences.

A two tiered level of description

Are these two necessary conditions sufficient, then, to show that the best life is the just life? I think that if we re-examine the works of Plato and Aristotle we may find some problems concerning what the motive of the just action becomes; yet, I do not think that these problems are insurmountable.

Some critics have found Plato's view that justice, or concern for the well-being of others, is constitutive of our own well-being to be morally repugnant. H.A. Prichard argues in 'Duty and Interest' that if justice is advocated on the grounds that it is advantageous to the just person, it is thereby reduced to a form of self-interest.[34] In that case it will not really be justice which is being advocated. The just person, at least as is conventionally understood, is a person who shows concern for others because of his concern for others, who keeps his promises simply because he has promised, who pays his debt because he owes it and who refrains from lying simply because it would be dishonest. He is essentially different from someone who does these things because it will make him better off.[35] Prichard is arguing for the importance of performing duty for duty's sake and believes that Plato's position is in fact a form of 'moral egoism'. Moral egoism consists in a detachment of virtuous activity from circumstances, including the circumstances of others' need. As Richard Norman, notes our own happiness is surely an end, therefore, if virtuous activity is constitutive of happiness, and if this is a reason for performing it, do we not have to say of the virtuous activity also that it is an end in itself? Does this not automatically put us in the position of moral egoism?[36]

The claim that the self-seeking motive of just action renders it merely a form of moral egoism can be most readily demonstrated in the work of Aristotle. Aristotle, like Plato before him, had a conception of value in which certain activities were thought of as ends-in-themselves, amongst these being just action. Aristotle also conceived of human beings as social animals; he refers to human beings as *zoa politika*, which roughly translates as 'animals of the polis'.[37] Hence, Aristotle's claim that justice is constitutive of well-being is grounded partially in a conception of the social nature of human existence and therefore he satisfies our two necessary conditions.[38]

According to his explicit doctrine concerning the just life, Aristotle claims that the just man cultivates altruistic virtues very much as states of himself. This however leads to the morally problematic consequences to which Prichard referred. It would seem that altruism is not practiced with regard to the circumstances of need, but rather with regard to the opportunities that each situation offers for exhibiting generosity. Aristotle speaks approvingly of the megalophyschos or 'great-souled man' who "will refrain from giving to anybody and everybody, that he may have something to give to the right people at the right time, and where it is noble to do so".[39] It would be difficult to describe such behaviour as treating others as ends in themselves. Again he writes of the great-souled or magnanimous man:

> He does not run into trifling dangers, nor is he fond of danger, because he honours few things; but he will face great dangers, and when he is in danger he is unsparing of his life, knowing that there are conditions in which life is not worth having. And he is the sort of man to confer benefits, but he is ashamed of receiving them, for the one is the mark of a superior, the other of an inferior. And he is apt to confer greater benefits in return; for thus the original benefactor, besides being paid, will incur a debt to him, and he will be the gainer by the transaction.[40]

It is precisely the tenor of this passage which led philosophers such as Bertrand Russell to describe Aristotle's doctrine of the great-souled man as the doctrine of a prig.[41] It seems that the *megalopsychos* is merely concerned with his own state of mind, or state of grace as it were, rather than the objective conditions of others.[42]

Of course, Aristotle's attitude is rather extreme, but it does highlight an underlying problem discernible in doctrines which claim that the just life is the best life.[43] The problem here seems to be connected to the emphasis upon ends, rather than upon the nature of the activities in themselves. It would appear that the circumstances of others' need becomes merely an opportunity for the just person, in Aristotle's sense, to act justly and thus fulfil themselves, rather than the activity being a response to the circumstances of need of others.

It would seem then that theory, constrained solely by the requirements of recognising that persons are social beings and who may have an internal telos, could quite easily degenerate into Prichard's vice of moral egoism; that is, the vice of merely regarding the misfortunes of others as a means for the realisation of our own well-being. Yet as it stands the *megalopsychos* has satisfied all of the conditions specified thus far for generating an argument to demonstrate the intrinsic value of moral action. In attempting to avoid the vice of moral egoism it is worth considering a further condition which Richard Norman has proposed in this context. He suggests that if we operate with a two-tiered level of reasoning, in which different questions are asked, it makes it possible to avoid treating others as mere means to one's own self-realisation when acting justly. On the one hand, we may ask the question, "What kind of life should I lead?", and on the other hand we may ask, "What action should I perform here and now?". Norman argues that provision of these two levels of reasoning enables us to avoid the morally egoistic conclusions reached earlier. It may be the case that my reason for trying to change my life in this way is that my life would thereby be enriched. But Norman argues that this change might lead to the cultivation of habits of thinking about others' needs in themselves, rather than about how any help proffered might enrich my life. In other words, I might become more the sort of person who, on particular occasions, helps others just because they need help.[44] Somewhat ironically, this is somewhat reminiscent of another Aristotelian doctrine in which the virtues are conceived of as habits of action.[45]

We may add a third necessary condition to our list of conditions required by a monistic internalist political theory which treats persons as ends in themselves. In addition to a social conception of the self and an internal telos, such a theory also requires that a two tiered level of reasoning be employed by the just agent.

The argument from subjectivity

In this next section, I shall employ some ideas drawn from Hegel's discussion of the Master/Slave dialectic in the *Phenomenology of Spirit* to generate an argument which purports to demonstrate how a concern for a person's interests in subjectivity could generate a kingdom of ends and thus a concern for justice.[46]

In the section 'Lordship and Bondage' of the *Phenomenology* Hegel begins with the notion that the Self is to be conceptually contrasted with the Other. The Self gains its identity from the Other.

> Self consciousness is to begin with simple being-for-itself, self equal through the exclusion from itself of everything else. For its essence and absolute object is "I"; and in this immediacy or in this (mere) being, of its being for self, it is an *individual*. What is "other" for it, is an unessential, negatively characterised object.[47]

Hegel notes at this point what we might call the 'problem of others'; that is, the problem generated by the fact that persons other than the individual consciousness exist in the world. "But the other is also a self-consciousness, one individual is confronted by another individual."[48] Here Hegel is referring to the fact that human beings are self-conscious beings. He then notes that human beings are social animals and that with regard to subjectivity our self-realisation requires a social context. He claims that self-consciousness achieves its satisfaction only in another self-consciousness.[49] In contradistinction to Descartes' 'cogito', according to which it is sufficient for an individual to think that he or she exists, in order to be, self-consciousness's satisfaction is found in other such entities according to Hegel. This is not to say that self-consciousness exists for others, but rather that it can only find its satisfaction in others.[50] Individual self-consciousness finds self in the outer world of others. Hegel suggests that self consciousness exists in and for itself when, and by the fact that, it so exists for another; that is, it exists only in being acknowledged.[51] In the development of 'Spirit', self-consciousness comes to realise that the Other, the object of its desire, is independent of it. It thus struggles and immerses itself in relations of domination.

Hegel believes that what is lost in relationships of domination—that is, in relationships in which there is complete disregard for the Other—is the capacity to receive the recognition which we essentially desire. Hegel employs the analogy of the Master and the Slave to illustrate his point. According to Hegel, the Master requires from his Slave not only service, but also recognition and acknowledgment. He needs to confirm his own power and dignity as a free agent. This requirement is self defeating however. By the very fact that the Master compels the Slave to obey his orders, he can set no store by any recognition which he extracts from him, for that recognition is not freely compelled. In short, the Master can only be recognised as a free person, if he live in the company of free persons.

The object over which the Master has achieved his mastery is not an independent consciousness, but a servile one in which he can not recognise himself; the required reflection of independent consciousness is distorted by the subjugation which has been the condition of its attainment. Despite his victory, the Master has no external object in which his free and independent consciousness can be mirrored back at him and hence sustained.

According to Hegel then, we are not only social animals with regard to our material needs, but also with respect to subjectivity, for our sense of self is embedded in the social context. Moreover, Hegel believes that we are specific sorts of social animals who require to treat others in certain ways in order to realise ourselves, for in the sphere of subjectivity, our interests can only be properly met via reciprocity and the treating of others as ends in themselves. As the French philosopher Alexander Kojeve notes, the Master's position is an existential impasse. Kojeve suggests that the master was on the wrong track; after the fight which made him master, he is not what he wanted to be in starting the fight, namely, a man recognised by another man. Therefore, if human beings can only be satisfied by recognition, the person who behaves as the Master does, will never be satisfied.[52] (Here one may be reminded of Aristotle's claim that the person whose life is structured around honour is mistaken because honour is a derivative good. Honour is valued only when it is accorded by the good and for good reason.[53])

Hegel implies that the person not involved in satisfying the two essential prerequisites of bothering about others as ends: i) recognising the other's otherness and; ii) acting beneficially toward the other as an end in himself, and who treats others as mere means, involves himself in a contradiction which prevents him from satisfying himself. As Charles Taylor notes concerning the Master/Slave dialectic:

> The contradiction underlying this is the following: men strive for recognition, for only in this way can they achieve integrity. But recognition must be mutual. The being whose recognition of me is going to count for me must be one that I recognise as human. The operation of reciprocal recognition is therefore one that we accomplish together.[54]

Hegel argues that it is only when the Master treats the Slave as an equal that he will receive the recognition he desires. Accordingly, the Master's goal of recognition can only be achieved when he ceases to treat the Slave as a mere instrumental means.

What is contained in this passage from *The Phenomenology of Spirit* is a potential explanation of how the maximal thesis might be fleshed out. An abstract theory of how people should be treated might be generated from a conception of the good which includes a recognition of our interest in subjectivity. Thus a monistic account of distributive justice can be generated.

Nonetheless, there are a number of problems with using the Master/Slave dialectic in this way. For Hegel's example to be capable of generating reasons why individual good requires just action, it must be the case (i) that the Master feels dissatisfaction with the recognition which he receives from the Slave and (ii) that the Master experiences dissatisfaction as dissatisfaction (i.e it needs to be the case that the Master is aware that the form of recognition he receives is inferior when compared to that which he could otherwise have received). In order for this to be so, there needs to be some criterion of *authenticity*; in order for the Master to feel dissatisfied he must authentically evaluate the praise which he receives. However, it seems plausible to me that the Master may in fact be capable of deluding himself about the recognition received from the Slave; that he in fact feels quite satisfied with himself. By inauthentically examining the Slave's recognition, he is thus quite content with his own self-consciousness.

Empirical observation would seem to confirm this claim about the Master's capacity for self-delusion. Acts of 'Bad Faith'—of the kind Sartre ascribes to the waiter who slavishly satisfies customers demands—are still received enthusiastically by many customers, who believe themselves to be special persons because of the very attention they receive from such slavish waiters.[55] It is not inevitable that the inauthentic recognition of slaves and employees will ultimately be felt as unsatisfactory so long as the recipients are capable of self-delusion. Secondly, we might well question whether the Master/Slave dialectic generates the universality that the maximal thesis requires. Consider the following story. A group of highly-placed businessmen meet on a regular basis at the Melbourne Club which is a highly exclusive club. All of the members are captains of industry. In the environment of the club they treat each other as equals or as close to equals as we morally-frail human beings are capable. Thus, in the confines of the club they are recognised by equals and receive all of the recognition that they require. However, at work they act disdainfully toward their employees. They do not need to treat their employees as equals, nor as ends in themselves, in order to receive the praise and recognition of free and equal agents. They treat their workers with disdain and yet, unlike the Master in Hegel's story, gain the recognition they require from social interactions at their club. In a way these men are reminiscent of Aristotle's great-souled man; the *megalopsychos*. The megalopsychos is quite content with the company of those whom he considers equals.[56]

This, then, would seem to indicate that use of Hegel's Master/Slave dialectic does not furnish us with *universal* reasons for treating others as equals. Hegel's example merely contains the implication that we should treat some other people as equals, but not all other people as equals. Thus, it is doubtful whether the maximal thesis can be generated via arguments from subjectivity.

There seems, then, to be some general problems with the various arguments, used in the pursuit of the maximal thesis, examined thus far. Firstly, given that the maximal thesis relies upon a social nature of the self, it is also possible that concern not be shown for those who one does not interact with. Let us assume that the Melbourne Club problem outlined above does not have the argumentative bite I have assumed it possesses; thus in order for us to realise ourselves, we must treat all persons whom we interact with as ends in themselves. It is still difficult to get *universal moral concern* out of such arguments. This may not seem morally problematic to everyone. Some readers might want to question why the treatment of those we do not interact with should concern us. So long as every one who does interact with others requires a kingdom of ends in order to realise themselves fully in those interactions, then we should be able to achieve the desired universality. However, this is goes to the heart of the problem. While in feudal societies individuals were only capable *ceteris paribus* of affecting those with whom they directly interacted, in modern world economies, we may affect people whom we will never meet. For instance, a farmer in Dubbo on rural Australia might decide to spray his wheat with a deadly pesticide. The wheat is then eaten by people in far-away cities such as Melbourne and Sydney and may well poison people whom the farmer will never meet. While he might well treat all of those whom he interacts with as ends in themselves, he does not treat these urban dwellers well. In the modern world it is possible to affect directly and significantly people whom we will never meet. Thus, this also seems to render these maximal arguments problematic given their reliance upon the social nature of the self; that is, their reliance upon the claim that people realise themselves in social interaction.

Secondly, it would seem that at the level of basic needs, such as adequate food, adequate clothing and adequate shelter, it is very unlikely that our interests will be most fully realised under conditions where all other people are treated as ends in themselves. While it may be true that interests in subjectivity might be best realised within a kingdom of ends, it cannot be true of all of our interests. Thus, there will always be a residual element of interest realisation which does not require a kingdom of ends, to which in fact the kingdom of ends is quite antithetical.

Finally, we might well wonder whether much of the previous discussion concerning the maximal thesis involves a fundamental misconception about the kind of justice which is at issue. While it may be possible to derive all of justice from the human good via the resolution of the problem of why it is that we should be moral if we think of justice as a virtue of individuals, does that possibility remain when one considers justice as a virtue of social institutions and arrangements? Have we imported an issue which is relevant to justice as a virtue of individuals to the analysis of justice as a virtue of social institutions and arrangements? It seems quite plausible that a case could be made that such a mistake has been made. On the other hand, it might be claimed that given the concern with individual human good, it is relevant to derive principles about how the State should treat its citizens from rules concerning how persons should treat other persons. Nevertheless, this doubt about the connection between justice considered as a virtue of social institutions and arrangements and the question of why persons should be moral provides further reasons for being sceptical of endorsing the maximal thesis.

Thus, although these objections are in no way decisive, they provide sufficiently strong reasons for abandoning the maximal project. Hence I will opt for the foundationally-pluralist minimal thesis. However, it should not be thought that the arguments laid out in this section are exhaustive of the possible ways in which one might argue for the maximal thesis, nor that all of the possible counter-responses that adherents of the maximal thesis might make have been outlined. It is simply that the arguments presented demonstrate serious problems associated with the maximal thesis and because of these difficulties it is the less adventurous minimal thesis which I shall adopt.

The minimal thesis

The internalist strategy which I shall employ herein, then, is the foundationally-pluralist minimal thesis. Given that it is unlikely that we can adequately demonstrate how the good will account for the realm of external relations, we need some further ground of obligation. Thus two foundational bases will be used: (i) a neo-Aristotelian conception of the good and; (ii) the deontic Kantian principle of Respect for Persons as Ends. I shall assume that these two conceptual elements provide sufficient normative data for the generation of principles of distributive justice.

In opting for the minimal thesis, I am adopting what might be called an *enkratic* approach.[57] In ancient Greece the term '*enkratic*' was used to describe a person who has learned how to control his desires, so that the performance of virtuous acts is not rendered impossible by those desires, but the desires themselves have not yet been transformed by the virtues. (In ancient Greece *enkrasia* was contrasted with the term *akrasia*, which roughly translates as 'weakness of will'). Thus to some degree the enkratic person acts virtuously, in spite of, rather than because of her desires. And such a person will experience the exercise of virtue and justice in general as a matter of negative psychological constraint. But this will not be the case for the *virtuous* person, who differs from the enkratic in that she no longer takes pleasure in what is contrary to virtue, and indeed takes pleasure in the exercise of the virtues themselves.[58] *Ex hypothesi*, for the virtuous person there is no distinction between the good life and the moral life. Accordingly, principles of how others should be treated can be derived from his or her own conception of the good.

Summary

In the preceding chapters I argued that an account of the human good is a necessary component of a theory of distributive justice. However, this left open the question of what other theoretical components might be required. In this chapter I have suggested that it is unlikely that an abstract theory of how persons should be treated can be derived from any plausible account of the good. Hence I leave Glaucon's challenge for all intents and purposes unanswered.[59] It is unlikely that we will be able to bridge the gap between the good life and the just life. An alternative ethical foundation is therefore required. Thus the conception of the good is to be supplemented by an abstract account of how people are to be treated which is not derived from the human good.

The task remaining is to provide: i) an account of the good and; ii) an abstract theory of how people should be treated. In the next two chapters then, I shall be concerned with outlining the two normative basic components of my theory; firstly a neo-Aristotelian value theory and secondly the Kantian principle of respect for persons as ends.

Notes

1. Interestingly, Urmson divides monistic theories into two categories; the *mononomic* and the *hierarchical.* The mononomic are those theories which lack a plurality of first principles or primary reasons for action. The mononomic have only one fundamental normative ground. On the other hand, Urmson claims that there may also be hierarchical monistic theories. These are theories which may have a plurality of first principles or primary reasons, but which have priority rules or some decision procedure for determining on which to act. According to Urmson, Rawls' lexical ordering of his two principles of justice would count as an example of hierarchical monism. There is some doubt as to whether we should accept that what Urmson calls the hierarchically monistic are genuinely monistic. Be that as it may, in this dissertation, when monistic theories are discussed, what is being referred to are what Urmson has labelled the mononomic. See Urmson (1974-75).
2. "Let us assume that each person beyond a certain age and possessed of the requisite intellectual capacity develops a sense of justice under normal circumstances.", Rawls, 1972, p.312.
3. Stephen R. Munzer writes: "The theory is 'pluralist' in that it contains several irreducible principles that sometimes conflict; when conflicts occur, priority rules can resolve some, but not all, conflicts." Munzer, 1990, p.3.
4. Of course, the maximal thesis is not monistic in all respects. As was noted, it must use empirical data about human society and the world in order to generate fully blooded theories of justice.
5. Plato, 1974, Part One Book 2, ch.4, [354-362].
6. We should not think of Glaucon's challenge as an example of a 'Prisoner's Dilemma'. Glaucon supposes that persons agree to justice in response to a Prisoner's Dilemma-type situation in which each would lose more at the hands of the others than she would gain at their expense. For a useful discussion of this see Gauthier, 1986, p.307.
7. We may contrast both of these approaches with the Kantian project, in which an attempt is made to derive an answer to the question of why it is that we should be moral out of reason. Kant argues that it is rational to be moral; he claims that the Categorical Imperative is an imperative of reason and therefore we should sacrifice self-interest to morality whenever the two conflict. For an examination of Kant's ethical views, see chapter one.
8. David Gauthier's refers to this position as 'the thesis. See Gauthier, 1967, pp.460-75.
9. Baier, 1958, p.314.
10. Ibid., p.309.
11. "If all men are moral, all will do better than if all are prudent.", Gauthier, 1967, p.469.
12. David P. Gauthier expresses the mutual advantage theorist's attitude toward deontology when he

writes: "Why, they ask, do we speak the language of morality, impressing upon our fellows their duties and obligations, urging them with appeals to what is right and good, if we could speak to the same effect in the language of prudence, appealing to considerations of interest and advantage.", ibid., p.460.

13. See ibid., p.469.
14. It may well be asked why it is that I talk of mutual advantage theory, when most of what is being discussed would normally be thought to fall under the rubric of the social contract tradition. There are two reasons which I believe justify focussing on mutual advantage theory, as opposed to social contract theories: firstly, social contract theory encompasses more than just the grounds of moral obligation, providing solutions to problems of political obligation and the origins of political society; and secondly, the social contract tradition is not an undifferentiated whole, encompassing, as it does, a wide variety of divergent philosophical doctrines. For a useful discussion of the various strands of thought which comprise the so-called Social Contract tradition, see Kymlicka, 1991.
15. Barry, 1989, p.163.
16. Locke makes just this very point when criticising Hobbesian contractarianism. He writes: "....an Hobbesist.... will not easily admit a great many plain duties of morality."; Locke cited Dunn, 1969, pp.218-19.
17. Gauthier, 1986, p.17.
18. Gauthier here seems to have in mind Locke's criticism of Hobbes, which focuses on the way in which contractarian morality could lead to the exploitation of the lower classes of society.
19. Ibid., pp.17-18.
20. There are some similarities here with rule-utilitarianism. For a useful discussion of the varieties of utilitarianism see Lyons, 1965.
21. Aquinas, 1911-42, la2ae 102, 6.
22. Kant, 1963, pp.239-40.
23. "According to Glaucon, then, there is an *external* relation between justice and benefit. According to the Socratic view, the relation is an *internal* one." Norman, 1983, p.58.
24. Plato, 1974, Part 9, Bk.6 ch.5, [553b-554e].
25. Much of what follows is substantially derived from Anthony Kenny's article 'Mental Health in Plato's Republic'. Cf. Kenny, 1973.
26. Ibid., p.2.
27. As Kenny notes: "Once the three parts of the soul have been introduced in Book Four, the way is open for the identification of justice with mental health. Justice in the state meant that each of the three orders was doing its own proper work.", ibid., p.7.
28. Kenny notes on the topic: "Justice is produced in the soul, like health in the body, by establishing the elements concerned in the natural relations of control and subordination, whereas injustice is like disease and means that the natural order has been subverted.", ibid., p.8.
29. Plato, op. cit., Part 5, Bk.4 ch.4, [445b].
30. Galston, 1980, p.280.
31. Popper, 1945, p.78.
32. Plato, 1969, [63a].
33. Cf. Aristotle, 1969, Bk.X ch.7, [1177a28-b].
34. Prichard, 1968.
35. See Norman, op. cit., p.56.
36. Ibid., pp.61-62.
37. Aristotle's position here is rather ambiguous. For the most part in the *Nicomachean Ethics* he envisages the virtues being exercised within the social context, at the end of Book X, Aristotle introduces the idea that the hermetic life of contemplation is in fact the best life. He writes: "..... the wise man can no less than the just one, and all the rest, requires the necessaries of life, but given an adequate supply of these, the just man also needs people with and towards whom he can perform just actions, and similarly with the temperate man, the brave man, and each of the others: but the wise man can practice contemplation by himself, and the wiser he is, the more he can do it. No doubt he does it better with the help of fellow workers: but for all that he is the most self-sufficient of men.", Aristotle, 1969, Bk.X ch.7, [1177a28-b].

38. Alan Brown writes of Aristotle: "For Aristotle, pursuit of the good life required that a man care for others. Primarily, the good life is a life of virtue and virtue requires that a man care for others and, ultimately, that he be just. But a life of virtue is only a fully good life in a good society ... and a good society is one devoted to the good of its members. Accordingly, the fate of others matters in two ways — directly through virtue, and indirectly through our need to promote the end of the good society." Brown, 1986, p.155.
39. Aristotle, 1969, Bk. IV ch.1, [1120b3-4].
40. Ibid., Bk.IV, ch.3, [1124b6-12].
41. Russell, 1979, pp.187-88.
42. John Casey notes of the modern reaction to Aristotle's *megalopsychos*: "The kindest thing that now seems to be said about the *megalopsychos* is that he is the crystallization of an aristocratic ethic prevalent in Aristotle's time, which Aristotle is not able to transcend". Casey, 1990, p.200.
43. Richard Norman writes of Aristotle: "This commits him to saying that if virtuous activity is not wanted for the sake of further consequences, then it must itself be an end, something which we aim at. This already has the effect of detaching the virtuous activity from the circumstances (including other people's needs) which require it: the circumstances become an opportunity to achieve the end of performing the virtuous activity, instead of the activity being a response to the circumstances." Norman, op. cit., p.61.
44. Ibid., p.62.
45. Aristotle, op. cit., Bk.II ch.5, [1105b5-1106a17].
46. It is assumed that use of Hegel's example would not commit one to his idealist theory of history, in which it is asserted that history is *Geist's* movement toward self-consciousness, nor to his idealist ontology.
47. Hegel, 1977, p.113.
48. Ibid., p.113.
49. Ibid., p.110.
50. Here we might usefully compare Hegel's work with that of Sartre. Sartre claims that we make ourselves in the presence of the Other. See Sartre, 1966, pp.301-400.
51. Hegel, op. cit., p.111.
52. Kojeve, 1969, pp.19-20.
53. Aristotle, op cit., Bk.1 ch.5, [1095b23].
54. Taylor, 1975, p.153.
55. Sartre, op. cit., pp.101-03.
56. Bertrand Russell writes of Aristotle's ethical views: "There is in Aristotle an almost complete absence of what may be called benevolence or philanthropy. The sufferings of mankind, in so far as he is aware of them, do not move him emotionally; he holds them, intellectually, to be an evil, but there is no evidence that they cause him unhappiness except when the sufferers happen to be his friends." Russell, op. cit., p.195.
57. In referring to the minimal thesis as '*enkratic*', I am speaking metaphorically; for if it is the case that justice is a virtue of social institutions and arrangements, then it is difficult to see how the State's treatment of its citizens could be described in terms of the controlling of desires. Nevertheless, the term is useful because it alerts us to the fact that our principles concerning how persons are to be treated are not derived from the good.
58. See McIntyre, 1988, p.112.
59. It should be noted that the various solutions examined in this chapter are in no way exhaustive of the ways in which one might attempt to answer the question "Why should I be moral?".

Section Two
The normative elements of distributive justice

4 A neo-Aristotelian theory of value

Human interests and the good life

I shall begin my discussion of value and the good life in general with some simple observations about human beings (I know no better way to begin). Human beings are born, grow up, grow old and die. We form friendships, plan for the future, raise children, barrack for football teams, learn languages and are capable of a wide variety of emotions, from pride to anger, from pity to love, from remorse to jubilation. We may say that there are distinctively human issues which concern and perplex us. Human beings are concerned *inter alia* with their own mortality, their relationships, the future, their environment, aging, their physical appearance, their relative standing in the community and their financial situation and so on. Underpinning such diverse considerations is a concern for the good life. In ancient Greece this was considered to be the central moral problem; yet it is an issue which twentieth century philosophers have, on the whole, shied away from.

It is this classical concern with the good human life which I shall consider in this chapter. What is the good life? While human existence is full of grief, ill health and unwanted social changes, how should a person go about living the best possible life? In this chapter, I shall outline a neo-Aristotelian theory of what the good life consists in. Good lives, as we shall see, involve *well-being* or *flourishing*. Unifying the apparent diversity of elements which are the central components of good lives, such as achievements and satisfactions, companionship and romantic attachments, intimacy and the fulfilment of plans, is the fact that all of these entities can be said to involve the flourishing of human interests. Furthermore, I shall assume that all of these human interests are objective in the way that the components of good health are objective. Thus, what I provide in this chapter is a naturalistic account of value in which value is located in the existence of objective human interests.

Human interests

Human beings, it can be said, have a nature best characterised using the interconnected Aristotelian notions of *ergon* and *telos*. Persons have an 'ergon'; that is, a characteristic functioning or work. The ergon of an entity is that particular entity's work or characteristic activity. For instance, the ergon or work of a musician is the making of music, just as that of an axe is to cut.[1] However, what is the ergon of a human being? This seems a much more complicated question which can only be plausibly answered in a metaphorical sense. The ergon of a human being—metaphorically speaking—is ultimately that which only human beings can do. Growth and reproduction we share with plants and animals; and sensations we share with animals.[2] Therefore, neither growth nor reproduction can be said to be the distinctively characteristic work of human beings. Instead the ergon of a human being is to be a *rational animal.* It is only human beings who have powers of rationality; this is our distinctive capacity.[3] Rationality is a capacity which human beings possess, which is not shared with either plants or lower animals. Thus our human ergon in this metaphorical sense is to be animals who act rationally. As we shall see as this chapter unfolds, this human ergon primarily involves a particular complex of activities.[4]

Human beings can also be said to have a 'telos'. A telos is, in general terms, a goal or aim. For example, if a person's goal is to climb Mount Everest, then this, in a contingent sense, is my telos. However, in discussing the human good we are not concerned with mere *contingent* goals, such as the desire to climb Mount Everest, but rather with what I shall call our necessary goals. The necessary or proper goal of a human being is to realise his or her ergon in the ways described above; to bring about that which is characteristic of him or her, which is his or her being as a rational animal. It is that which a person must achieve in accord with his or her inherent nature. The proper goal for an individual is to be that which he is, by his essential nature, committed to seeking. This is the full actualisation and development of his or her powers. Let us put this schematically:

1. the telos or goal of a thing is whatever is aimed at;
2. human beings must aim to realise to bring what is their essential nature;
3. the nature of human beings is their ergon;
4. therefore, the proper goal must be to fulfil this ergon.

My conclusion here is obviously rather vague. Much of this chapter will consist of an attempt to explicate what is relevantly characteristic of human beings.

It should be noted that the use of the notion of a human telos is not uncontroversial. In the writings of Aristotle, the word referred to the 'end term' of a process or more specifically the purpose or final cause. Assumed within Aristotle's account was the idea of a grand plan and implicitly an abstract grand planner.[5] For Aristotle, human beings had a function, just as an artefact, such as knife or clock had a function; and just as the knife's form is shaped by its function, so too is a person's being determined by their function.[6] Such teleological views of human nature are, of course, generally out of favour in a post-Darwinian world. However, we need not adopt such teleological metaphysics, nor must we adopt the view that reality is ordered by goals, purposes, values or final causes in adopting the idea that human beings have a telos and using this idea as the basis of our ethics. It is possible to remove it from associations with the idea of grand design. Instead I take the term to mean something like 'characteristic functioning'; characteristic functioning which we may want to claim has arisen due to a fluke of evolution. What it thus means to realise oneself is to bring about this inherent characteristic functioning. This is why I say that the notion of an *ergon* must be understood metaphorically

Furthermore, we may say that value resides in the realisation of this telos or characteristic functioning and thus the good involves the realisation of human nature. This idea that the good involves the realisation of our telos is the central tenet of neo-Aristotelianism, as I employ the term in this book. It is basic in terms of moral evaluation; other questions of value or valuing may be assessed in relation to it. Hence, the value of a knife must ultimately be derivative of the role that it has to play in human flourishing.

However, a further question which needs to be addressed concerns what this telos consists in. Let us try to give the idea of the human telos greater content. Human beings are essentially *interest-bearers*; that is, they are beings or agents to whom it is possible to ascribe interests. By this I do not mean to focus on the human capacity for being interested in activities and objects, but rather on the idea that there are certain objects and activities which are good for human beings. Of course, this not to say that human beings are the only bearers of interests, for all beings with a nature, including animals and plants, are interest bearers, but merely to acknowledge that we are but one of a number of beings to whom it is possible to ascribe interests. Such human interests include such things as autonomy, cooperation, knowledge, communication, skill-development, health and friendship. These interests, which we can characterise as objective properties of human agents, have the capacity to exist either in a state of flourishing or well-being (which Aristotle referred to as *eudaimonia*) or in a state of disease. Value, therefore, resides in the flourishing of interests or the realisation of the potential for flourishing.

Good lives and the flourishing principle

Value, then, for human beings resides in the realisation of human nature and the realisation of this nature involves our realisation of our potential for flourishing. Thus value resides in the sensuous movement from potentiality to actuality of our potential for flourishing; interest realisation being the process of movement of such potentialities to actuality. This leads us to the conclusion that value resides in a particular process of transformation of potentiality.[7] From these claims about value it is possible to formulate the *Flourishing Principle*, which states that:

The goodness or badness of any state of affairs is dependent upon the flourishing of human interests; that is the good involves the realisation of human interests.

This principle involves a developmental view of value which is consequentialist, i.e. according to which the rightness or wrongness of an action is, in part, determined by consequential states of affairs.[8] (However, as we shall see it also involves the claim that actions in themselves may constitute valuable states of affairs.[9]) These human interests can be divided into three broad categories of interests, these being;

1. the interests in subjectivity;
2. the basal interests;
3. the eudaimonian interests.[10]

These distinct categories are all constitutive elements of human flourishing or self-realisation and, while not exhaustive of human interests, these categories cover the greater portion of normatively significant interests.[11] The basal interests concern our material need to survive and reproduce our individuals selves as ourselves; the interests in subjectivity concern our capacities for self-reflection; and the eudaimonian interests reflect our need for a developed creative existence. Full human flourishing requires the flourishing of interests in all three of these categories.

Finally, all three categories of interests: a) involve some level of cooperation as a means of realisation; b) might be realised within the 'economic sphere' or in the external sphere (that is, they may be realised at work or outside of work)[12] and; c) might be thought of as either intrinsically or instrumentally valuable. This final point concerning the instrumental value of human interests is underpinned by the further claim that various interests are causally related to one another and thus some interests are valuable not only in themselves, but also because they make possible the realisation of other interests. For instance, satisfaction of the basal interests in food enables a person to pursue eudaimonian activities, such as designing aeroplanes. I shall explore some of these connections in greater detail as the chapter unfolds.

Good lives and the social context

Human interest realisation does not occur in a vacuum, rather it exists in the context of the natural and social world. A further issue which should be addressed then concerns the relationship between human interest realisation and the social context. In what sense is human interest realisation dependent upon the social context?

On the initial evidence presented thus far, there does not seem to be any reason to presume that human beings are necessarily social beings. It is possible, for instance, to imagine beings who are interest bearers and yet who do not require society. For example, swamp men who spontaneously emerge out of mangrove swamps and who have no need for other beings of like kind or for processes of socialisation might well furnish a bizarre fictional example of such interest-bearers. Such beings would obviously realise themselves without society.

My concern here is with specifically *human* interest bearers. Human nature, I would want to claim, is such that full human interest realisation requires human society: it is a platitude about human existence that we can only fully flourish within human society. This is the sort of view held by Aristotle who believed that the two great purposes of collective existence were preservation and the attainment of the good life. It is a claim which has also been made by Hegel[13] and Marx[14] as well as other philosophers of the Hegelian school. In fact, the English Hegelian, F.H. Bradley, goes so far as to claim that our very being is not only dependent upon social being, but that it is *interpenetrated* by social being, by which he means that we are what we are solely by virtue of our social relations.[15] This may be true (although it is hard to know how one would make good such a claim), but it goes no way toward showing that society is a sufficient condition of full interest realisation. It would, for example, be quite possible for opponents of Bradley to argue that our being is such that it is totally penetrated by social relations, but that this does not imply that it is impossible for humans to realise themselves outside of the social context. Robinson Crusoe's 'being' might have been interpenetrated by sociality and yet he still may have been able to live a flourishing life on his own.

Alternatively one might contrast this social view of human nature with the Stoic ideal of '*autarkeia*'. The Stoics advocated a form of self-sufficiency, in which humans transcended their normal limitations and attained a higher more godlike form of existence. The ideal Stoical person (or *autarkes*) is supposed to need and want nothing outside the immediate control of his own will. Self-sufficiency is a characteristic of happiness as a goal of human life. For that very reason the autarkes has to shun all worldly goods and pleasures and free himself from dependence upon other persons.[16] Accordingly, Stoicism treats this ideal of autarkeia as the standard against which all goodness must be measured[17]. Wealth, success and power (and even love and friendship) turn out not to be good things for human beings because the desire for such things is incompatible with self-sufficiency. Equally, love and friendship cannot be considered to be personal goods because they make a person's happiness dependent on the presence and happiness of others.[18]

However, I do not think these counter-examples make a nonsense of my claim that full human interest realisation requires society. It is hard to imagine Crusoe living a fully human life: while solitary hunting and fishing may seem idyllic, there would be many distinctively human activities denied him. Moreover, it cannot truly be said that a fully socialised adult, such as Robinson Crusoe, realises himself totally independent of the social context. His speech, his capacity to use tools, his knowledge of hunting and fishing and his understanding of his requirements for shelter, as well as hygiene rules, are all products of human society; they are all products of a human social context. A more relevant example here would be children brought up from birth by animals.[19] While many of their interests may be fulfilled, it would be difficult to call them truly human persons (and here the empirical evidence would seem to vindicate such a claim[20]). This connection between human flourishing and sociality is most evident in the realm of subjectivity; self-esteem and self-identity seem to be intimately tied to community and the recognition of others.[21] The need for the recognition of others is, but one, aspect of the general fact that our interests are socially realised. Alternatively, if we reconsider the Stoic ideal it represents a conception of the good life which is contrary to human nature. While freedom from dependence upon others would release us from the compromises which social life forces upon us, in actuality it would only do so at the expense of full human flourishing. The Stoic ideal overlooks the fact that human interests are only properly realised in the social context. In summary, then, human beings can be said to be socially dependent beings for whom social cooperation is a central component of interest realisation.

I noted earlier that human interests can be divided into three broad categories. In the following three sections I wish to examine these categories in greater detail.

The basal interests

The term 'basal interests' refers to those interests which involve the daily 'reproduction' of our individual selves as living and active beings.[22] The basal interests are interests which are connected to our need to survive and to provide the grounds of further interest realisation. These basal interests include *inter alia* our interests in basic needs such as food, companionship, shelter and sex. Additionally, goods which prevent injury and harm may be said to be basal goods. Translated into the modern industrial context the basal interests would include: i) adequate nutrition and shelter; ii) sanitary safe and unpolluted living and working conditions; iii) exercise, rest and other features of a healthy lifestyle; iv) preventative, curative and rehabilitative medical services.[23] Our basal interests are defined in terms of the role which they play as necessary preconditions of any other interest satisfaction, for it is imperative that our basal interests be satisfied to *adequate* levels before it is possible to pursue other kinds of interests, such as those realised in artistic achievement or sporting activity. A person who is starving and who spends her evenings sleeping on the streets, is unlikely to have the energy to compose sonatas or to play volleyball. Adequate basal interest satisfaction is required for persons to pursue *truly human lives*, beyond mere subsistence; that is, for us to transcend the realm of mere survival.

It is partially this role that basal interests have to play in enabling other interests to be realised that gives them their normative significance. Basal interest satisfaction is of great importance because it enables us to pursue other interests. Thus our primary moral concern should be with the satisfaction of these interests, for the very reason that they enable us to be persons in the fullest sense. This is a way of saying that we cannot lead flourishing lives unless our basal interest requirements are satisfactorily met and that therefore this category of interests should be accorded special moral and political consideration.

Some resonances can be found between this claim about the basal interests and the work of Aristotle. Aristotle argued that human beings first associated to satisfy their animal needs. Only after they secured the means of self-preservation for species as well as for individual, could they develop the more sophisticated activity of political communication.[24] According to Aristotle, people were able to govern themselves because they were not only ruled by instinct, but also possessed the faculty of '*logos*' which for our purposes we might translate as reason. This *logos* was able to be activated because human beings' needs for self-preservation and self-reproduction were met. Here Aristotle seems to be alluding to the fundamental role that sustenance plays in human affairs. It is possible to interpret Aristotle as asserting that by developing society and more efficient means of sustaining ourselves, human beings become more capable of leading developed existences.

Furthermore, it is also the case that a minimal level of basal interest satisfaction is a precondition of survival *per se*. For instance, if we have neither food, shelter nor companionship, then we will, in the fullness of time, die.[25] Basal interests are, in this minimal sense then, also the preconditions of human survival. However, this precondition is assumed in the ability to pursue other interests. In order to pursue other interests it is, of course, necessary that we are alive. What is of moral significance about the basal interests is their role in allowing persons to live *truly* human lives.

Another salient feature of the basal interests—and one in which they differ from our other categories of interests—is that their satisfaction does not necessarily require the interest bearer to be actively involved in their realisation. If one takes, for example, a person's basal needs in relation to sustenance, it is possible to see that this is an interest which may be realised intentionally or non-intentionally by the interest-bearer. Think of an unconscious person who is being drip-fed. Here the basal interests of the person in question are being satisfied, even though she is not *actively* involved in their realisation. Similarly, the child fed by his mother has his basal interests satisfied by the intentional agency of another person. Such examples tell us something about the basal interests; the basal interests can be realised without the active intentional agency of the interest bearer and, in some instances, this must necessarily be the case for there are certain conditions of basal interest satisfaction, such as the provision of sunlight, which lie outside human control.[26]

The eudaimonian interests

Human beings also possess what we might call eudaimonian interests. The term 'eudaimonian interests' is used here to describe interests realised by a whole range of creative and cooperative activities which involve the exercise and development of skill; from chess playing and surfing to architectural design and the practice of theoretical physics; from acting and writing novels to philosophy and the act of designing aeroplanes. All of these activities may realise our eudaimonian interests.[27]

In order for any of these activities to realise eudaimonian interests, they must necessarily involve *activity processing*; that is, they must involve activity in which there is an interactive relationship between theory and practice.[28] This interactive relationship provides human activity with a sense of narrative.[29] For example, take a landscape painter; let us call him 'Jim'. Jim paints his landscapes according to a specific theory he entertains concerning certain colour combinations of paint and the psychological effects that these induce in the viewer. Yet, in actualising his theory, Jim discovers problems and weaknesses. He thus modifies his theory and then puts his new theory of colour into practice. This process is repeated again and again, as Jim the painter develops his skill and actualises his potential for both painting and eudaimonian activity. For another example, think of a billiards player; let us call her 'Jane'. Jane spends her time attempting to perfect a complex cannon shot: she continually practices the shot and in so doing develops manual skills, which are the product of this interaction between practice and non-propositional theory.

The eudaimonian interests, then, involve human activity which is informed by theory: employing theory which may be either *explicit* (i.e. of a propositional nature) or *tacit* (i.e. of a non-propositional nature). The painter's activity would be an example of activity guided by a certain quotient of explicit theory, while that of the billiards player is an example of activity guided by tacit theory.[30] On my account, it is not just mere activity which realises eudaimonian value, but specific kinds of activity which involve continual interaction between theory and practice.

Moreover, two different aspects of the eudaimonian interests can be distinguished: (a) the *instrumental-strategic* and; (b) the *practical-rational*. While the 'instrumental-strategic' refers to that aspect of action which is directed toward means, the 'practical-rational' refers to that aspect which is directed towards the ends of activity.[31] (This distinction has its origins in the work of Aristotle, Hannah Arendt[32] and that of the early Habermas).[33] Both of these two aspects of the eudaimonian interests involve activity processing and both may be exercised within the 'economic sphere' and externally to it.[34]

(a) The instrumental-strategic aspect

Instrumental-strategic activity processing involves the exercise of skill. It involves a developmental interaction between a person's activity and her perspective on the best means of accomplishing that activity. The example given earlier of the landscape painter illustrates clearly what is meant by the instrumental-strategic aspect. Here we have an example of a practice in which the primary developmental component resides in the person's increased capacity to determine the *means* of achieving specified ends. The eudaimonian element in this case (at least as described) is derived from Jim the painter developing his technical dexterity: developing his control over the means of realising specific artistic ends. The more that he engages in what may be referred to as 'eudaimonian' painting, the more his control of the means of achieving his goals increases.

This aspect of the eudaimonian interests enables us to understand more fully why some kinds of factory work are diminishing.[35] A factory worker, engaged in what may be called paradigmatic repetitive factory work, has no theoretical input into the transformation of her practice. Unlike, for instance, an architect, painter or musician, no matter what she thinks, whether she thinks about her work or her garden, whether she is drugged, drunk or sober, her thought will have little significant effect upon transforming her work activity.[36] The pattern of her daily work will in this case only be transformed when a mechanical engineer or a time and motion study devises a more efficient manner of productive movement. Thus, this form of activity is typically devoid of opportunities for the actualisation of the eudaimonian interests.

(b) The practical-rational aspect

The instrumental-strategic aspect does not exhaust the eudaimonian interests. Consider an architect whose instrumental-strategic aspect of the eudaimonian interests is satisfied. In his work he has the opportunity to engage in open-ended activity in which his theory and practice interact and in which it is possible to develop latent talents. Imagine also that this architect, who is a member of the Tasmanian Wilderness Society, works for a company that has recently taken a contract with the Tasmanian Hydro-Electric Commission. The architect is given work designing dams: dams to which as a member of the Wilderness Society he is violently opposed. Thus, while he develops his architectural skills, he has little or no say over the goals or *telos* of his activity.[37] What this example serves to illustrate is another aspect of eudaimonian interest realisation which consists in the practice of determining the proper goals of instrumental activity. Therefore, in the example provided above, the Green architect's eudaimonian interests are not fully realised for the very reason that the practical-rational aspect is frustrated. It is important to note however that his practical-rational aspect would be frustrated regardless of whether he agrees with the project or not, simply because he has no input into the determination of the ends of his activity. Even if his views were in accord with those of the Tasmanian Hydro-electricity Commission, he would still fail to realise an important aspect of the eudaimonian interests because of his exclusion from decision making concerning the goals of the collective activity in which he is involved.

Full eudaimonian interest realisation, then, requires that the practical-rational aspect also be satisfied, in a sense through participation in the decisions concerning the ends or goals of activity in which one is engaged. (It is, we may say, an argument in favour of democratic decision making in the workplace as well as in other areas of public life).

Here one is reminded of Protagoras' in favour of democracy arguments in the Platonic dialogues. While Socrates argued that the activity of governing should be under the control of expert philosopher-kings, Protagoras believed it to be important that all persons participate in the process of determining the ends of social activity. Protagoras believed that although all people share in the capacities to make good citizens, they do not so by nature, but acquire these skills by instruction and practice. According to Protagoras, democratic decision-making enables people to develop these skills.[38]

In the foregoing I have assumed that there is some sort of connection between *developed existence* and *happiness*. While it is difficult to quantify, there does seem to be some empirical truth in this claim. It is evident from the way that children enjoy developing their capacities, satisfying curiosity and acquiring physical dexterity, that it is true that persons enjoy developing themselves. In general we believe that it is preferable to develop and exercise our powers and potentialities.[39] However, this does not mean that the developed existence is good only if it brings happiness. Here we may concur with Mill and say that it is better to be a human being dissatisfied than a pig satisfied. Of course, there are limits to this as well. William Galston notes that a "highly developed insight into the misery of others may make life unbearable" and illustrates this with the claim that the senses are of dubious worth in a concentration camp.[40] My focus on developed existence involves a denial of the fact that there are some innate abilities that ought not to be developed—for example, our capacity to be mass murderers—nor does it commit me to the view that only the developed and happy life has any worth. Life retains some worth even if an individual life is stunted and wretched. Nevertheless, that individual may sensibly decide at some point that life has become altogether worthless.[41] However, what I would want to deny is any blanket claim that the development of intellectual capacities contradicts the requirements of human well-being.

The interests in subjectivity

Finally, I turn my attention to a set of interests which I will refer to herein as the 'interests in subjectivity'. This term will be used to circumscribe all of those interests which are connected to our self-conscious and self-reflective nature. Human beings form conceptions of self; we are the sorts of beings who contemplate something we unreflectively call the 'self'. Some philosophers, such as David Hume, have argued that the self is illusory.[42] However, for my purposes it does not matter whether this self exists in the way that we think it does, or whether it is in fact illusory, for we do as a matter of fact concern ourselves with the self and continually attempt to form conceptions of the self. We attempt to generate an identity or self-image. Human beings are self-reflective beings who form conceptions of themselves which play a central role in their lives.[43] It is this self-reflective capacity to which the term 'interests in subjectivity' refers. The interests in subjectivity, then, involve *inter alia* such things as self-esteem, pride, self-respect and narcissism and connects with such human foibles as our fear of death, our desire for status and our love of praise.[44]

Human beings are not only concerned with self, but are concerned with it in particular ways. We desire to form a conception of the self, a self-image, which enables us to feel 'good' about ourselves. (It is difficult to make this point in a non-circular way; but I think we all have some intuitive grasp of the theoretical terrain). No one cheerfully tells themselves that they are useless or that they are the vilest scum.[45] Indeed, we often delude ourselves in order to generate a *favourable* conception of self. Moreover, the way in which we view ourselves fundamentally affects how we interact with others. The act of realising this favourable conception of self we can refer to as the realisation of *subjectivity* and the term 'interests in subjectivity' refers to the various means by which we may generate favourable conceptions of self. However, this should not be confused with self-obsession. The flourishing of our interests in subjectivity requires not that we think about ourselves more—which would be a recipe for personal disaster—but rather that we relate to our self in specific kinds of ways. In short, then, human beings are amongst other things self-conscious entities who attempt *ceteris paribus* to construct favourable conceptions of self, favourable subjectivity, and accordingly our flourishing requires the flourishing of these interests in subjectivity.

We might usefully further divide the interests in subjectivity into three subgroups; self-respect, self-esteem and self-image. All three notions are interrelated but conceptually distinct. I make no claim that these are exhaustive of the interests in subjectivity; they merely pick out three conspicuous aspects of human self-evaluation.

Self-identity

I shall begin by considering the idea of self-image (or self-identity). Human beings conceive of themselves in terms of a characteristic (or set of characteristics) which they believe to be central to who they *really* are. This we may call self-image. Self-image involves an overall vision of oneself. It is a defining idea of who a person believes that they essentially are. Persons might say of themselves, for instance, that they are miners, rock musicians, parents, Collingwood Football Club fans, models, athletes or a number of the above simultaneously. We are the sorts of beings who form conceptions of what kind of person we essentially are or would like to be. Furthermore, this self-image is not fixed or immutable. Typically our self-identity is in a constant state of change; change which comes about as we re-evaluate our projects, our central concerns and accordingly who we think we are. We may connect this changing self-image with the idea that human lives have a narrative structure, i.e. our self-image changes as our lives progress. Some of that narrative of our lives is derived from our changing understanding of ourselves. In creating our conception of self, we partake in a narrative, attempting to make ourselves who we think we want to be.

It should also be noted that self-image may be attained via identification with the collective or by differentiation from it. For instance, a person might construct their subjectivity by identifying themself with some collective. A person might consider the fact that she barracks for the Collingwood Football Club or that she is an Australian citizen to be central components of her identity. In identifying herself with this collective she attains a particular self-image and realises self-esteem. Alternatively, she might ground her conception of self in opposition to collective groupings. Self-identity might be gained by differentiating herself from the collective.

This particular interest in subjectivity can also be exercised within the economic sphere or outside of it. A person's conception of self might be derived from their profession or job and thus lead him to proclaim proudly "I'm a butcher", "I'm a miner" or "I'm an actor".[46] This kind of self-identification we may call 'vocationalism'.[47] Alternatively, self image might be exercised outside of the economic sphere and thus lead persons to self-identify by proclaiming "I'm a motorbike rider", "I'm a bushwalker" or "I'm a fan of a certain rock band".

Self-respect

Let us shift our attention to the notion of *self-respect*. One view which immediately suggests itself is that self-respect is some kind of favourable opinion of oneself.[48] However, this is hardly satisfactory. Self-respect is a *specific* kind of favourable opinion of ourselves. It involves our respect for our own intrinsic worth and importance as persons.[49] It involves the belief that one's projects and goals are worth pursuing, simply for the reason that they are one's own. Self-respect is independent of one's capacities, achievements, attributes or moral status, other than one's being as a rational animal. Self-respect, we may say, is respect due to one's status *as* a person, rather than because of the person that one is; or to put the point another way, it is because I am a person that I am worthy of respect, not because I am the person I am.

On this account, self-respect is a universal virtue, in the sense that it is a virtue which can be realised by all persons.

Here one is reminded of the Kantian doctrine that persons have intrinsic worth. In the *Groundwork* Kant characterised 'dignity' (which for Kant would be the proper *ground* of self-respect, just as we owe respect to others because they are rational beings) as an unconditional and incomparable worth.[50] One way of interpreting Kant here would be to say that this worth is independent of any contingent facts about oneself. Thus, for example, whatever has dignity has value independently of any effects, profits or advantage which it might produce. Similarly we may say of self-respect that it is recognition of one's value or worth, independently of any contingent facts about oneself, other than the basic fact that human beings are rational animals.[51]

Self-respect is also non-comparative.[52] Given that self-respect is independent of other persons or of one's own capacities, skills and attributes (with the exception of those capacities which are requisite for one to be a rational animal), then it follows that we do not gain self-respect by comparing ourselves with such contingent aspects. In this regard it is quite unlike respect for someone else which usually implies the belief that that person is above the ordinary. Self-respect does not have these connotations. Elizabeth Telfer notes of self-respect that it seems to be "a man's belief that he attains at least some minimum standard, and the emotion which goes with this, if any, is something like peace of mind".[53] This minimum standard is the recognition of the fact that one has worth regardless of any contingencies concerning one's status in the world.[54]

Of course, it goes without saying that my account is not the only account of self-respect to be had. Some theorists have defined self-respect in terms of the recognition that one is a being worthy of fair treatment. Larry L. Thomas, for example, argues that each person is deserving of fair treatment (although it is hard to know how one could be deserving of unfair treatment) in virtue of the fact that he or she is a person and labels this sense of worth which corresponds with having this conviction 'self-respect'. He argues that no matter what a person's abilities are and no matter what a person's moral character is like, he should not lose sight of the fact that he is deserving of fair treatment in any case.[55] Thomas' account, however, seems to me to involve a confusion. Self-respect is primarily an attitude toward oneself, a recognition of one's worth, rather than a belief about how others should relate to one.[56] What is true, however, is that one consequence of a person possessing self-respect is that she expects fair treatment. Approaches such as Thomas' confuse what might well be a consequence of a person having self-respect with its definition.

Self-respect, then, is the recognition that one has worth *independent of any contingent facts about oneself* other than one's being a rational animal. Such self-respect is an important component of good human lives. Full human flourishing requires that people have such self-respect. In order for us to live the best human life, it is important that we are self-respecting, for without self-respect, there are many important interests that we are unlikely to realise. A servile life, in which one fails to exhibit the proper self-respect, is to be condemned not only because of its demonstrative failure to recognise one's unconditional worth, but also because it prevents persons from realising interests which they may have otherwise realised.[57] It is for this reason that we may agree with R.S. Downie and Elizabeth Telfer when they argue that undue submissiveness is a sign of moral deficiency.

With regard to the role that self-respect plays in the good life, my account is similar to that of Rawls.[58] Under self-respect Rawls includes a person's sense of his own value, his secure conviction that his conception of the good, his plan of life is worth carrying out as well as a confidence in one's ability, so far as it is within one's power to fulfil one's intentions.[59] Rawls takes self-respect to be a primary good; it is something which is required no matter what one's plan of life. "Without it", he remarks, "nothing may seem worth doing, or if some things have value for us, we lack the will to strive for them".[60] Here Rawls makes an important point about the role that self-respect plays in the good life. It is a universal means to the pursuit of our projects; it is a means to the realisation of other interests. Self-respect, then, is, at the very least, *instrumentally* necessary if we are to flourish.

Self-esteem

Self-respect may be usefully contrasted with self-esteem. Self-esteem concerns not simply a belief in one's own worth, but rather a belief in one's worth in relation to personal or community standards of achievement or capacity, ideals and the commendations of other persons.[61] It is recognition of one's status as a person with regard to capacities, skills, attributes and moral standing. (It is interesting to consider the etymological origin of the word 'esteem', which derives from the Latin verb 'aestimare' meaning to assess oneself, one realises that self-esteem has connotations of self-assessment.) Self-esteem is self-assessment of oneself in relation to the kind of person that one is.

Furthermore, there are a wide variety of capacities, attributes, or activities which may be 'objects' of esteeming. For instance, one's self-esteem may be derived from one's sporting ability, one's mathematical prowess, one's beauty, one's social skills or one's artistic or mechanical skills. Alternatively it may be derived from tasks which one has set oneself. David Hume makes a related point when he notes the wide variety of entities which may cause one to feel 'pride'. He writes:

> To begin with the causes of pride and humility; we may observe, that their most obvious and remarkable property is the vast variety of *subjects*, on which they may be plac'd. Every valuable quality of the mind, whether of the imagination, judgement, memory or disposition; wit, good-sense, learning, courage, justice, integrity; all of these are the causes of pride and their opposites of humility.[62]

Similarly, self-esteem may be grounded in a vast array of qualities.

Self-esteem is closely connected to self-identity; how we see ourselves is related to who we think we are. Moreover, generally we form our identity in relation to those activities and attributes from which we gain high self-esteem. Thus, although conceptually distinct there is a significant overlap between self-esteem and self-identity.[63]

Self-esteem should be distinguished from self-respect. It differs in terms of the role that one's status *as a person,* i.e. one's capacities, skills or attributes, play in its realisation. Moreover, while self-esteem might in some quarters be considered a vice, it is difficult to see how self-respect could ever be so considered. In his article 'How to distinguish Self-Respect from Self-Esteem', David Sachs argues that one way of distinguishing between the two phenomena is to observe that whilst it makes perfect sense to talk of a person having too much self-esteem, e.g. she is arrogant or conceited, that it does not similarly make sense to talk of a person having too much self-respect.[64] Or simply claiming that someone has too much self-respect, does not mean the same as saying that a person has too much self-esteem. "If a person is disabused of an unduly high estimate he has of himself" Sachs writes, "he gets rid, perhaps at some cost in dismay or chagrin of a misconception of himself; and this is likely desirable." However, surrendering some of one's self-respect is not the same. In such instances one is not being "disabused of any misconception or falsehood", but rather is subjecting oneself to a form of abuse.[65] No longer esteeming oneself for things which one once felt proud of, such as one's arithmetical ability, is not the same as losing one's self-respect. I also want to argue that self-respect is more fundamental to the good life than self-esteem. Without self-respect we can not be said to flourish, yet a person may well flourish and yet lack high self-esteem.[66]

A further distinction may be drawn at this point. We can distinguish between those forms of self-esteem which involve comparison of one's worth with reference to the achievements, capacities or attributes of others from those which does not involve such interpersonal comparison. For example, one may make a resolution to run five miles every morning and feel good about oneself if one lives up to this ideal or alternatively have low self-esteem if one fails to live up to it. Here self-esteem need not refer to the activities of other persons. This kind of self-esteem we might usefully refer to as 'non-competitive self-esteem'. Alternatively, self-esteem may be founded upon competitive comparison with others. For instance, one might gain self-esteem through winning first prize in an athletics competition. In this case, it is the fact that one's person's skill is superior to that of others with respect to the relevant criteria that provides one with high self-esteem. This manner of gaining self-esteem may be referred to as 'competitive self-esteem'. If one considers oneself more beautiful than others, more muscular, more loved or more clever than others, then one is enjoying competitive self-esteem, rather than the non-competitive variety.[67] Competitive self-esteem involves the pursuit of world-glory, of goods, capacities, attributes and skills which enable one to compare oneself favourably with others. Hume writes of interpersonal comparison that it "is in every case a sure method of augmenting our esteem of any thing. A rich man feels the felicity of his condition better by opposing it to that of a beggar."[68] Hume, of course, makes no mention of how the beggar in question might gain self-esteem.

Kant drew a similar distinction to the one provided above between self-respect and self-esteem. He claimed that we should recognise the existence of two forms of self-esteem; one which involves comparing oneself with other people and the second which involves comparing oneself with the 'Idea of Perfection'.[69] The first captures what I have called 'competitive self-esteem' and the second would appear to be similar, at least in some respects, to non-competitive self-esteem (although the Idea of Perfection is clearly a concept with theological origins).

Some writers have suggested that self-esteem is *necessarily* competitive. They have claimed that while self-respect might be attainable by all, self-esteem is a *relational* virtue and thus of necessity can only be enjoyed by a proportion of the population at any one time and it is enjoyed at the expense of others in the community. Such theorists would presumably deny the existence of the non-competitive variety of self-esteem. According to such philosophers, we can only gain self-esteem by considering ourselves better than others and thus those who are worse than others at what ever is considered valuable cannot gain self-esteem, at least with reference to that object of esteeming. Robert Nozick is one such thinker. In *Anarchy, State and Utopia* he acknowledges, somewhat disingenuously, that it would indeed be a wonderful thing, if everyone could be an Aristotle, a Goethe or a Marx, as Trotsky had envisaged.[70] These standards of excellence would presumably lead to higher estimations of self by the general community. However, Nozick argues that even if everyone achieved this standard, that little self-esteem would be generated because people do not gain self-esteem via their common human capacities by comparing themselves to animals who lack them. Nozick suggests that we do not say to ourselves, for instance, "I'm pretty good; I have an opposable thumb and can speak some language".[71] Nozick's argument here is that the achievement of universal self-esteem cannot be a realistic moral goal.[72] If true, then this would seem to place some limitations upon human flourishing; human beings would appear to be locked in an ineliminable struggle of one-up-manship.

I think that this strongly relational view of self-esteem, according to which self-esteem *can only be attained* through interpersonal comparison, is mistaken. Anthony Skillen suggests in *Ruling Illusions* that a secure sense of one's own worth is not always dependent upon thinking of oneself as better than others.[73] Self-esteem, he argues, might be fostered by knowing that one has the respect of those one respects, or alternatively by the thought that one is engaged in a worthwhile project. In these cases, he claims, one is not measuring oneself against others. Skillen cites the example of a boat builder who is pleased with the boat he has produced, so long as it performs its required task. Such a boat builder does not need a reserve army of incompetents in order to feel good about himself.

Nevertheless, here too a note of caution should be sounded. While it is a fact that it is *logically* possible for all to achieve standards which satisfy them in the manner of which Skillen speaks, it is also true that such logical possibility does not entail that the State *necessarily* has the capacity to ensure that all persons achieve high self-esteem. One reason for this incapacity is that there are those who are morally and psychologically incompetent, and thus no matter what ideals they set themselves, they always fail them. Secondly, if one takes seriously the idea that persons aspirations are at least partially socially determined, then one must also reach the conclusion that it is unlikely that all can achieve the sorts of standards that society sets.[74] Larry L. Thomas makes a similar point in 'Morality and Our Self-Concept', arguing that the social institutions of a society cannot be arranged so as to be conducive of everyone having equally high self-esteem. He claims that if James' formula for self-esteem—according to which self-esteem is a ratio between expectations and achievements—is correct, then the inevitable conclusion seems to be that equally high self-esteem among all persons is not possible, given that the following propositions are correct: (i) the social institutions among which we live influence the ends which we come to value, (ii) these institutions place a comparatively greater value upon many ends which, as it happens, only the well-endowed can successfully pursue, and therefore, (iii) not all persons come to aspire towards those ends which are within their reach.[75] If Thomas is correct, then we should conclude that there are limits to the extent to which the State should be held responsible for ensuring that all reach equally high self-esteem

Before proceeding to the next section, I shall make some final remarks about the interests in subjectivity. Firstly, the flourishing of our interests in subjectivity is *intrinsically* necessary for human flourishing in that it is important, in itself, that we feel good about ourselves. It is thus intrinsically valuable. The interests in subjectivity are also *instrumentally* valuable; that is, they are valuable as a means to other intrinsically valuable ends. This is because our conception of self has a role to play in determining whether or not we satisfy some other interests. It is our conception of self which, to some extent at least, either encourages us to pursue other interests or which inhibits us. Rawls makes a similar kind of point about the instrumental value of self-esteem in *A Theory of Justice* when he claims that it is one of the 'primary goods'. For Rawls self-esteem is a component of what is required if one is to be capable of following a rational life, regardless of what one's conception of the good consists in.[76] Again this kind of point, concerning the instrumental value of subjectivity, has also often been made by members of the feminist movement, who have often focussed on the way in which women's subjectivity has prevented them from realising interests which they might otherwise have pursued.[77] Women's conception of self has historically been such in most instances that there have been many activities which women have not considered pursuing, even though they would have been quite capable of performing them. This would include activities as diverse as rock-climbing, priesthood, carpentry and engineering.

The tyranny of the basal

In the brief final section of this chapter, then, I want to explore an issue concerning the relationships between the various categories of interests. Do any of the categories have 'lexical priority'? I argued earlier that an *adequate* level of basal interest satisfaction was a necessary condition of the realisation of other forms of flourishing. I shall refer to this necessity hereafter as the 'tyranny of the basal'. The tyranny of the basal is comprised of two components: i) the fact of physical necessity which prevents us from pursuing other interests unless satisfied and; ii) the compromises that this requirement of satisfying physical necessity forces upon us. Our basal interests are tyrannical in a way that means that the satisfaction of the basal interests should be given priority over the other interests, until such time as they are satisfied to levels sufficient for other interests to flourish. In this sense, adequate levels of basal interest satisfaction are to be given normative priority. They possess what William Galston calls an *urgency*.[78]

However, this is not to say that our ethical aim is constituted solely by the satisfaction of the basal interests. It is important to go beyond the basal interests and realise the full range of activities of which human beings are capable. To be confined to the mere satisfaction of the basal would indeed be a dreadful life. We would be condemned simply to the 'filthy business' of materially reproducing ourselves. Here one is reminded of Hegel, when he wrote: "To be confined to mere physical needs as such and their direct satisfaction would simply be the condition in which the mental is plunged in the natural and so would be one of savagery and unfreedom, while freedom itself is to be found only in the reflection of mind into itself, in mind's distinction from nature, and in the reflect of mind in nature."[79] One need not take on board Hegel's idealist language in order to be sympathetic to his assertion that a life spent merely satisfying one's biological needs would be a dreadful life. Hannah Arendt makes a similar point when she argues that poverty is abject because it puts people under the absolute dictates of their bodies, that is, under the absolute dictates of necessity.[80]

We should also note the distorted forms of communication and cooperation that the tyranny of the basal brings about. The obsequiousness and servility of shoe shine boys in third world countries is an example of the way in which a failure to satisfy adequately one's basal interests may lead one to accept forms of domination, servility and oppression.

The 'tyranny of the basal', then, refers to the important role that basal interest satisfaction has to play in human flourishing and in human lives. The nature of our dependence upon the satisfaction of basal interests is such that unless these interests are satisfied, people will be forced into compromising situations. Think of the Biblical story of Esau who sold his birthright in order to satisfy his hunger.[81] Or again consider the plight of those resourceless workers in third world countries who must take hazardous jobs in areas such as mining and industry in order to support themselves and their families.[82] In this sense, the level of basal interest satisfaction influences the degree of choice we have when making decisions. Unsatisfied basal interests are tyrannical in that they force us to take steps which we would, in all likelihood, not have made if our basal interests had been satisfied. Unsatisfied basal interests prevent us from pursuing courses of action other than those required to meet such needs.

It has, of course, been the hope of many theorists of poverty that technical innovation and consequent abundance might do away with problems of basal scarcity; and thus enable human beings to ignore the demands of the basal in their decision making.[83] The hope was that technology would allow all persons to override this tyranny. However, we cannot rely on technology alone. As I shall argue in §3, greater emphasis should also be placed upon the generation of distributive principles whose formulation takes into account the tyranny of the basal.

Finally, it should not be inferred from my claim of the important role that basal interest satisfaction has to play in human life that therefore basal interest satisfaction constitutes our final ethical or political aim. Ultimately, our moral goal should be directed toward the realisation of the other categories of interests. We should aim to realise the full range of human potentialities. Of course, there is nothing new in such a claim. The ancient Greeks took labour which is grounded in biological necessity to be the lowest form of human activity.[84] The truly virtuous man did not engage in activity which was determined by brute necessity. (However, the fact that such freedom from the realm of necessity for aristocrats such as Aristotle was predicated upon the labour of enslaved foreigners and local workers was a fact not generally taken into account by such ancient Greek theorists). Our ultimate ethical aim should be the universal transcendence of the tyranny of the basal, a transcendence which liberates all persons to pursue a wide range of creative and cooperative activities.

Summary

In this chapter I have outlined a neo-Aristotelian account of value which will be one of the two normative postulates employed in the generation of principles of distributive justice. I suggested that there are three broad categories of interests which, while not necessarily exhaustive, encompass the most important human interests. This three-fold classification will take on greater significance in §3 in which distributive goods and principles will be classified according to this taxonomy.

To be sure, there are many aspect of the good life not covered here. For instance, I have made no mention of intersubjective relations, e.g. love and friendship, nor the role of narrative in the good life. Equally, I have not discussed the relation between one's stage of life and the good life as a whole, that is, the roles and goods to be enjoyed at differing stages of one's life. I could, of course, go on. To explore these issues adequately would be a project in itself. I shall assume that the discussion of the good life provided here is *good enough* for my purposes with respect to social justice. I turn now to my second normative postulate, the Kantian principle of respect for persons as ends.

Notes

1. Aristotle, 1969, Bk.1 ch.7, [1097a15-1098a20]. Cf. Ross, 1964, p.191.
2. Op. cit., Bk.1 ch.7 [1097a13-1098a20].
3. Ibid, Bk.1 ch.7 [1097b25-1098a15].
4. We should note that this emphasis upon activity is particularly Aristotelian, when we consider Aristotle's insistence that eudaimonia was a kind of activity; that is, that it is not any kind of pleasure, though pleasure accompanies it. Ibid, Bk.1 ch.5 [1095b6-1096a15].
5. In Aristotle, the idea of a grand planner is rather abstract; it only becomes personalised as God in the works of Aquinas.
6. We should distinguish the idea of 'function' from that of 'purpose'. A pig's liver has a function, but not a purpose, unless one believes in a grand designer. The function of an entity is the role of that entity in a system. Darwinism leaves function intact; it is 'purpose' which is restricted by the Darwinian project. See Nagel, 1961.
7. There is a perfectionist aspect to the ideas of this thesis in the sense that the flourishing of human interests is taken as an ideal towards which we should aim. It provides a commensurable standard against which actions and states of affairs might be judged. But, as I note in the introduction, this does not mean that I am committed to the view that all of our interests can and will harmonise with one another. In many instances, the development of one set of interests will impede the development of others.
8. If carried into the realm of moral philosophy proper this flourishing principle would involve the claim that the rightness or wrongness of any action is dependent on the extent to which it is conducive to the realisation of human nature.
9. Aristotle thinks that actions which are of value in themselves are the most important. See op. cit., Bk.1 ch.7, [1097a15-34].
10. William Galston also provides a neo-Aristotelian account of value. However, he divides value up into four distinctive components; the worth of self-preservation; the worth of developed existence; the worth of happiness (viewed as subjective satisfaction) and the worth of rational action. There is some overlap between Galston's categories and the account provided here. See Galston, 1980, p.7.
11. It is important to distinguish my use of the term 'self-realisation' from its current use in contemporary pop psychology. In realising one's nature, it is not a matter of realising one's 'true' self; but rather of realising some of the potentials that we have. Thus, rather than there being a true self to be realised, there are a number of different worthwhile selves which may be brought

about.

12. The distinction I draw between the external sphere and the economic sphere will take on greater significance in chapter eight 'The Eudaimonian Sphere'.
13. See Wood, 1990.
14. Marx writes: "Only in community [with others has each] individual the means of cultivating his gifts in all directions; only in the community, therefore is personal freedom possible.", Marx and Engels 1970, p.83.
15. Bradley writes: "To know what a man is (as we have seen) you must not take him in isolation. He is one of a people, he was born in a family, he lives in a certain society, in a certain state. What he has to do depends on what his place is, what his function is, and that all comes from his station in the organism.", Bradley, 1962 paragraph 19.
16. See Slote, 1983, pp.132-3.
17. See Zeller, 1962, pp.223-77.
18. This ideal of self-sufficiency can also be found in the works of Thoreau, 1983.
19. For an ancient mythic account of non-social human life see *The Epic of Gilmagesh* (Saunders,1972, pp.30-31). In this story, the wildman, Enkindu, is socialised through his attraction to a woman.
20. See Lane, 1976.
21. John Rawls writes: "Now our self-respect normally depends upon the respect of others. Unless we feel that our endeavours are honoured by them, it is difficult if not impossible for us to maintain the conviction that our ends are worth advancing.", Rawls, 1972, p.178.
22. In referring to them as 'basal' interests, it is important that they not be confused with what Feinberg calls 'basal reasons'. For Feinberg, the basal reasons are the grounds on which desert claims are made. See Feinberg, 1970.
23. See Daniels, 1981, p.158.
24. Aristotle, 1959, [1252b25-1253a25].
25. Locke, in formulating his theory of property rights, acknowledges that humans have minimal requirements of sustenance and that if these cannot be obtained that it is acceptable to override property rights. In extremis, this may justify him taking the surplus goods of others for his own use. However, Locke rather optimistically believed that in a prosperous property-owning society, such redistribution would be required very rarely. For a useful discussion of this see Waldron, 1988, p.251.
26. There is some similarity between the basal interests and what human need theorists, such as Norman Daniels, in 'Health Care Needs and Distributive Justice' call 'needs'. Like the basal interests, Daniels' 'needs' are objectively ascribable. Secondly, Daniels argues that they are objectively important; that is a special weight is attached in a variety of moral contexts and "we do so independently of the weight attached to them and competing claims by the relevant individuals". Finally, Daniels notes that these needs are necessary conditions for the achievement of our goals. At this point there would seem to be a great deal of conceptual conjunction between the basal interests and needs. One might ask, why bother with the idea of basal interests, why not just talk about needs? Indeed, this is a pertinent question. However, close examination reveals some differences. In Daniels' system needs are differentiated from other moral categories in that they are part of normal species functioning, whereas other moral categories are not. However, this distinction cannot be made in the context of the basal interests. All of the categories of interests, not just the basal interests, are considered to be important components of our species-being. Their realisation is central to our proper functioning. Thus, the basal interests are different in as much as they are part of a different theoretical context. See Daniels, 1981, pp.146-79.
27. This is not, I would argue, a totally inappropriate usage of the term 'eudaimonia'. Aristotle argues in the *Nicomachean Ethics* that the good life involves the use of reason in activities. As J.O. Urmson notes of eudaimonia: "...the most complete preliminary account of eudaimonia will be that it is activity involving the use of reason, at a high level of excellence and throughout a complete life.", Urmson, 1988, p.18.
28. By 'dialectical' I do not mean an interaction of opposites, but rather an interactive process where component elements in turn transform one another. Theory and practice are not opposites or contraries.

29. There are similarities here with Nerlich's description of values in *Values and Valuing* where he writes "....subjective values are the products of a dialectical transformation of lower-order desires under the pressure of higher order ones....", (p.17). This concern with dialectical transformation of desires leads him to say: "Some sports and games are better than others in expanding the general physical capacities (strength, alertness, precision of movement, speed of response or inventiveness in tactics) of those who play them...The game or sport is a good one if it really does strengthen, sharpen and expand our capacities in playing it", Nerlich, 1989, p.186.
30. What is meant by 'tacit' theory is best understood by thinking of the way in which we recognise faces and family resemblances without having any explicit propositional theory concerning what specific facial characteristics belong to certain family groups. Alternatively, to illustrate what is meant we may quote Wittgenstein: "Compare *knowing* and *saying* how many feet high Mont Blanc is - how the word 'game' is used - how a clarinet sounds. If you are surprised that one can know something and not be able to say it, you are perhaps thinking of a case like the first. Certainly not of one like the third.", Wittgenstein, 1967, Part 1. 78.
31. Kant makes a distinction between technical skill, prudential reasoning and morality. "Willing according to these three kinds of principles is also clearly distinguished by dissimilarity in the necessitation of the will. To make this dissimilarity clear, I think that they are most suitably named in their order when they are said to be either rules of skill, counsels of prudence or commands (laws) of morality.", Kant, 1981, [416], p.26.
32. Hannah Arendt's critique of utopian thought begins from the Aristotelian distinction between making and acting. 'Making' aims at the production of a product or end, separable from the process of production, that provides both the justification and standard of judgement of that act. 'Acting' does not produce a separable product; the end of acting is the act itself. Through action human beings achieve their fullest development, and each individual is revealed as unique. See Arendt, 1959, pp.175-236. Cf. Galston, 1980, p.27.
33. See Habermas, 1971.
34. Gorz, 1989.
35. We should note that not all factory work is repetitive. There have been many attempts to make factory work less repetitive and more stimulating and challenging. See S. Wood, 1989.
36. Marxists have traditionally thought of this kind of activity as alienated labour. Such a term may indeed be equally appropriate. However, what actually constitutes a lack of alienation has never been clearly outlined. For a discussion of the idea of alienation see Ollman, 1971.
37. There are similarities here with Aristotle. "Every art and every inquiry, and similarly every action and pursuit, is thought to aim at some good; and for this reason the good has rightly been declared to be that at which all things aim.", Aristotle 1969, Bk.I Section I.
38. See Plato 1956, [318a-328d].
39. As William Galston notes: "We exist as beings of a certain kind, endowed with organs of sense, practical abilities and intellectual capacities. These facts carry with them an evaluative force: in general we believe that it is preferable to develop and exercise these powers and that their full development constitutes the norm through which partial realisations are judged.", op.cit., p.61.
40. Ibid, p.94.
41. Ibid, p.94.
42. Hume focussed on the elusiveness of the self to introspection. This elusiveness, he argued, was the result of the fact that there is no self other than the bundle of experiences; there is no substance. Hume, 1946, Bk.I Part IV sec.VI.
43. "T'is evident, that pride and humility, tho' directly contrary, have yet the same OBJECT. This object is self, or that succession of related ideas and impressions, of which we have an intimate memory and consciousness.", Hume, 1946, Bk.II, Part I, sec. II.
44. For a useful discussion of various emotions of self-evaluation see G. Taylor, 1985.
45. Of course, we must note that according to the rule of St. Benedict the highest spiritual stage is attained when one truly believes that one is the worst of all men. Aquinas defends this position arguing that *for all you know* you are the worst person in the world. See de Vogue 1983. Cf. Aquinas, 1991-42, 2a 2ae 161, 6.
46. Hegel makes a similar point concerning the relation between self-image and vocation. For a discussion of this see Norman 1976, p.53.

47. It is an unfortunate fact that in *A Theory of Justice* Rawls overlooks the role of work in the realisation of one's self-image and one's sense of worth.
48. See Telfer, 1968, p.114.
49. Elizabeth Telfer distinguishes between *conative* self-respect and *evaluative* self-respect. Conative self-respect refers to such claims as "self-respect prevented me" or "he did it out of self-respect"; whereas evaluative self-respect is what Telfer calls the 'favourable opinion' version of self-respect. It is then the evaluative account which I am concerned with. See Telfer, 1968, pp. 115, 117, 119.
50. Kant, 1981, [436], pp.41-42.
51. Kant is a strange figure to invoke here, since he argues for the importance of humility and claims that true humility *humilitas morales* is accompanied by exaltation and self-esteem. See Kant, 1991, part 2 section 1.
52. Interestingly, Rousseau contrasted self-respect with egoism. He believed that while self-respect was a natural feeling which emerged from our instincts for self-preservation, egoism was a product of society. See Rousseau 1938, p.197.
53. Op. cit., p.114.
54. There are, of course, questions concerning whether one's moral status should be considered irrelevant to one's self-respect. If one has committed some heinous crime, and one recognises it as being such a crime, should one keep one's sense of intrinsic worth. This is an interesting, yet difficult question.
55. Thomas 1978, p.268.
56. See Hill 1982.
57. As Thomas E. Hill Jnr. notes: "Servility, as often revealed in grovelling, flattery, simpering and self-disparagement, is condemned because it symbolises an attitude which does not place the dignity of one's own humanity above all price". op. cit., p.55
58. It is important to note that Rawls does not really distinguish between self-respect and self-esteem. It would appear that he uses the terms interchangeably. For instance, see Rawls 1972, pp.178-79 & p.234. Stephen Darwall also makes this point. "To some extent Rawls' remarks in *A Theory of Justice* suffer from a confusion of self-respect and self-esteem.". Darwall, 1977-78, p.48.
59. Op. cit., p.440
60. Ibid., p.440
61. Of course my usage of these terms may be challenged. Actual examination of the every day use of these terms reveals a startlingly diverse list. From the point of view of ordinary language, however, my schema is no more problematic than any other putative schema. Given that these terms are used in a myriad of incommensurable ways, any schema will necessarily be as problematic in this respect as any other.
62. Hume, 1946, Book II, Part I, Sect.II, pp.278-79.
63. An interesting alternative way of characterising self-esteem can be found in the work of William James. In his essay 'The Consciousness of the Self', James defines self-esteem as the ratio of a person's successes to his or her aspirations. He claims that self-esteem may be thought of in the following manner: self-esteem = successes/aspirations. (Here we should probably be careful about attempting actually to perform the mathematical equations involved. The ratio is interesting as a way of illustrating what we mean by self-esteem, not as a formula for actually measuring people's self-esteem. Now, what obviously follows from James' formulation of self-esteem is that all persons would have reasonably high self-esteem if their abilities and aspirations generally matched one another; for such persons would be generally successful in pursuing the goals toward which they aspire. This formulation of James' is clearly compatible with the account provided here which involves assessment of contingent factors about oneself in relation to standards, ideals and other persons. See James, 1950, p.310. An interesting question which might be asked of James' formula is whether it is meant to include life-long aspirations or only short term ones.
64. Sachs, 1981, p.347.
65. Ibid., p.349.
66. One person who has tried to argue that lack of self-respect is a vice is Thomas E. Hill. See Hill, 1973, pp.87-104.
67. Mill refers to something similar to competitive self-esteem when he writes: "... the pride which derives gratification from the abasement of others...", Mill, 1972, p.147.

68. Hume, 1946, Book II, Part I, Sect.XI, pp.315-16.
69. Kant, 1963, p.216.
70. Nozick, 1974, p.241.
71. Ibid., p.243.
72. Cf. Sullivan, 1989, p.238.
73. Skillen, 1977, p.49.
74. Hume notes how our sense of self is socially determined in *The Treatise*, when he writes: "But beside these original causes of pride and humility, there is a secondary one in the opinion of others, which has an equal influence on the affections. Our reputation ..... character, our name are considerations of vast weight and importance; and even the other causes of pride; virtue, beauty, all riches; have little influence, when not seconded by the opinion and sentiments of others.", Hume 1946, p.316.
75. Thomas, 1978, p.259.
76. It should be noted that in his later works Rawls abandons this instrumental understanding of the primary goods. While in *A Theory of Justice* the primary goods are characterised as being that which is required for the following of a rational plan of life; in the later writings it provides an account of what the moral person in a well-ordered society would prefer. For a discussion of this see Rawls, 1982, pp.159-85.
77. See, for instance, Weedon, 1987.
78. Op.cit., p.96.
79. Hegel, 1991, 194R (explanatory notes).
80. Arendt, 1973, p.54. We may also turn to Norman. "Poverty and material deprivation make it difficult for people to lift their sight above the desperate struggle for survival. A greater degree of material affluence changes that; people can then direct their attention elsewhere, can turn their thoughts and energies to new possibilities.", Norman 1987, p.44.
81. Genesis 25: 29-35.
82. For a discussion of the economic unfreedom of the propertyless, see Cohen 1988, pp.239-54.
83. See Airaksinen,1985.
84. See Bernstein, 1980, p.239.

5 Respect for persons as ends

The formula of an end in itself

In this chapter I shall outline the second of the two normative postulates to be used in generating principles of distributive justice, *viz.* the 'principle of respect for persons as ends'. This is a principle concerned with the ways in which the State should treat its citizens; and I shall derive this abstract account of the State's obligations towards its citizens from a general account of how persons should be treated.[1]

In his canonical work, the *Groundwork of the Metaphysics of Morals*, Kant outlines the Categorical Imperative, which he takes to be the one fundamental principle of morality. Whilst Kant thought the Categorical Imperative to be one unified principle, he also suggested that it can be formulated in numerous ways. The second of these formulations, which he refers to as the 'formula of an end in itself', reads as follows:

> Act in such a way that you treat humanity, whether in your own person or in the person of another, always at the same time as an end and never simply as a means.[2]

This principle is often simply referred to as the principle of 'respect for persons'.

I intend to employ a similar principle as the basic normative rule concerning how persons should be treated. I shall make use of what I call the Principle of Respect for Persons as Ends (hereafter to be referred to as the R.F.P. Principle) which can be stated in the following manner:

> All persons should be treated as ends and never simply as means.

This rule, which expresses a concern for the essential *worth* of persons, places limits upon the ways in which people may be treated. Persons must not be treated as mere means, but rather, they must always be treated as ends as well. It thus limits what persons and institutions may do to other persons in the pursuit of their own individual and collective goals.[3] Moreover, not only does the principle place limits upon the ways in which individuals and groups might pursue their own ends, transferred to the political realm it also provides a mandate for the State to promote the ends of citizens.[4] As the chapter proceeds, I shall attempt to say more precisely what the principle entails.

One of the distinctive aspects of this rule is that it regards all persons as being equally deserving of this respect. It involves an acknowledgment that all persons have ends which are their own and which should be respected equally. Simply in virtue of being a person, every person is equal in worth with all other persons.[5] This focus on the worth of all other persons is the central reason that Kant's principle is sometimes referred to as the principle of *moral equality*.[6] Indeed, Roger Sullivan suggests that Kant's theory is an ethics of moral egalitarianism and that this is nowhere more clearly evident than in this second formula.[7] Sullivan argues that 'respect' is radically different from the notion of 'honour' which rests only on societal roles and prudential distinctions. Respect, according to Sullivan, is an attitude due equally to *every* person *simply* because each is a person, a rational being capable of moral self-determination, regardless of social position, occupational role, learning, wealth or any other special qualities or talents he or she may or may not possess.[8] When Kant discusses the respect that we owe others, one of his primary concerns is that we do not confuse the *moral* attitude of respect with the *prudential* honour and respect traditionally accorded the aristocracy and the powerful.[9] We gain a sense of this in the following passage:

> The only reverence to which I am naturally obligated is reverence for the law as such; and to reverence the law is man's universal and unconditional duty to others, which each of them can demand as the respect originally due him. But it is not a duty to hold other men as such in honor or to give them some service in this way.[10]

The principle of moral equality requires us to recognise that all other persons have objective value; but in no way countenances servility.

Such an attitude toward persons gives rise to some important political implications. If taken as the *modus operandi* of government, the idea of moral equality would rule out many social forms. For instance, it would rule out societies which institutionalise relations of domination and subordination. This implicit political element is not unintended in Kant's formulation; there is a political context to which much of Kant's work refers. As Sullivan notes, many of Kant's remarks were directed explicitly at the peasants who had been acculturated to believe that they should recognise and be content with their lowly and degraded place in society. Kant makes the comment that "one who makes himself a worm cannot complain if people step on him".[11]

Before continuing, it is important to distinguish the R.F.P. Principle I use from Kant's formulation of respect for persons. There are a number of ways in which it differs. Firstly, Kant considers his principle of 'respect for persons' to be derivative: it is derived from the first formulation of the Categorical Imperative. However, I take the principle of 'respect for persons as ends to be philosophically *primitive*, in the sense that the principle stands without reference to any further grounds of justification. Secondly, unlike the Kantian formulation, the principle outlined here is not taken to be philosophically *fundamental*; it is not assumed to encompass the whole of morality. On the contrary, it is assumed that, at the very least, a conception of the human good is required to resolve moral problems. This again distinguishes it from the Kantian system in which the Categorical Imperative, in all of its various formulations, is assumed to be the single principle of morality from which all other moral principles may be derived.[12]

What it means to be treated as an end

Respect for persons has been defined as treating persons not simply as means, but always as ends. But what does this phrase mean? R.S. Downie and Elizabeth Telfer note in *Respect for Persons* that our familiarity with the Kantian formula of Respect for Persons blinds us to the fact that there is something odd about talking of people as 'ends'.[13] Furthermore, the demand that persons should not be treated as mere means is rather vague. What does the rule that we should treat persons as ends and never simply as means tell us about the kinds of actions which are morally acceptable?

In some works of moral philosophy, the principle has been explicated via analysis of the term 'respect'.[14] Therein the writers in question attempt to give content to the second formulation of the Categorical Imperative by examining what the notion of respect might signify. Some explicate the idea of respect in terms of 'sympathy'; thus the principle is interpreted as an exhortation to have an attitude of sympathy towards other persons. Alternatively, others have argued that the principle should be understood as imploring us to have reverence for other human beings.[15] Under both of these approaches, the central issue becomes the achievement of the right frame of mind when confronted by other persons. This is, of course, a plausible way of interpreting the Kantian formula. However, I am not at all convinced of the value of these approaches. It seems to me that analysis of the formula *itself* would be a more fertile manner of explicating the Kantian principle. Replacing 'respect' with 'sympathy' or 'reverence' seems to be merely postponing clarification rather than providing it. Accordingly, in this chapter, the principle will be clarified by analysing what the proposition that persons should be treated as ends and never as mere means involves.

Close scrutiny of the R.F.P. Principle reveals that this 'formula of humanity as an end in itself' is comprised of two central elements:

(i) the claim that persons should not be treated as mere means and;

(ii) the claim that persons should be treated as ends.[16]

However, we do not need to treat these ideas as *entirely* separate questions. Given that being treated as a mere means is *contrary* to being treated as an end, then, the answer to what it is *not* to be treated as a mere means, will also partially tell us what is involved in being treated as an end. Of course, this is not the end of the story. Thomas Hill argues that the meaning of (i) depends upon the meaning of (ii) and that (i) will always be satisfied if (ii) is satisfied.[17] Furthermore, he argues that (ii) goes beyond (i); that is, the requirement to treat humanity as an end demands more than just avoiding treating human beings merely as a means. Hill cites Kant's discussion of the examples of the imperfect duties of developing one's talents and of giving aid to the needy, which do not refer to the idea of using someone as a means, as evidence for this particular claim.[18] Whether Hill is right about this is difficult to ascertain, for the relationship between the ideas of treating persons as mere means and treating them as ends is a complex one. What we can say though is that there does seem to be something intuitively correct about Hill's claim that 'as an end' is a technical term for the appropriate *additional* ways to treat humanity when using it as a means. Nevertheless, this should not prevent us from examining both aspects of the formula, for the very reason that (i) does appear to shed light on (ii).

Let us begin, then, with the idea of treating a person as a means. A paradigmatic case of treating persons as mere means would be as follows. Suppose an army commander decides to use some of his soldiers to form a human bridge to enable other soldiers to cross marshy ground. Here the soldiers are being used as means to some military goal, with complete disregard for their well-being. Treating someone as a mere means would include *inter alia* using them as a means to some military goal without any concern being given for their health and safety. The soldiers used as bridges would be mere means.

A second less outrageous and more mundane example of a person being treated as a means is furnished in the following story of two supposed friends. Two middle-aged men—let's call them Fred and Alby—live in a small country town. Fred is the local real-estate agent and Alby is a retired bank clerk who is particularly lonely, but who has inherited a prime block of land near the centre of the town which Fred would like to subdivide into housing blocks. With the aim of acquiring this land, Fred begins visiting Alby on the week-ends, pretending to enjoy his company, conferring praise and what appears to be friendship upon him. Under the illusion that Fred is his friend,

Alby sells the land to Fred. However, as soon as he does so, Fred no longer visits Alby and their so-called friendship comes to an end.

This story provides a clear example of a person being treated as a means. It accords with our everyday understanding of 'using' people, and which we would, in the normal run of events, consider to be vicious. The R.F.P. Principle would seem to rule out such exploitation, just as it would rule out the army commander's decision to use some of his men to make a bridge for other soldiers, because, in general, it deems the treatment of others as means to be morally unacceptable.

In the political realm we may consider Marx's description of the conditions in which nineteenth century industrial labourers were forced to work, as constituting what might also be considered a paradigmatic case of persons being treated as means.[19] Marx argued that all mechanisms for increasing the productivity of human labour are achieved at the expense of the health, working conditions, and job satisfaction of the working class.[20] Marx was concerned here with the ways in which the industrial proletariat are treated as mere conduits to the reproduction of capital with scant regard for their health and well-being. The force of Marx's critique comes from the fact that we recognise that these workers are being treated as instrumental means to the goals of the capitalist class, i.e. his critique gains its argumentative force from the fact that we do not believe that people should be treated instrumentally.

However, the discussion thus far might be said to be rather idealistic for the very reason that we cannot rule out all instances of instrumental treatment. If we think carefully about contemporary social life, it soon becomes apparent that social life necessarily requires that we treat others in an instrumental manner; that is, that we treat them as means to our ends (and this is particularly true in the commercial realm). Human society would be impossible if people could never make use of one another. For instance, every time I go to a shop, I make use of the shopkeeper; every time I ride on a train, I make use of the driver; and every time I watch a film, I make use of the actors and film makers. Commercial transactions require that persons be treated as means. Therefore, making use of others would seem to be central to human action in the social context. Does this provide a pragmatic refutation of the idea of the principle of respect for persons?[21]

Moreover, one might argue that we can expand this idea of the necessity of instrumental treatment well beyond the commercial realm and claim that all human behaviour involving others is instrumental. On this account, forms of behaviour, which might normally be thought of as constituting paradigmatic cases of benevolent activity, are revealed to be instrumental in fact. For instance, it might be claimed that a mother in wanting a child and then giving birth to one, is actually using that child as a means to her end; or alternatively, that the philanthropist—the person who works amongst the starving and ill—uses these people as a means to make himself feel pious. The corollary of this view would be *psychological egoism*, which asserts that persons are essentially self-seeking. Given that people are self-seeking, then their interactions with others must, of necessity, be instrumental. Without wishing to debate the merits of psychological egoism in detail, we might simply say that this is an exceptionally cynical view of human nature. I am inclined, therefore, to restrict myself to the claim that there will necessarily be instrumental treatment in the economic realm and that this is morally acceptable because of the overall good it brings about. The higher purpose which justifies treating others as means in the economic sphere is the fact that such treatment enables us to live in a society which has significant social production.

We might be tempted to ask whether the social necessity of instrumental treatment of others makes a mockery of the Kantian formula. The answer to that line of inquiry is simply "No". Kant was well aware of such difficulties and attempted to circumvent them. He did not claim that we should never use others as means; rather in the Kantian formulation—and in the formulation advocated in this chapter—the injunction is tempered by the modifier 'merely'. We should not regard others *simply* or *merely* as instruments to our own ends. Thus, according to Kant, in social life we must treat others as ends as well as means.

To be sure, *prima facie* nothing about the Kantian injunction commits him to the belief that one must live in society. As it stands the principle does not rule out withdrawing from society; however, once one is involved in social interactions then one must treat others as ends and never merely as means. However, Kant himself argued elsewhere that sociability was a duty. In the *Metaphysics of Morals* he argues that "it is a duty to oneself as well as others not to *isolate* oneself", but rather one must use one's moral perfection in social intercourse.[22] However, we should not become too embroiled in fine details of Kantian scholarship at this point, for the R.F.P. Principle employed here is Kantian in spirit only and it is a central contention of my theory that human beings can only fully flourish in the social context. More importantly to the issue at hand, however, is the fact that simply adding 'merely' to the injunction, without extensive explanation, does not really enlighten us as to what counts as morally legitimate action. What does it mean to never treat a person simply as a means? How can a single act at the same time be both an example of means-treating and one of ends-treating? Should we think of it then as referring to sets of actions rather than single actions?

One way in which we may explicate this proviso is to think of it *quantitatively.* On this interpretation, any action would be judged according to *how much* it involves treating another person as an end and how much as a means. Thus, judgement of the moral status of the action would be a matter of degree. Accordingly, we would weigh up the extent to which an action involves treating a person(s) as an end and how much as a means and then adjudicate as to whether it was morally acceptable. Alternatively, we might think of it as referring to sets of actions, some of which are end-treating and some of which are examples of instrumental treatment. On this interpretation, the R.F.P. Principle commands us to weigh up how many of the actions are end-treating and how many are means-treating and if the ratio of means to ends is above the acceptable level, then that set of actions is morally unacceptable.

However, there is something absurd about this latter interpretation. It construes the Kantian principle in an unlikely utilitarian manner. Moreover, it does not appear to capture what it means to treat a person as an end, for the very act of calculating the degree or amount to which we treat another person as an end seems antithetical to treating persons as ends. There are good reasons, then, for rejecting this interpretation of the R.F.P. Principle.

A second way in which one might make sense of the role which 'merely' has to play here would be to cash the principle out in terms of a 'bastardised' version of Davidsonian action theory, recognising that there may be more than one legitimate intentional description of any single action. In his article 'Agency', Donald Davidson focuses on the seemingly paradoxical phenomenon of there being various plausible descriptions of actions other than the intentional description relevant to the intention which motivated the action. For instance, Hamlet intentionally kills the man behind the arras, but he does not intentionally kill Polonius. Yet Polonius is the man behind the arras, and therefore Hamlet's killing of the man behind the arras is identical with his killing of Polonius. Thus while Hamlet intends to kill the man behind the arras, he does not intend to kill Polonius. Yet they are one and the same action. Is his murder of Polonius intentional? In considering the problem Davidson urges us to consider an action to be intentional if some description of it is intentional. He claims that "a man is the agent of an act if what he does can be described under an aspect that makes it intentional."[23] The action is intentional because there is one description of it under which it is intended. What is significant for us about Davidson's discussion is his claim that there are a number of true descriptions of an action and that so long as one description is intentional, then, the action is intentional. As well as differentiating between intentional and non-intentional descriptions of an action, Davidson also notes that there may be a number of different intentional descriptions of a single action. In the one action I may flip a switch, turn on the light and illuminate the room.[24] All of these are legitimate descriptions of this single act; the point here being that a single action may have a number of different legitimate descriptions.[25] It is not as if my describing the action as the flipping of a switch necessarily implies that describing it as the act of illuminating the room is incorrect. (For the sake of simplicity, I shall assume from this point onwards that when we talk of 'action-descriptions' we are referring to 'intentional action-descriptions').

Analogously, if we apply this idea of there being a number of true intentional descriptions of any action to the problem of how the R.F.P. Principle should be interpreted, we may come to say that some of the action-descriptions may count as instrumental treatment and some as treating persons as ends. This enables us to focus on single transactions rather than sets of actions. In order to illustrate this, let us consider the commercial transaction which occurs between myself and 'Nick', the local milk-bar owner from whom I buy chocolate. In buying bars of chocolate I am treating him instrumentally because I am using him as a means to my goal of obtaining chocolate. However, at the same time I am paying him money; which involves recognition of his ends. This latter description is a description of my action under which Nick is treated as an end.

We may say that so long as one (or more) of the intentional descriptions of my action counts as treating the relevant person as an end, then the action is morally acceptable. According to this interpretation of the R.F.P. Principle:

> an action is morally acceptable if and only if one (or more) intentional descriptions of the action involves treating the person as an end.

My commercial interactions with Nick the shop-keeper are morally acceptable, according to this interpretation because one of the descriptions of my action involves treating Nick as an end.

However, while this interpretation of the R.F.P. Principle does make sense—to some extent at least—of how commercial transactions might count as respecting persons as ends, it is still problematic. If we think carefully about various human interactions, we find that many seemingly heinous acts might be said to have at least one possible intentional description under which the act would count as treating persons as ends-in-themselves. For instance, take the case of an invasion of the traditional lands of rainforest Indians by ravenous, money-hungry goldminers. The goldminers not only mine for gold, destroying the rainforests which the Indians have lived in for millennia, they intentionally introduce various diseases to the Indians, as well as beating and humiliating these traditional owners of the land. However, they do also bring with them the trappings of Western civilisation as they build towns around their goldmines. Thus, although the Indians' lifestyle and health has been destroyed, according to this particular interpretation of the R.F.P. Principle provided above, it is possible that their action might well be considered to be morally acceptable because there is at least one description of their action which may count as end-treating; namely that what they are doing is bringing civilisation to these putatively primitive peoples. And indeed they are.

This quasi-Davidsonian treatment of the R.F.P. Principle would need to be modified so that such acts cannot be said to be examples of end-treating. One way of doing so would be to invert the definition, so that instead of arguing that what is required is a *single* description which *counts* as end-treating, we argue that there should be *no single* intentional description of the action which is *contrary* to treating persons as ends. Thus, the goldminers' action would no longer be morally acceptable because there is at least one description of their action which is contrary to the Indians being treated as ends-in-themselves. At the same time, according to this line of thought, if we apply the criteria to the commercial transaction between myself and Nick, we find no action description, on the face of it at least, which is contrary to his being treated as an end. There would seem to be nothing about my using him as a means to obtain chocolate which is, of itself, contrary to Nick being treated as an end. The R.F.P. Principle then is modified to read:

> an action is morally acceptable if and only if no single action description is contrary to the person being treated as an end.

When we say that a person should not be treated simply as a means, we are demanding that there should be no description of what is occurring which is contrary to that person being treated as an end.

However, while this negative account of the principle has some merits there are again still some difficulties. These problems arise out of the seemingly infinite way in which one might describe an action. It is hard to think of any action which it is impossible for someone to think of a description of that act which is contrary to persons being treated as ends. For instance, if we think about what many would consider the paradigm case of end-treating, the Parable of the Good Samaritan, it might be claimed that the Samaritan's action is contrary to end-treating because the Israelite that he helps may be shamed by being helped by a Samaritan, to the extent that afterwards he decides to commit suicide. We need to fix the relevant descriptions of actions, such that we do not leave ourselves open to such counter-examples.

In this context, it is worth considering in some detail a paper entitled 'Humanity as an End in Itself' by Thomas E. Hill Jnr. in which the Kantian principle of respect for persons is explicated in terms of irrational conflicts of will.[26] In attempting to lay out what might be involved in the Kantian injunction to treat persons as ends and not as mere means, Hill makes *inter alia* the following points about the Kantian principle of respect for persons:

i) it is a supreme condition limiting the use of every means:

ii) it has precedence over other reasons for action:

iii) it entails that persons are the grounds of self-determination:

iv) it entails that persons should be subject to no purpose, unless it is in accord with a law that might arise from the will of the person affected.

It is this final point which I wish to take up in some detail. Hill argues that in the second example employed by Kant to illustrate the Categorical Imperative—which concerns a lying promise—he implies that one at least partially satisfies the requirement to treat humanity as an end, if one treats persons as "beings who must themselves be able to share in the end of the very same action". For example, a lying promise is wrong because the man whom I seek to use for my own purposes by such a promise cannot possibly agree with my way of behaving towards him and so cannot share the end of the action.[27] Hill believes that it would be absurd to argue that one should not use a person's services unless that person quite literally shared all of one's ends in doing so; for example, to say that carpenters employed to build an opera house must have among their goals the increased enjoyment of opera. The point is that, in so far as they are used as means, they must be able to adopt the agent's ends, under some appropriate description, without irrational conflict of will.[28] What Hill is claiming is that an appropriate interpretation of Kant's respect for persons principle involves asking whether the persons whom one is acting toward could *possibly* adopt the goal of the action performed, without such irrational conflict. It is not necessary that they share the actual goal. Hill claims that if the carpenters are in need of work and are decently paid, "they can without irrationality adopt the immediate end of building an opera house, whether they care for opera or not."[29] This might be contrasted with goals which one could not possibly share, such as building one's own gallows.

In explicating the Kantian principle in this way, the crucial issue becomes *irrational* conflicts of will. To be sure, it is possible to imagine a person who willingly agrees to build their own gallows; however, Hill claims that such an action would constitute an irrational determination of the will. Just as one cannot rationally will suicide, one cannot will any end that is contrary to one's status as a rational agent. He claims that in the *Critique of Practical Reason*, Kant states as the condition of treating a person as an end that his autonomy as a rational being be subjected to no single purpose unless it is in accord with a law that might arise from the will of the person affected.[30] Here the restriction on the purposes or ends to which a person may be subordinated is more explicitly the compatibility of such purposes with laws which the affected person, as a rational being, could accept.[31] According to Hill, the question which must be asked of any maxim of action is whether the agent could *rationally* share in the end or goal of the action to which he is subjected, with the added proviso that it is not necessary that the person actually share the goal, but that it would be possible as a rational agent to share it.

While Hill is primarily concerned with explicating the Kantian version of the principle of respect for persons, I think that his work is of use in elaborating the R.F.P. Principle. The idea of talking about goals that the agent could share as ends of his own provides a useful way of talking about treating people not as mere means, but as ends in themselves. However, I would want to modify it slightly. Rather than grounding appropriate action in rationality, I shall use the idea of the human good and rather than talking of acts which are contrary to being treated as an end, as we did earlier, I shall be concerned with acts which are contradictory to the conditions of that person's flourishing. We may talk of goals which the agent could possibly have without contradicting the conditions of his own flourishing. Thus, we may reformulate the R.F.P Principle in the following manner:

> An action is morally acceptable if and only if the goals of the action to which persons are subjected are goals that those persons could adopt as their own without contradicting the conditions of their own flourishing.

By modifying the principle in this way, it is possible to make sense of what it means to say that we should treat a person as an end, and not as a mere means. It does not matter whether the person affected is a means to some end under certain descriptions of the action, nor that the goal of the action is one which she would contemplate as an end, so long as the goal of the action is one which the subject could take on as her own without violating the human good. If we apply this abstract account of morally acceptable behaviour to our earlier example of the manipulative real estate agent, we find that Fred's treatment of Alby is unacceptable for the very reason that Alby could not adopt as his own the goal of Fred's action without undermining the conditions of his own flourishing. Alby could not adopt the goal of himself being duped without the adoption of that goal being detrimental to his own well-being. Similarly, the bridge-soldiers could not adopt the goals of this action without possibly undermining the conditions of their own flourishing. If we apply this formulation to the political context, it reads as follows:

> The social treatment of a person as an end and not as a mere means involves ensuring as far as is practicable that the goals of the action to which they are subjected are goals that they could adopt as their own without contradicting the conditions of their own flourishing.

What it means to flourish is to be cashed out in terms of the neo-Aristotelian value theory laid out in chapter four. One important point should be made about this interpretation; it requires a conception of the good in order to substantiate what would count as violating the conditions of one's flourishing. It is dependent upon a conception of the human good, rather than an account-of what the rational person would or would not do.

Some objections to the foregoing formulation of the R.F.P. Principle

What I have outlined, then, is an account of what the R.F.P. Principle involves which is intended to demonstrate how treating persons as ends may be compatible with various socially necessary instrumental actions. Against my account, with reference to the examples of socially necessary instrumental action, it might be argued that we cannot provide a way of distinguishing these supposed examples of end-treating from actions which should be thought of as purely instrumental; and thus if we cannot distinguish them, then this makes a nonsense of the idea that we have shown how actions may be both instrumental and end-treating at the same time. I shall call this the 'Objection from Indistinguishability'.

Let us illustrate this objection by reconsidering my interactions with Nick the milk-bar owner from whom I buy chocolate bars. I argued that I treat him as an end by buying chocolate from him, rather than stealing it from his shop. However, contrast this with the moral status of my action when I buy chocolate bars from an automatic vending machine. In this case it would be very difficult (on initial appearances at least) to argue that I treat the vending machine as an end in itself. Yet, on the evidence presented, there seems to be no difference between my act of buying chocolate from Nick and my act of buying it from a vending machine. It is true that I say "good morning" to Nick when I enter his shop, but this is no part of the act of buying the chocolate; I could still buy the chocolate from him, and under our earlier description treat him as an end, without even acknowledging his existence. If my interaction with Nick cannot be distinguished from an interaction which patently is merely instrumental, then how can I maintain that I have treated Nick both as an end and as a means? Does this not create problems for my account of what is involved in treating a person as both a means and as an end at the same time? Am I deluding myself in thinking that I am treating Nick as an end, when in fact I am simply treating him as a mere means.

One way of responding to this 'Objection from Indistinguishability' would be to question whether it in fact matters when we compare the treatment of persons with that of inanimate objects that we cannot distinguish action which is both end-treating and instrumental from purely instrumental action. The vending machine cannot be treated as an end because it does not have ends of its own; however, if it did have ends, such as the end of accumulating wealth, then we would be treating it as an end by buying goods from it. Accordingly, the problem lies not with my action, but rather with the subject towards whom I act. However, this is a rather weak response. If I am truly treating Nick as an end, then we should be able to distinguish my action from that which is purely instrumental.

A second way of responding would be to ask whether it is, in fact, simply a machine with which we are interacting. Can we in actuality *buy* any thing from a machine? While we may obtain commodities from a machine by placing money in the appropriate slot, do we not actually buy the goods from the person who owns the machine? Does the lack of actual human contact mean that we are not really buying goods from a vendor? If this is indeed the case then we treat the vendor as an end by placing money in the slot and not attempting to obtain the goods without paying by fiddling with the machine. I think that this is the right line of response. The 'Objection from Indistinguishability' can be defused by demonstrating that whilst we do not treat the vending machine as an end, we do in fact treat the vendor as an end when we buy his goods rather than steal them, for the force of this objection comes from the fact that it is absurd to talk of vending machines being treated as ends in themselves. It seems to me that this second line of argumentation provides a refutation of the Objection from Indistinguishability.

We may wish to strengthen this response to the objection by arguing that not only is it a fact, *as it were*, that there is a person involved in this commercial exchange, but that it is a fact of necessity because the very notion of 'buying' is itself analytically connected to relations between persons. According to this line of argumentation, conceptual analysis reveals that it is necessarily the case that 'buying' involves persons because that is what buying is; a relation between persons.

However, if for some reason these arguments do not convince the reader that there is a relevant difference involved, there is a third way of responding to the objection which would involve demonstrating *counter-factually* the difference between my interactions with Nick the milkbar owner and those with the inanimate vending machine. Let us reconsider my interactions with Nick and the vending machine and imagine that I am in a hurry and that in both cases the service is slow. What distinguishes my end-treating of Nick and my instrumental treatment of the vending machine is what I would do in response to this slow service. In the case of the slow-responding vending machine I might give it a hard kick (though not hard enough to do any structural damage), hoping to hurry the machine along and at the same time venting my frustration. This would be quite consistent with treating the machine as a means. However, when buying chocolate from Nick, even though I might feel like giving him a kick when he takes along time to serve me, I do not do so because it would not be consistent with treating him as an end in himself. The two cases can be distinguished counter-factually, by considering what I would do under differing circumstances.

The Objection from Indistinguishability fails then because: i) we do in fact treat someone as an end (namely the vendor) when we buy goods from a vending machine and; ii) that even if we eliminate the vendor, we may distinguish counter-factually the way that I would treat Nick from the way that I would treat the vending machine in certain relevantly similar circumstances.

Respect for persons as ends and the minimal thesis

I claimed in chapter three that a conception of the human good was not sufficient to generate adequate principles of distributive justice. In that chapter I argued that any particular conception of the human good would be compatible with such a wide variety of incompatible theories of distributive justice, and therefore we cannot really claim to be able to generate principles of distributive justice *solely* from a theory of the good. Thus, I argued that the theory of the good required supplementation with an abstract or formal theory of how people should be treated. (In effect I argued that there exists a gap between theories of the good and theories of distributive justice which can only be overcome with supplementation by an abstract deontic account of how others should be treated). The purpose of this chapter was to supply such an account.

What I need to show then is that the R.F.P. Principle is capable of supplementing our theory of the good in such a way as to enable us to generate adequate theories of justice. It is probably easiest to attempt this task negatively: that is, it is probably easiest to show that the R.F.P. Principle rules out various theories of distributive justice which intuitively at least appear repugnant.

Let us begin by considering what kinds of State activity our R.F.P. Principle would rule out *morally*. In chapter three I argued that political theory grounded solely in a conception of the human good was compatible with a wide variety of institutional arrangements, many of which we might consider to be far from desirable. For instance, a theory of the human good, *prima facie*, would seem to be compatible with a social organisation in which some members of that society are systematically tortured, misled and exploited. However, with the addition of the R.F.P. Principle, as elaborated above, this is no longer the case. The R.F.P. Principle would rule out a wide variety of such acts, simply because they are illegitimate ways of treating persons. For instance, it would rule out torture, murder and enforced slavery because it is difficult to see how such acts could be construed as ways of treating persons as ends. Those persons upon whom these acts are perpetrated could not share the goals of such acts without contravening the conditions of their own flourishing. It would also rule out actions such as that of the tank commander who uses his soldiers as human bridges for his armoured tanks.

Furthermore, given that the Principle of R.F.P. deems certain forms of treatment to be illegitimate ways of treating people, it follows that it would rule out certain social forms which institutionalise such morally illegitimate forms of behaviour. For instance, slave societies would be discounted because slaves are not allowed to follow their own ends, but rather must predominantly serve the ends of their masters Their lives are consumed with the task of being means for their masters' ends. Thus slave societies would be ruled out for the very reason that these are societies which institutionalise the treatment of persons as mere means.

However, it is not enough that we discuss what the R.F.P. Principle rules out morally. We need to demonstrate what distinctive and determinate *distributive* principles it generates or at least how the addition of this principle narrows the scope of principles which our theory of the human good might generate. With this task in mind consider a distributive theory which is solely oriented toward the production of excellent individuals through the diversion of social resources to the talented. Such an account of distributive justice in its most extreme form would involve the claim that distributive resources should be allocated only to those individuals who are extremely talented; and if this means that some persons who are not so talented miss out on resources altogether and subsequently starve to death, then, so be it. According to this distributive theory, the only important distributive concern is the fostering of excellence. Now, given that on my story, part of what it is to be an end is to be recognised as a bearer of basal interests, then the R.F.P. Principle would rule out such a distributive theory. (To be sure, on the evidence presented thus far, a less extreme version which recognises the importance of ends other than the promotion of excellence, may not be ruled out; however for the sake of argument, let us stick to the strong thesis which is concerned solely with excellence.)

We can see then how, in theory at least, the R.F.P. Principle might rule out at least some undesirable distributive principles; i.e. how it 'fills the gap', so to speak, between an adequate theory of the human good and an adequate theory of distributive justice, by enabling us to rule out various distributive theories and social forms. However, we cannot as yet fully demonstrate how the R.F.P. Principle makes determinate distributive principles derived from the good, because the way in which the principle works will be partially determined by the account of the human good employed. It is, after all, an *abstract* account of how people should be treated. Thus the extent to which the R.F.P. Principle narrows the range of distributive principles which our conception of the good gives rise to will become more apparent when we combine it with our neo-Aristotelian theory of value. The task of properly demonstrating how the R.F.P. Principle restricts the range of distributive principles, which our account of the human good generates, will have to wait until §3.

Summary

In chapter three, I argued that accounts of the human good were not sufficient as grounds of justice simply because they were too indeterminate to generate adequate principles of distributive justice; it was argued that a theory of the human good cannot determine distributive principles within anything other than a broad range. Thus in this chapter, in attempting to bridge the gap between the good and the distributively just, our second fundamental normative principle, the R.F.P. Principle (which states that persons should always be treated as ends and never simply as means) has been formulated. This principle is intended to provide theoretical criteria for the generation of substantive principles of distributive justice.

However, while the principle of respect for persons (usually the Kantian version) is often cited in various philosophical discussions of moral and political issues, it is rarely acknowledged that what the principle actually entails is rather ambiguous. In this chapter the R.F.P. Principle has been explicated in terms of the relationship between descriptions of actions and the conditions of the flourishing of persons. I have argued that:

> An action is morally acceptable if and only if the goals of the action to which persons are subjected are goals which those persons could adopt as their own without contradicting the conditions of their own flourishing.

If we translate this interpretation into the realm of the obligation of the State to its citizens, we may say that the R.F.P. Principle involves the claim that:

> The social treatment of persons as ends involves ensuring (as far as is rationally possible) that the goals to which persons are subjected are goals which these persons could adopt as their own without contradicting the conditions of their own flourishing.

Whilst not the final word on the issue, it is hoped that this explication of the R.F.P. Principle clarifies (at least sufficiently for the purposes of a work in political theory), what it means to treat a person as an end and not merely as a means. For the State to treat its citizens as ends and not as mere means entails that it ensure (within its capacities) that the goals of the actions to which the citizens are subjected are goals that the citizen could adopt as his or her own, without contradicting the conditions of his or her own flourishing. Furthermore, it is intended that this principle, when employed in unison with neo-Aristotelian value theory, will enable us to generate substantive principles of distributive justice; that is, that it sufficiently narrows the range of distributive theories which our neo-Aristotelian account of the human good will generate. Having outlined the two foundational normative principles, I now shift my attention to issues of distributive justice.

Notes

1. As was the case with the first of these normative postulates, the neo-Aristotelian conception of the good, this principle is taken to be philosophically *primitive* in the sense that it is not justified by reference to further philosophical reasons. The 'buck stops', so to speak, with this basic principle. Thus I will not be concerned with the problem of the grounds from which the principle might be derived, but rather with what the principle entails.
2. Kant, 1981, [429], p.36.
3. The principle, at least as it stands, does not necessarily rule out the idea of beings other than persons being treated as ends in themselves; indeed we may wish to extend end-treating well beyond persons. Be that as it may, our immediate concern is with the treatment of persons.
4. It is particualrly interesting to note that one of the reasons Rawls provides for introducing his veil of ignorance is to ensure that all persons will be treated equally as ends; no one having an advantage (derived from social position and natural advantage) over any other person. See Rawls, 1972, pp.11-22.
5. Kant, 1981, [451], p.52.
6. Ronald Dworkin notes that a whole variety of forms of equal treatment are logically compatible with the idea of moral equality. See Dworkin, 1977, p.135.
7. Sullivan, 1989, p.197.
8. Op. cit. [434-35], pp.230-31.

9. Ibid., [467-68], pp.258-59.
10. Ibid., [468], p.259.
11. Ibid., [437], p.232
12. It also distinguishes the R.F.P. Principle from the work of such theorists as R.S. Downie and Elizabeth Telfer who attempt to defend the foundationally monist view that respect for persons is the ultimate single principle presupposed in all of our ordinary judgements of social morality. Downie and Telfer, 1969, p.38.
13. Op. cit., p.13.
14. See, for instance, Cranor 1982.
15. See Atwell, 1982.
16. Cf. Hill, 1992, pp.41-42.
17. Ibid., pp.41-42.
18. Ibid., p.42.
19. We should note that many Marxists would find the idea that Marx held moral beliefs to be an anathema for the very reason that Marx argued at a number of points that the whole of morality was ideological. Yet, the passage quoted from *Capital* would seem to indicate that Marx did indeed have strong moral convictions; indeed it is hard to understand why he was so opposed to capitalism, if he did not morally condemn its treatment of the working classes. However, we do not have time to discuss this issue fully. For discussions of Marx's views on morality see Wood, 1971-72, pp.244-82; Lukes 1985; and Nielsen 1989.
20. Marx writes: ".... all methods for raising the social productiveness of labour are brought about at the cost of the individual labourer; all means for the development of production transform themselves into means of domination over, and exploitation of, the producers; they mutilate the labourer into the fragment of a man, degrade him to the level of a machine, destroy every remnant of charm in his work and turn it into a hated toil, they estrange him from the intellectual potentialities of the labour process in the same proportion as science is incorporated in it as an independent power; they distort the conditions under which he works, subject him during the labour process to a despotism the more hateful for its meanness; they transform his life-time into working-time, and drag his wife and child beneath the wheels of the Juggernaut of capital.....", Marx, 1977, p.645.
21. Of course, this recognition of the importance of instrumental treatment in social life is not problematic for mutual advantage theorists, for the very reason that their project involves building systems of moral and political theory out of the foundational belief that it is acceptable for sets of people to treat each other merely as means. See chapter three 'The human good, justice and others' for a discussion of mutual advantage theory.
22. Kant, 1991, [477] p.266.
23. Davidson, 1980, p.46.
24. See ibid., 1980, p.4.
25. We should note that some true intentional descriptions are better than others, As Stephen Clark notes 'he is testing for dry rot' is a more adequate description of events than 'he is sticking a knife into the wall', if that is why he is sticking the knife in. Thus one description will be overridden by another. See Clarke, 1975, p.152
26. Op. cit.. We should note here that Hill does not adopt what I have labelled a 'Davidsonian' account of action, talking as he does of *the goal* of an action, rather than *the goals.*
27. Kant, 1981 [429], p.36.
28. Op. cit., p.45.
29. Ibid., p.45.
30. Of course, this does not mean that Kant rules out punishment. For when one commits a crime one negates the normal rules of treatment. An individual's unlawful deeds render that person deserving of a loss in happiness. The criminal owes society a debt to restore the reciprocal contractual relationship between obedience to the law and the benefits received from living under the law. For a useful discussion of this see Sullivan, 1989, pp.243-44.
31. Op. cit., p.45.

Section Three
Distributive justice

6 Distributive justice and the principle of equal well-being

Introduction

I have argued that the generation of principles of distributive justice requires both an account of the human good and an abstract account of how people should be treated. However, even these two normative elements are not sufficient for the generation of substantive distributive principles; rather they need to be combined in the context of information about the nature of the problem of distributive justice and other empirical facts about the world for which these principles are to be framed. We should also consider the kinds goods it is that these distributive principles are to allocate.

In the first half of this chapter, then, I shall consider the nature and scope of distributive justice. What are theories of distributive justice about? What kinds of goods do distributive principles apply to? Can we provide a useful taxonomy of the different kinds of distributive goods? In the second half of the chapter, I turn my attention to the derivation of a general principle of distributive justice. In earlier chapters, I outlined a neo-Aristotelian conception of the good and asserted that the Kantian principle of respect for persons should be the formal principle used to define how people should be treated. In this chapter, I argue that an egalitarian principle of justice can be derived as an abstract distributive ideal if the principle of respect for persons is combined with a neo-Aristotelian theory of persons. This is the 'principle of equal well-being'. I suggest that this principle functions, in the first instance, as a regulative ideal rather than as a concrete distributive principle for the allocation of actual goods (for reasons which I will reveal as we proceed). What I propose, then, is a form of 'egalitarian pluralism', in which a variety of distributive principles (some of which are not egalitarian) are employed, all of these being governed by an overall egalitarian regulative ideal.

Distributive justice: its nature and scope

From prior discussions, we may compile a number of salient features of distributive theory, at least as the topic is to be dealt with herein. Firstly, the problem of distributive justice concerns the distribution of distributive goods. The aim of a theory of distributive justice is to generate a principle (or set of principles) for the allocation of distributive goods. A theory of distributive justice might advocate principles which are, for instance, need-based (according to which goods are allocated according to need), egalitarian (according to which goods are distributed equally), meritocratic (according to which goods are distributed to those who deserve them), or pluralistic (according to which different goods are distributed according to a variety of principles). Secondly, I treat distributive justice solely as a virtue of social institutions and arrangements. However, this is not intended to be exhaustive of the plausible ways in which one might legitimately use the term 'distributive justice'. It is quite legitimate to talk of just persons and just situations. However, I restrict my usage to discussion of social institutions. Thirdly, as I pointed out in chapter two, the problem of distributive justice assumes *conflict* amongst persons over distributive resources. In contemporary society that conflict occurs primarily because of scarcity.

In discussing what distributive justice consists of, let us now consider some cases which concern the *scope* of distributive justice, particularly when justice is conceived of as a virtue of social institutions and arrangements. Consider the following cases in which (intuitively at least) it seems odd to talk of distributive injustice at least when that term is defined as a virtue of social institutions and arrangements.

i) A professional golfer is walking along a golf course when a small bullet size piece of a fragmenting comet hits her in the leg and breaks her leg in two. She is thus forced to buy a wooden leg and abandon her golfing career.

ii) A man grows up in an isolated community. For reasons which are difficult to ascertain, he comes to be known as 'Stinky'. He is generally disliked for no other reason than the nickname given to him. As a youngster, he is the butt of schoolyard jokes and as he grows older has increasing difficulty finding acceptance in his community. A local councillor becomes aware of his plight and puts a motion through the local council banning the use of all derogatory nicknames in the community. However, the locals still secretly refer to him as 'Stinky' and, more importantly, refuse to be friendly.

I think that both of these examples demonstrate the limits of distributive theory when treated as a virtue of social institutions and arrangements. The first example concerns a situation in which what happens to the person in question is the fault of no person or institution. It is a form of cosmic misfortune, if you like. Within the ambit of cosmic misfortune we may include such hardships as being born physically and mentally handicapped. Aristotle recognised the role of cosmic factors in human affairs when he noted that "the man who is very ugly in appearance or illborn or solitary and childless is not very likely to be happy".[1] In genuine cases of cosmic misfortune there can be no blame: these cases are not the province of distributive theory, at least as understood herein. However, principles of distributive justice might well be expected to contain provisions for the establishment of systems of compensation for those who are affected by such cosmic misfortune. Social institutions might provide for the comet-struck golfer, even if they are not responsible for her misfortune. I should also stress that while it is true that cases of cosmic misfortune demonstrate the limits of distributive theory, they should not be seen as providing permanent barriers, for as technology advances many cases of cosmic misfortune will become issues of distributive injustice. For example, in earlier times if one became afflicted with diseases such as cholera, it was *ceteris paribus* just bad luck. However, in contemporary industrial societies—in which there exists plentiful means of curing and preventing such afflictions—any person who dies of cholera because of lack of medical resources might well be said to be a victim of distributive injustice, rather than cosmic misfortune.

The second case, which I shall dub the 'Problem of Stinky', demonstrates once again the limits of the social organisation of just states of affairs. Grant it that distributive justice is a virtue of social institutions and arrangements, then the limits of distributive justice are also the limits of possible action by social institutions. In Stinky's case, we have a situation in which the state has limited powers to reorganise the relevant states of affairs: no matter what governments do, it is difficult to ensure that no single person will be victimised by others in his or her community. In effect, cases such as the Problem of Stinky demonstrate the limits of distributive justice when characterised as a virtue of social institutions and arrangements. Ultimately, the overall justice of human societies will rely upon individuals and communities. William Galston notes that "in the last analysis, one must agree with Rawls that the quest for a purely institutional or procedural solution to the practical problem of obtaining justice is futile."[2] He claims that every community must rely in the end on its members possessing a rudimentary sense of fairness and equity. Here we might concur with Gandhi, who is supposed to have once said rather scathingly that everybody is looking for a system so perfect that no one has to be good.[3] Further, most people would probably consider interference by social institutions into all aspects of the social lives of persons to be excessively intrusive. That people should be able to associate freely is an important human good. As J.S. Mill notes: "We are not bound, for example, to seek his [another person's] society; we have a right to avoid it (though not to parade the avoidance), for we have a right to choose the society most acceptable to us."[4] Our rights of freedom of association might well exclude some forms of interference by the State in the social interactions of persons.

My two toy examples do not exhaust the possible constraints upon distributive theory. However, they do provide a sense of why it is that we should not expect principles of distributive justice to deliver flawless social conditions.

The circumstances of distributive justice

In *A Theory of Justice* John Rawls claims that the circumstances of justice are the normal conditions under which human cooperation is both possible and necessary.[5] He then divides these into the *objective* and the *subjective* circumstances. The objective circumstances include such facts as it being the case that many individuals co-exist in the same time and place, that human mental and physical capacities are roughly equal and that conditions of moderate scarcity obtain; while the subjective circumstances are the relevant aspects of the subjects of cooperation, *viz.*, of persons working together. According to Rawls such circumstances are a reflection of the underlying fact that human society is marked by both an identity and conflict of interests. There is an identity of interests because social cooperation makes possible for all a better life than would have been the case if each individual were to try to live solely by his own efforts. Yet, on the other hand, there also exists a conflict of interests since human beings are not indifferent as to how the benefits produced by collaboration are distributed, for in order to pursue their ends they each prefer a larger to a lesser share.

However, whilst I agree with Rawls' central claim that human society is marked by both a conflict and an identity of interests, I do take a different approach to the issue of what the relevant circumstances of justice might be. In considering this issue, I focus instead on the empirical circumstances which must be taken into account when generating distributive principles. Accordingly, the distributive principles derived from the two normative principles will differ according to the empirical circumstances in which they are combined: decisions about distributive justice must occur within a particular empirical context. What I outline in this section, then, are some important empirical assumptions about the world in which distributive principles are to be enacted; and these assumptions will guide my later formulation of principles of distributive justice.

Scarcity

One contingent fact which should be taken into account is scarcity. We can distinguish two kinds of scarcity; *hard scarcity* and *moderate scarcity.* Hard scarcity refers to conditions in which resources are so scarce that they cannot be distributed to all persons, i.e. we are talking about conditions in which resources cannot be allocated universally. Moderate scarcity, on the other hand, refers to conditions in which it is possible for all to receive some amount of the good in question, but in which supply is not so plentiful that all of the interests a particular good might satisfy can in fact be satisfied. These two kinds of scarcity are to be contrasted with conditions of *abundance*, i.e. with conditions of plenty in which all potential interests which a good might satisfy, can be satisfied.

Whilst distributive issues become less problematic in conditions of material abundance, it would seem that for the foreseeable future we will continue to be confronted by conditions of moderate scarcity. Our productive forces are not in such a state of development that conditions of universal bounty are likely to arise in the near future. It is interesting to note that both Rawls and Hume think that principles of justice apply only to conditions of moderate scarcity. However, in contrast to these thinkers, I suppose that conditions of hard scarcity do admit of questions of justice. As William Galston notes, justice is altered—but not suspended—in conditions of hard scarcity.[6]

A continuing realm of necessity

Secondly, I assume that human beings will continue to inhabit a realm of necessity in which it is necessary, for the foreseeable future, for at least some people to work in order to ensure that human beings both survive and flourish. As I noted earlier, human beings are sensuous beings who are in no small part governed by the 'tyranny of the basal'; that is, we are beings who must provide for our basic needs of food, shelter and so on, before we are capable of pursuing other interests. If this fact about human nature is considered in the light of the growing recognition that the goal of achieving material abundance is probably nothing more than a utopian dream, then it would seem to be the case that the realm of necessity is not just a passing moment of human history, but instead will continue to be a central feature of human existence.

Of course, this claim about the continuing necessity of work is not uncontroversial. Some critics, such as for instance Andre Gorz, claim that we are on the verge of post-industrial society.[7] Gorz thinks work is soon to be transcended. However, I think that we should eschew his approach on the grounds that the idea that work will be absolutely transcendence is excessively utopian.

A continuing technical division of labour

I assume herein that at present a technical division of labour—by which I mean the division of work into small minute tasks—is required for the production of what we might call the 'necessaries' of life for all persons. Some utopian thinkers have argued that the conditions which would enable us to abolish the technical division of labour are almost at hand, and others that the abolition of the technical division of labour is a moral imperative. However, I think that neither of these options is feasible, at least in the near future. Moreover, such a continuing division of labour is problematic in that in all likelihood it ensures that self-developmental autonomous activity will continue to be scarce.

A continuing necessity for large scale productive units in industry

In order to produce the means of materially reproducing the human population, it will continue to be necessary that production of these goods be undertaken in large scale units. Whilst small scale productive units are to be preferred because of the intimacy and the opportunities for eudaimonian interest-realisation which they provide, we must acknowledge the continuing economic necessity of large scale ones.

Distributive goods: a neo-Aristotelian conception

In the previous section I outlined four contingent aspects of the world for which distributive principles are to be framed. As we shall see, these empirical circumstances will help shape the kinds of principles of distributive justice which are actually generated. I want now to consider the distributive goods to which the principles of justice shall apply.

To implement a theory of distributive justice fully, one must not only have an account of how goods should be allocated, but also a conception of which human goods it is that these distributive principles are to distribute. While the generation or postulation of distributive principles does not require commitment to any particular account of distributive goods, nonetheless it is an important issue which should be addressed.

Philosophers have been divided about how we should categorise distributive goods, as should be evident from the following survey. In the *Nicomachean Ethics* Aristotle divides distributive goods into three categories: namely, wealth, honours and the other things that fall to be divided among those who have a share in the constitution.[8] David Hume, taking a different approach, draws a distinction between *internal* and *external* goods—the internal goods being the advantages of our bodies—and then limits the scope of distributive justice to the external ones.[9] Hume resists the idea that possessions acquired by good fortune and industry should be included in the distributive pot, so to speak.[10] In *Spheres of Justice*, Michael Walzer provides a broad list of distributive goods which, *contra* Hume, include possessions acquired by good fortune and industry. Walzer draws a list which includes *inter alia* wealth, knowledge, physical security, commodities and jobs.[11]

There is, it would seem then, a wide divergence in opinion as to what goods distributive principles are to allocate. This divergence not only concerns how the various distributive goods are to be categorised—that is, how we cut them up—but also the sorts of goods to be included in the list of distributable goods. I take an entirely different approach from the ones outlined above. As we shall see, on my account goods are to be divided into three different categories, all of which are derived from my earlier account of human interests.

Let us begin by distinguishing between human goods and distributive goods. This distinction is an important one because distributive principles apply only to distributive goods. Human goods are essentially means to human interest realisation and thus for every human good there must be corresponding interests to be realised. Human goods are objects with which we are concerned because of the possibilities they offer for the satisfaction of human interests. For instance, food is a human good because it satisfies our basal interests. Prizes and honours, on the other hand, enable the recipient to enjoy self-esteem and thus realise interests in subjectivity. Money—in the form of wages—enables us to buy other goods which realise human interests. There are, in fact, no goods which do not realise some human interests. Of course, some goods, such as oil for instance, only become goods when we become aware that they might realise some interest – in earlier pre-industrial times oil was merely dirty water. Such phenomena simply confirm the intrinsic relationship between goods and interests. Once we become aware of the interests which might be realised, then the item becomes a human good. We can further illustrate this relationship between human goods and human interests by noting that we do not concern ourselves with the distribution of things which either do not affect human existence or do not produce measurable effects.[12] For instance, the existence and distribution of metals in far-off galaxies is currently of little relevance to our needs.

Not all human goods are distributive goods. Think of friendship and companionship.[13] Whilst undeniably human goods, they are not distributive goods in so far as they cannot be distributed by social institutions. Whilst parents, for instance, might distribute love and affection—often unequally I might add—to their children, the State cannot and could not distribute these goods without substantially transforming them; this is a way of saying that there are *pragmatic* constraints upon some human goods becoming distributive goods. William Galston is adamant that justice cannot be said to regulate the sphere of private sentiments and attachments. "We cannot be obliged to love, except when our acts and promises have created a situation within which love may be presumed. In the sphere of love, needs and merits may have an effect on our sentiments, but they are not claims that we must honour."[14] He suggests that this is partially because we do not have full control over the "direction and intensity of sentiments" and partially because universal standards are out of place here.

There are many other goods which evade distribution—at least partially—by social institutions. Consider honour. Whilst we can distribute honours, the decisions of social institutions cannot determine with any degree of certainty who is honoured in a society. Think of the *Stakhanov* phenomenon in the Soviet Union of the nineteen thirties. Stakhanov was a coal miner of reputedly exceptional strength, who was said to have produced more coal than required by the official quota. Stalin chose Stakhanov as a role model for the workers of the Soviet Union. Good Soviet citizens were urged to emulate Stakhanov's feats and Stakhanov prizes were awarded to those workers who outperformed their workmates. However, the mere fact that these prizes were awarded by the State did not ensure that the recipients of the Stakhanovite prizes were respected by their workmates. In fact, anecdotal evidence has it that the Stakhanovites were ostracised from, and in many cases harassed by, their workmates.[15] Here again the State could not control the allocation of the goods in question. I shall refer to goods which evade—for all intents and purposes—patterned distribution by the state, as *distributively wayward.*

Societies might well wish to place moral constraints upon the state allocation of certain goods. Sex, for instance, is both a human good and a potential distributive good. We can imagine societies in which the State considered it to be its duty to ensure that all of its citizens were sexually satisfied (the mechanics of which I leave up to the imagination of the reader). However, sex is not usually considered to be a distributive good. The allocation of sex is not typically thought to be the proper province of the state – it is not considered to be a human good to which distributive principles of any kind should apply. Herein, the major human goods which are morally constrained in this way are the 'naturally provided' components of human physical well-being, such as our eyes, hands, lungs and hearts. These are contrasted with what we might call the 'socially provided' components, such as food and water. The State has no role to play in the distribution of eyes, hearts and hands. (It is important to note at this point that the issue of morally-constrained distributive goods is separate from the issue of whether some goods, such as pornography or drugs, should be banned. What is at issue is whether certain human goods should be ones to which distributive principles apply, not whether people should be allowed to have them. Questions of moral prohibition are not central to the problem of distributive justice.)

I intend to categorise distributive goods herein according to the sorts of human interests they realise. Accordingly, then, I divide distributive goods into the basal goods, the goods of subjectivity and the eudaimonian goods, and it is to these various spheres of goods that different distributive principles shall be applied. In addition to these goods, there are also what we might call 'derivative' goods which have an instrumental role to play in the realisation of one or more of these three categories of interests.[16]

The basal goods would include in their number different forms of food, shelter, basic income, clothing, sanitation, medical supplies, search and rescue equipment, medical services, life-preserving technology and machinery and procedures which help to prevent injury in the workplace and the home. The eudaimonian goods would include all of those goods which enable us to realise eudaimonian interests; i.e. goods which facilitate the development of our capacities for creativity and innovation. Thus, they would include amongst their number certain professional jobs, education, leisure time, resources to develop skills—such as photographic equipment and a darkroom for the person who wishes to develop photographic skills—as well as artistic scholarships. Finally, the goods of subjectivity would include all those goods which enable us to realise our interests in subjectivity. Amongst the list of goods of subjectivity would be such things as literary prizes, status goods (such as Jaguar motorcars or yachts), military honours, fashionable records, citizenship, positions of eminence and authority (such as governorships and corporate directorships) and fame. All of these are goods which enable one to gain both self-respect and self-esteem.

My taxonomy provides us with a broad account of distributive goods. This is important. Of course, there are many theories of justice which employ much more economistic accounts of what it is that distributive principles have to regulate. However, there are good reasons for eschewing such accounts; distributive goods are not just those entities which are registered as Gross National Product. Distributive goods include a wide variety of entities; from sporting prizes to income, from jobs to jacuzzis, from food to council homes.[17] The point here is that distributive goods should not just be restricted simply to material commodities.

The observant reader will have noticed that my neo-Aristotelian categorisation of distributive goods leaves open the possibility that certain goods might well fall into two separate, or even all three, distributive categories. For instance, some goods (such as food) might realise basal interests; however, if consumed in a different context (for example at a dinner party), these goods might also simultaneously realise other interests, in the sphere of subjectivity – here I am thinking that one of the reasons for holding such parties would be to gain some self-esteem. Alternatively, a helicopter owned by a millionaire might merely be a status good – a rich man's week-end plaything. Yet, if it is used as a search and rescue vehicle to recover lost bushwalkers or cattlemen, then it would become a basal good. Goods can belong to more than one category. However, this is not particularly undesirable. It simply means that our 'line of cut' is not perfect and hence the particular category to which a good is to be assigned will depend upon its usage.

Before leaving the topic, there are some final points I would like to make about distributive goods. Firstly, while some human goods evade distribution by social institutions, there are also other goods which constrain the capacity of social institutions to determine the overall allocation of even *distributive* goods. For instance, the good of high office might well enable the holder to acquire other goods such as overseas holidays, government cars, office equipment, as well as influence over economic decisions which affect his own financial fortunes. This sort of capacity to acquire other goods was very much the sort of power enjoyed by high-ranking members of the Communist Party in the former Soviet Union. Equally, it is also enjoyed by high ranking public servants in many capitalist nations. Michael Walzer notes that it is just this very form of corruption which was one reason which motivated the Roman Catholic church to ban their clergy from marrying; if they did not have family onto whom they might pass material goods and power, then it was thought that this would lessen the occurrence of corruption.[18] Equally, if higher education is a good which only some receive, then such education confers upon its recipients the chance to obtain a wide variety of goods to which non-tertiary educated people do not have such ready access. For example, a tertiary education can provide one with knowledge about other health or financial matters and this knowledge can contribute to one's standard of life, improving one's well-being in comparison with others who do not possess such information. I shall call goods which enable the holder to acquire other goods I shall refer to—somewhat facetiously—as 'locomotive' goods. They are goods which have causal powers such that they enable their possessors to acquire other goods. While the causal powers of capital have long been noted, many other goods, such as land, education, beauty and political office also have causal powers. Such locomotive goods limit the capacity of social institutions to distribute human goods, in ways which bring about *specific patterns* of human interest realisation.

Secondly, there are some goods which are intimately linked to particular distributive patterns such that they can only be the goods that they are if they are distributed according to these principles. Their pattern of distribution is in a sense *logically implied* in their very nature. For instance, sporting prizes can only be the sorts of goods which they currently are, if they are distributed meritocratically to the most deserving athletes. A sporting trophy which was allocated randomly by, for instance, selecting a name out of a hat, would no longer be the same good as a trophy which is distributed to, for instance, the fastest sprinter. Similarly, romantic love can only be romantic love if it is allocated freely. Egalitarian allocations of one's sexual favours would not count as examples of romantic sexual love. Thus, it would seem that there are some goods which can only be the goods that they are if they are distributed according to particular distributive principles and patterns.

Thirdly, there may be some human goods which are such that we can only distribute their *preconditions*. In such cases, the good itself is not capable of being distributed. This is especially true in what I call the sphere of subjectivity. For example, self-esteem is a human good, yet we cannot distribute self-esteem *per se*. All that we can allocate are various distributive goods such as public honours, which are the preconditions of self-esteem.

Finally, I should say something, albeit briefly, about negative distributive goods or distributive burdens. I have not as yet considered the place of unpleasant or onerous activities, such as military service and garbage collecting or other burdens such as bad housing conditions, in distributive theory. Where do these things—which David Miller calls 'disadvantages other than punishments'—fit in my neo-Aristotelian conceptual schema?[19] This is not a frivolous question, for distributive justice concerns not only the distribution of goods, but also of 'bads'. Many of the most difficult issues in political theory concern how burdens such as military service should be distributed amongst the citizens of a nation. Herein, I shall follow David Miller in assuming that burdens are simply negative benefits and thus do not give rise to independent theoretical problems.[20] Bad housing, on this line of thinking, would simply be considered a negative basal benefit.

Respect for persons and distributive principles

In deriving principles of distributive justice, the principle of respect for persons has an important role to play herein. In this section, I want briefly to consider the various uses to which the principle of respect for persons has been put by some important political philosophers. (This provides some important theoretical background for later discussion.)

The principle of respect for persons has a long history of use in political philosophy, and more specifically in the realm of distributive theory. Yet, as we shall see, there is no strong consensus as to what sorts of distributive principles it may generate. One initial point to make about the principle of respect for persons is that no distributive principle follows deductively from it alone. Distributive principles cannot be generated deductively merely from this principle of moral equality. Furthermore, it would also be foolish to assume that a commitment to moral equality would necessarily commit one to distributive equality. All that the principle of respect for persons involves is the idea that people should be treated as ends, and never merely as means.

Much Kantian scholarship in this area has focussed on questions of whether the principle of respect for persons can be derived from the categorical imperative. My concern however is somewhat different. My main claim is that this principle of moral equality is distributively empty unless supplemented with a conception of the good. Without a conception of the human good, no distributive principles can be derived from the principle of respect for persons. This claim may be partially vindicated by observing the wide range of political philosophies which claim to be grounded in the principle of moral equality. There are a wide variety of political doctrines which claim to derive their legitimacy from this third formulation of Kant's Categorical Imperative.[21] For instance, many egalitarians have argued that the justification of the principle of distributive equality is that it is derived from respect for persons.[22] Accordingly, redistribution would be justified with reference to the principle of respect for persons. Meritocratic principles are also said by some theorists to be derived from morally egalitarian bases. In giving people what they deserve, we are treating them as ends and not merely as means.[23] Equally, the libertarian philosopher, Robert Nozick, also claims that his entitlement theory of justice—according to which persons' rights to their legitimate private property are inviolable and any welfare redistribution is morally illegitimate—is derived from the Kantian principle of respect for persons. Finally, at one point in *A Theory of Justice* John Rawls seems to imply that his 'difference principle' is in fact equivalent to the Categorical Imperative.[24]

Observation of the wide variety of political philosophers who employ this Kantian principle might well prompt one to think that this phenomenon demonstrates the rather slippery and abstract nature of the principle. However, some theorists make different use of this phenomenon. For instance, Ronald Dworkin claims that not only do a wide variety of political philosophies gain their legitimacy from the idea of moral equality, but that *every plausible theory does so.*[25] According to Dworkin, modern political theories do not have differing foundational values. On Dworkin's view, every plausible political theory has the same ultimate value which is equality.

Clearly, this claim is false if by egalitarian theory we mean a theory which supports an equal distribution of income. However, there is another, more abstract and more fundamental, idea of equality in political theory, namely the idea of treating people as equals which can be expressed in a number of ways. According to Will Kymlicka, a theory is egalitarian in this more basic way if it accepts that the interests of each member of the community matter and matter equally.[26] Put another way, Kymlicka claims that egalitarian theories require that social institutions treat their citizens with equal concern and respect.

However, while Kymlicka acknowledges that there is a tendency for political theories to be grounded in the principle of respect for persons, he does not defend Dworkin's contentious claim that *all* modern political philosophies can be said to be ultimately derived from the principle of respect for persons or from some related principle of moral equality.[27] This would seem quite judicious, given that counter examples to Dworkin's thesis can readily be found. For example, think of David Gauthier's work *Morals By Agreement.* Therein, Gauthier argues that justice merely consists in mutual agreement between those agents capable of contracting.[28] Accordingly, those agents incapable of bargaining—such as the severely handicapped or the aged—miss out on being objects of concern on Gauthier's story. Dworkin would be hard pressed to demonstrate how such a theory of justice could have the principle of moral equality as its fundamental value.

Why it should be the case that so many philosophers make use of the principle of respect for persons is quite a perplexing question and not one which I intend to answer here. Nor do I have a firm answer on why the principle gives rise to such a diverse range of distributive principles. However, my intuition on the latter question is that the theorists in question employ different accounts of the human good. If this could be demonstrated, then this would be further grist to the internalist mill.

From respect for persons and the human good to equality

I turn now (finally!) to the generation of an overarching principle of distributive justice. I shall begin with the formal principle of respect for persons as ends and our account of the human good. The reader will recall that the conception of the good to be used herein is a neo-Aristotelian one, which has at its core the Flourishing Principle. This principle states that what is good are those actions directed towards human well-being or the flourishing of human interests. If the principle of respect for persons is combined with the flourishing principle, then the 'principle of equal well-being' is generated. This principle states that social resources should be directed toward the equal realisation of the well-being of all persons. The argument can be outlined in the following deductive schema:

1. Each person matters in their own right; that is, they are to be treated as ends in themselves, not merely as means.
2. What matters about each person is their flourishing or well-being.
3. If persons are to be treated as ends in themselves, then it is their flourishing which should be of theoretical and practical concern.
4. Each person is to be treated so as to realise the good, in each person. Human well-being should be *equally* realised in *each* person.

The principle of equal well-being—which is derived from the Kantian principle of respect for persons as ends and neo-Aristotelian value theory—commands that human well-being should be equally realised in each person. Here I follow Thomas Nagel when he argues that if people are equal in the relevant respects, then *ipso facto* that constitutes a reason to distribute benefit to them equally.[29] Persons are equally ends in themselves—which is the relevant respect—and thus should be treated distributively in ways conducive to the realisation of their well-being. The principle of equal well-being is a principle of *distributive equality*, as opposed to political equality or legal equality. According to this principle, the distribution of social benefits and burdens should be organised so as to realise the well-being in each person equally.

The circumstances of justice and egalitarianism

As stated, the principle of equal well-being is still rather abstract. How should it be concretely implemented? The easiest mode of implementation would be for the regulative ideal of equality to operate as a concrete distributive principle at all levels of distribution in society; i.e. the most obvious mode of implementation would be for all goods to be distributed according to egalitarian principles. However, there are a number of problems for this form of universalist egalitarianism. The circumstances of justice outlined earlier in this chapter, in conjunction with a number of other factors concerning human goods (such as the fact that some goods cannot be distributed directly by social institutions and arrangements), provide practical constraints upon the possibility of implementing universal egalitarianism. As we shall see, while the egalitarian project can be implemented universally in the basal sphere, it cannot be realised so easily in either the sphere of subjectivity or the eudaimonian sphere.

Let us reconsider some of the factors which have a bearing upon the implementation of egalitarian distributive principles. Firstly, one of the circumstances of distributive justice is the fact that for the foreseeable future there will be a realm of necessity. This means that human beings will continue to have to work in order to sustain and reproduce themselves. Secondly, there are some tasks which are necessary for human existence, which are, by their very nature, non-eudaimonian – a good example of which would be cleaning the toilet. Once one has cleaned a toilet a couple of times and learnt the basics of the task, it is unlikely that there will be any great gains to be had in one's level of skill. The work offers little opportunity then for eudaimonian interest realisation. The existence of such work in a society means that while some persons have the opportunity for eudaimonian interest realisation at work, others will be condemned to a life of relative drudgery. The continuing necessity of such tasks means that in the eudaimonian sphere any attempt to implement the egalitarian regulative ideal of equality in a straight-forwardly egalitarian way will run into trouble. Thirdly, some work will be non-eudaimonian because of various contingent factors relating to modern production methods. Earlier I noted that the circumstances of justice were such that for the foreseeable future, work would (i) need to be organised in large scale units and (ii) require a technical division of labour so that the goods necessary for human existence might be produced. These contingent facts about work make any straight-forward attempt at implementing the regulative ideal of equality in the eudaimonian sphere problematic.

The intrinsic nature of the human goods of subjectivity also makes egalitarian distributions difficult. The human goods of self-respect and self-esteem are not, on the whole, distributable and hence they are not distributive goods in the ordinary sense. Social institutions can only allocate the preconditions or grounds of these human goods. For example, we can allocate honours and prizes, but not self-esteem. Finally, there are some human goods which enable their possessors to acquire other goods. Earlier I called these locomotive goods: status would be an example of such a locomotive good. If one has status in the society in which one lives, then a whole range of other goods will come one's way. Such transactions are outside of the control of social institutions.

In conjunction, these five factors provide substantial barriers to the successful and deliberative implementation of the principle of equal well-being. Let us examine these factors in greater detail in order to discover why this should be the case. Firstly, consider the eudaimonian sphere. Here we discover that the facts that (i) the realm of necessity will not in the near future be eliminated and thus most adults will need to work for a living and (ii) some kinds will be non-eudaimonian, leads us to the conclusion that not all persons can enjoy eudaimonian work simultaneously. If it is true that some work is necessarily non-eudaimonian and it is also true that work will continue to be a feature of human social life, then it must be the case that these eudaimonian goods cannot be distributed to all citizens simultaneously. We may say, then, that eudaimonian work is a scarce resource and cannot be universally distributed. (I shall say more about this in chapter eight.)

Secondly, if we consider the sphere of subjectivity, again we find difficulties with respect to the implementation of the egalitarian principle. If the *distributive goods* of subjectivity are mere preconditions for the realisation of the *human goods* of subjectivity, then there must be limits upon the extent to which social institutions can ensure egalitarian outcomes therein. What social institutions allocate are the *grounds* of goods such as self-respect and self-esteem. However, provision of grounds does not give one the power to ensure that the actual goods are distributed equally. (I shall expand upon this theme in chapter nine.)

Finally, the existence of what I earlier called (for want of a better name) 'locomotive goods' creates difficulties in general for the implementation of the principle of equal well-being: their existence means that it is unlikely that social institutions can absolutely determine the allocations and holdings of all distributive goods. Given that those who possess the capricious human goods of beauty and wit, for instance, are capable of acquiring some other human goods—regardless of how social institutions allocate—we must acknowledge the limited capacity of social institutions to implement the general conception in a fulsome manner.

Distributive pluralism and the general conception

While the principle of equal well-being outlined above might well be unproblematic at an abstract level, at a concrete level the existence of various constraints, as we have seen, leads us to the conclusion that such a principle cannot easily be implemented in a universal fashion.

In response to this problem, the strategy I shall adopt is as follows: (i) I shall divide distributive goods into different spheres according to the human interests which they realise and then (ii) I shall apply different distributive principles to each distinct sphere. The aim of division is to achieve equality in each sphere and ultimately to bring about equality overall. Hence, what I propose is a 'distributively pluralistic' approach. While my theory is egalitarian at a general level, at the particular level it is pluralist. The overall aim shall be to realise the principle of equal well-being in all spheres. In order to achieve this aim, I adopt a *distributively pluralist* strategy. This distributively pluralist strategy is, I believe, preferable to attempting to implement the principle universally for two reasons. Firstly, such a strategy acknowledges the fact that in some areas a straightforward implementation of equality is not possible, whereas in other spheres it is. Secondly, it recognises that in those areas where straightforward implementation is not possible, the consequent inequality which remains *is* significant and therefore some effort should be made to rectify such inequalities.

On my account, the principle of equal well-being becomes the 'general conception' of justice, providing an overall orientation for distributive policy.[30] It is a 'regulative ideal'.[31] In each of the three spheres of justice this general conception will generate different distributive principles, depending upon the specific conditions arising in each particular sphere. At a general level the theory is egalitarian, yet at the concrete level the theory is distributively pluralist.[32] The principle of equal well-being thus functions as a regulative ideal orienting the principles which determine the allocation of distributive goods in each of the spheres of justice.[33]

The egalitarian distributive pluralism advocated here differs from the pluralism advocated by Michael Walzer. In *Spheres of Justice*, Walzer argues that equality cannot be achieved merely by distributing goods equally. According to Walzer, there are many goods, such as romantic love, which either cannot or should not be distributed equally. Thus Walzer advocates what he calls 'complex equality' which involves the implementation of a plurality of distributive principles with the aim of achieving overall equality. Walzer contends that not all people can do well in every sphere, but hopefully all will do well overall.

Walzer thus deals with distributive issues in the context of what he also labels 'spheres of justice'; that is, in the context of broad categories of benefits and burdens to which different distributive principles apply. These spheres include spheres of membership, security and welfare, money and commodities, office, hard work, free time, education, kinship and love, divine grace, recognition and political power. By applying different distributive principles to each of these categories Walzer hopes that the overall aim of complex equality can be achieved.

The distributive pluralism advocated here, however, differs from that of Walzer in that: i) the spheres are not divided according to historically conditioned categories, but rather according to neo-Aristotelian value theory and; ii) the aim is to achieve equality, wherever possible, in each sphere, whereas in Walzer's system the aim is to achieve overall equality across the spheres. It is thus a distinctively different pluralism from that advocated by Walzer in *Spheres of Justice*.

Summary

The strategy to be pursued in the next three chapters is as follows. Firstly, the principle of equal well-being outlined in this chapter provides a regulative ideal for the allocation of distributive goods. Secondly, distributive goods are to be divided into three spheres, the basal sphere, the eudaimonian sphere and the sphere of subjectivity; and in each of these spheres of goods the principle of equal well-being will regulate the types of principles formulated to distribute the goods of that sphere. The principle of equal well-being will provide a regulative ideal for the kinds of distributive principles to be generated in each sphere. Thus, while the concrete distributive principles generated in each sphere will vary, I contend that the overall effect will be a form of equality.

Notes

1. Aristotle, 1969, Bk.1 ch.8 [1099b3-5].
2. Galston, 1980, p.279.
3. See Schumacher, 1979, p.72.
4. Mill, 1972, p.146.
5. Rawls, 1972, pp.126-28.
6. Cf. Galston, 1980, pp.119-20.
7. Cf. Gorz, 1982.
8. Aristotle, 1969, Bk. V ch.2 [1130b18-1131a6].
9. Hume, 1946, Bk.V ch.2 [1130b18-1131a6].
10. William Galston argues that Hume's distinction is ill-conceived because of the social factors which also influence the so-called 'internal goods', op. cit., p.113.
11. Hume, 1946, Book III Part II Section II, pp.487-88.
12. Walzer, 1983, p.3
13. Cf. Galston, 1980, p.110.
14. Aristotle writes: "But it seems strange when one assigns all good things to the happy man, not to assign friends who are thought the greatest of external goods.", op. cit., Book IX ch.9 [1169a35-b20].
15. Op. cit., p.282.
16. For a useful discussion of this see Walzer, 1983, pp.262-67.
17. Aristotle thought that a clear distinction could be drawn between derivative goods and intrinsic goods. "Clearly, then, goods must be spoken of in two ways, and some must be good in themselves, the others by reason of these.", op. cit., Bk.I ch.6, [1096b3-24].
18. Cf. Walzer,1983, p.3
19. Ibid., pp.147-8.
20. Miller, 1976, p.22.
21. Ibid., p.22, fn.6.
22. Andrew Mason argues that the idea that respect for persons requires the state to be neutral between different conceptions of the good life is an important component of contemporary liberal theory. See Mason, 1990, pp.433-52.
23. Cf. Kymlicka, 1990, pp.4-5.
24. Ronald Dworkin's thesis of endowment-insensitive/ ambition-sensitive distributions would seem to fit into this characterisation. See Dworkin, 1981, pp.185-246, 283-345.
25. Cf. Rawls, 1972, p.180.
26. Cf. Dworkin, 1977, pp.179-83.
27. Kymlicka, 1990, p.4
28. Nagel also makes the point that rights-based, equality-based and utility-based views of justice "share an assumption of moral equality between persons, but differ in their interpretations of it", Nagel, 1979, p.111.
29. For a useful review of Gauthier's work see Baier, 1988, pp.315-30.
30. Nagel 1972-73, p.354. Cf. Williams, 1973.
31. It is worthwhile at this point to recall the Rawlsian distinction between a concept and a conception of justice: "...it seems natural to think of the concept of justice as distinct from the various conceptions of justice and as being specified by the role which these different sets of principles, these different conceptions, have in common.", op cit., p.5.
32. A regulative ideal is an abstract principle which regulates the formation of substantive principles.
33. The principle of equal well-being is not a regulative ideal *per se*. It would be possible, in theory at least, to think of it as a concrete distributive principle. However, in the context of the various constraints upon egalitarian-implementation which have been outlined in this chapter, we find that the principle cannot be concretely instantiated and therefore it must be considered to function solely as a 'regulative ideal'.
34. J.R. Lucas advocates distributive pluralism, because he believes that no one principle can be used by the state to cover the distribution of all goods. "Social justice is difficult to apply even in

small-scale societies with limited purposes, like a gambling syndicate, a joint-stock company or an army. It becomes much more questionable whether it has any application when the society in question is the State, with its many, and sometimes incompatible, purposes; and many modern thinkers have sought to replace it altogether by Aristotle's third species of justice....In the end, I shall go half-way with them, and conclude in company with Aristotle, de Jouvenal and Nicholas Rescher, that no one principle of social justice can be applied through out a state - in modern terms, that no fair incomes policy is possible - but not for their reasons.", Lucas 1972, p.239.

7 The basal sphere

The principle of basal interest equality

In this chapter I shall apply the principle of equal well-being to the basal sphere. The reader will recall that the basal sphere consists of those goods which realise our basal interests. Amongst the basal goods we may include such things as food, shelter, and hygienic living conditions. By applying the principle of equal well-being to the basal sphere we generate the 'principle of basal interest equality' which can be stated as follows:

> within any specific social formation, all persons' basal interests are to be satisfied.

As a distributive principle, the Principle of Basal Interest Equality (hereafter referred to as the B.I.E. Principle) requires of social institutions—given the existence of adequate resources—that no person, within that specific social formation which social institutions and arrangements have jurisdiction over, should go without food, shelter or other basal goods.[1] This principle requires, *inter alia*, that we rule out distributions of basal goods based on meritocratic criteria, such as cleverness, virtue or physical prowess.[2] Similarly, with regard to the allocation of basal goods, distribution according to utilitarian criteria seems to be quite inappropriate. All persons have an equal right to adequate basal interest satisfaction.[3] Furthermore, if we consider the role that basal interests have to play in the realisation of the other categories of interests, then, it becomes apparent that the B.I.E. Principle should have *priority* over any other principles that may be generated by the regulative ideal.

I made the point earlier in chapter four that basal interest satisfaction is both: a) a precondition of human existence and; b) a precondition of the flourishing of human interests. Additionally, we should note that the satisfaction of these two preconditions requires different levels of basal interest satisfaction. Given that basal interests are the very grounds of human flourishing and that no other interests can be fully realised unless the basal interests are realised, then, it follows that the satisfaction of such interests should be accorded priority over all other distributive goals. We might characterise this priority in the following manner:

> the primary responsibility of social policy in relation to distributive issues, is to ensure that all persons' basal interests are satisfied.

The satisfaction of all persons' basal interests should take precedence over all other distributive goals.[4] Those individuals, or groups of individuals, who lack the requisite levels of basal interest satisfaction have a more urgent claim on distributive resources than those whose claims are based on other grounds. For instance, if a choice has to be made between allocating resources to the homeless for the provision of food and shelter, and allocating those resources to a group of opera enthusiasts who wish to build a memorial to Puccini, then, the priority of the B.I.E. Principle would mean that those resources should be given to the homeless.

The priority of the B.I.E. Principle is central to my account of distributive justice developed herein.[5] All persons require basal interest satisfaction in order to be *properly* persons. There are at least two important senses to this claim about the connection between basal interest satisfaction and personhood which we may discern. Firstly, persons require basal interest satisfaction in order simply to exist. Without some minimal level of basal interest satisfaction, without some minimal level of food, shelter and clothing, persons cannot survive. Secondly, basal interest satisfaction is necessary if the flourishing of other interests is to occur; that is, for persons to be fully persons. Given this pivotal role in human life, if human beings are to be fully persons, then this B.I.E. Principle should have priority over other rival principles of distributive justice. Respecting persons as ends in themselves requires that we accord priority to the B.I.E. Principle. If we are to respect persons as ends, then we must accord priority to ensuring that the conditions required for persons to be fully persons are met. In Kantian terms, if we will the end, then we will the means. If we wish to respect persons as ends, then we must ensure that they are capable of actually being ends, by ensuring as far as is practically possible that: i) they continue to exist and; ii) they are capable of realising other interests.

In short, the priority of the B.I.E. Principle commands of social institutions that all persons' basal interests be satisfied before social resources be directed toward the satisfaction of other interests. For instance, all persons' food, shelter and health needs should be met before other interests are satisfied[6]. This is in keeping with Thomas Nagel's rather abstract dictum that "an arrangement must be acceptable first from the point of view of everyone's most basic claims, then, from the point of view of everyone's next most basic claims".[7] If satisfaction of the requirements of the B.I.E. Principle entails that more affluent individuals must sacrifice their consumption of fine wine and French cuisine in order that the basal interests of all are to be adequately realised, then such sacrifice should be thought of as being merely part of the burden of justice. Similarly, according to the B.I.E. Principle, the satisfaction of basal interests must have priority in any decisions concerning distributive goods and this priority may well necessitate *sacrifices of redistribution*, i.e. where some persons' non-basal interests are sacrificed in order to satisfy the basal interests of the needy. Thus, distributive justice may require the sacrifice of redistribution *across persons across interests*.

Such sacrifice across persons across interests may, of course, require the establishment and maintenance of some form of welfare state as well as redistributive taxation in order to ensure that all persons' basal interests are satisfied; in conditions where persons' basal interests were not being met by other means, the B.I.E. Principle would justify such functions of the welfare state. However, it would be a mistake to think that the B.I.E. Principle involved a claim about the *necessity* of the welfare state or the claim that the welfare state is necessarily just. The B.I.E. Principle is, in abstract at least, neutral toward various social forms. The B.I.E. Principle entails that, *contingent* upon the existence of unsatisfied basal interests, redistributive sacrifice and welfare state functions should operate; that is, contingent upon the existence of basal need, then, the State should instigate sacrifice across persons across interests, which would in most cases involve taxation and redistribution oriented toward the satisfaction of basal need.[8]

The priority principle

I suggested in the previous section that the satisfaction of the basal interests of all persons should have *distributional priority*. However, as yet, the exact nature of this distributional priority is unclear. Two plausible interpretations come immediately to mind:

i) lexical priority; in which the satisfaction of basal interests always takes priority over the satisfaction of other interests and;

ii) conditional priority; in which the satisfaction of basal interests typically takes priority, but does not necessarily take priority in every possible case of conflict of interest.

The first interpretation of priority (lexical priority) is, of course, the kind of ordering which Rawls applied to his two principles of justice. According to Rawls, under his special conception of justice the liberty principle is lexically prior to the difference principle.[9] Rawls says of lexical ordering that "this is an order which requires us to satisfy the first principle in the ordering before we can move on to the second, the second before we consider the third, and so on." Hence, a principle does not come into play until those previous to it are either fully met or are found not to apply.[10] In the context of the current discussion, a lexical ordering would require that the B.I.E. Principle must take priority over all other possible principles of justice such that, whenever the ideal of satisfying the basal interests of all conflicts with principles which advocate the satisfaction of other interests, then, the ideal of satisfying the basal interests of all must take priority. Thus, in practical terms this means that disputed resources should be directed toward the satisfaction of basal interests as opposed to the satisfaction of other interests.

The second interpretation of priority, 'conditional priority', involves a much weaker sense of a hierarchical ordering. Here the satisfaction of basal interests generally takes precedence over the satisfaction of other principles; but, it does not take precedence in every possible situation.

On first sight, lexical priority might well be preferable for the simple reason of its economy. A lexical ordering is much easier to use for the reason that every time one is faced with a conflict between basal interests and some other claim upon distributive resources, then, one automatically distributes the resources to the basal claimant. As Rawls notes that a lexically ordering avoids "having to balance principles at all; those earlier in the ordering have absolute weight, so to speak, with respect to later ones, and hold without exception".[11] Conditionally ordered principles, on the other hand, do not hold without exception; thus *practical reason* must be brought to bear upon distributive decisions in order to decide which are the relevant exceptions.

For reasons of parsimony, then, it might well seem preferable to characterise the priority of the B.I.E. Principle in lexical terms, rather than in conditional ones. Thus, whenever a dispute arises concerning the allocation of certain resources between basal claimants and non-basal ones, then, the basal claimants would triumph.

However, there are serious problems with this interpretation. Consider the following scenario. Imagine a society—let us call it 'Camp Concentratamento'—organised along rigid military lines. The citizens of this society live in barracks run by army commandants. The commandants, who labour as hard as every one else, wake all of the citizens up at 4.00 a.m. to commence the working day. They toil all day until sunset, never relaxing (except for necessary meal breaks). Let us also imagine that all involved, both commandants and citizenry, are healthy, strong and enjoy full basal interest satisfaction.[12] Yet their lives consist of nothing more than a strict regimen of work and sleep. No matter how much they work, or how much surplus they generate, the citizens of this country never do anything other than toil, day after day. The surplus that they do generate is directed toward providing more and more basal goods. Surplus is never directed toward any goals other than ensuring the satisfaction of basal interests. We would surely be tempted to say that life in such a country would be equivalent to life in a concentration camp and, on the face of it at least, seems rather horrendous.[13]

However, as it stands, if the B.I.E. Principle is accorded lexical priority, then it would appear to countenance such a form of societal organisation. In Camp Concentratamento all persons' basal interests are satisfied and thus the sacrifice of other possible interests, which distributive resources might conceivably be directed towards,is justified. The reason that this problem arises, is the conceptual slack between: i) the maximum satisfaction of the basal interests and; ii) the point at which satisfaction of the basal is sufficient to ensure that all may begin to satisfy other interests. While basal interest satisfaction is required if persons are to satisfy other interests, the point at which basal interest satisfaction is sufficient to ensure that persons may begin pursuing other interests, is not the maximum level of basal interest satisfaction. There is no upper-limit as to how much social resource might be directed toward the basal interests; that is, there is no 'saturation' point, as it were. It would be possible to continue directing resources toward basal interest satisfaction *ad infinitum*, well beyond that requisite level which would enable us to satisfy other interests.

A similar point has also been made, using different terminology of course, by various theorists of poverty. Nicholas Rescher, for instance, notes the difference between welfare directed toward ensuring that persons survive and that directed toward ensuring that people live at a level of comfort which would enable them to share in the good things in life.[14] In a similar vein, Timo Airaksinen distinguishes between *relative* and *absolute* poverty. Airaksinen believes that absolute poverty is failure to reach a minimal level of subsistence (by my lights minimal basal interest satisfaction), whereas relative poverty reflects a failure to reach a level at which one can enjoy the good things of life.[15]

However, what these theorists do not discuss is the fact that there is no limit to the amount of resources which can be directed toward the provision of basal goods (or subsistence goods). For example, there is no limit to the amount of resources which can be spent on building better latrines, or on the provision of rescue equipment for bushwalkers. Equally, it would be possible to provide more and more helicopters to ensure that fallen bushwalkers arrive home safely or place safety nets around all mountain cliffs from which walkers could conceivably fall. There is no saturation point for the provision of such basal goods.

It would seem then that our principle of basal interest equality should be formulated in terms of conditional priority, even if this involves a much weaker sense of hierarchical ordering.[16] I shall reformulate the priority of our first principle of justice in the following manner:

> Basal interests should have conditional priority: that is, they should take precedence up to that level of basal interest satisfaction at which people are capable of satisfying other interests.

Basal interests should always be accorded priority, until such time as they are satisfied to a level that is sufficient for the realisation of other interests. Thus persons must have adequate housing, food, clothes and medical care.[17]

Some readers might object that the idea of 'adequacy' employed here is somewhat vague. For instance, it might be claimed that the malnourished are capable of watching television. Would this mean that the malnourished have reached an adequate level of basal interest satisfaction because they are still capable of pursuing interests other than the basal? I think that the answer to this question is quite simply no. When I talk of human beings having the material preconditions of pursuing other interests, what I mean is that they are capable of acting autonomously to some significant degree.

Merely being able to sit in front of television would not count as being capable of pursuing the morally relevant interests, and thus such capacity, in itself, would not count as evidence of the achievement of adequate levels of basal interest satisfaction.

'Giving your right arm' or non-external basal holdings

I have argued thus far that the B.I.E. Principle is; (i) conditionally prior to other distributive principles and, (ii) is a principle which may involve the sacrifice of redistribution across interests across persons. In this section I want to focus in some detail on the latter claim.

Under the right circumstances the B.I.E. Principle might well require redistributive sacrifice across persons across interests. For example, it may provide welfare redistributions. However, it would not allow the sacrifice of whole lives. By not merely sacrificing across persons, but by also sacrificing across interests, the sacrifice of whole lives is avoided. One charge which has traditionally been levelled at utilitarianism (and consequentialism in general) by deontic critics is that the application of such theory could lead to the sacrifice of whole lives. However, by sacrificing across persons across interests, the B.I.E. Principle is capable of avoiding such problematic conclusions. While it involves sacrifice—as all distributive principles must—it does not involve the problematic sacrifice of whole human lives.

An integral part of this strategy of sacrificing across persons across interests involves treating the pool of social resources as collective assets. In redistributing social resources across persons across interests, social resources are considered to be collective goods. In this regard at least I am in agreement with Rawls who treats social resources in the original position as part of a collective pool. I shall assume herein that goods have no entitlements attached prior to the deliberations of justice.[18]

One important question to ask at this juncture concerns what the limits of such redistribution should be. Are there any limits which should be placed upon the tendency to treat assets as collective goods? If parts of peoples' bodies are to be regarded as basal resources, then what is to stop us sacrificing across basal interests, and redistributing bodily parts to the needy? So long as people are not killed, what would be wrong with redistributing various bodily parts of persons who are more fortunate than others in this regard? For instance, what would be wrong with taking one eye from a fully sighted person in order to give partial vision to a blind person? (Indeed, this is a question which Robert Nozick asks of the egalitarian in *Anarchy, State and Utopia.*) If we subscribe to the sacrifice of redistribution in external holdings, e.g. in property and income, with the aim of ensuring that every persons' basal interests are satisfied, why not extend this welfare redistribution to bodily parts, or to what we may call 'non-external basal holdings'?

Nozick raises this problem in the context of his objections to Rawls' claim that natural assets and natural endowments should be treated as being part of the collective pool of resources which society has in its possession to distribute. According to Nozick, Rawls' view seems to be that everyone has some entitlement or claim on the totality of natural assets viewed as a pool, with no one having differential claims. The distribution of natural abilities is viewed as a 'collective asset'.[19] Rawls makes this claim because he believes that from the point of view of justice, the distribution of natural talents is morally arbitrary.[20] Nozick, taking a different tack altogether, asks why holdings should not partially depend on natural endowments. He is critical of the alternative to holdings being dependent in this way. Moreover, he argues that if we consider natural talents and assets as common assets, this inevitably leads us to the counter-intuitive conclusion that people are not the owners of their own bodies. Nozick argues that if we take arguments concerning the redistribution of assets seriously, then, we must entertain the suggestion that people may not actually own parts of their own bodies. Consider the following passage.

An application of the principle of maximizing the position of the worst off might well involve forceable redistribution of bodily parts ("You've been sighted for all these years; now one - or even both of your eyes - is to be transplanted to others")[21]

On what grounds, Nozick asks, are such cases to be ruled inadmissible? On what grounds can it be claimed that the fundamental principles of justice need apply only to the fundamental institutional structure of a society? If we find the idea of eye redistribution horrific and subscribe to self-ownership in our bodies, why not recognise self-ownership of external resources in ways that would prohibit the general sacrifices of redistribution? Alternatively, another way of asking this question is, if we subscribe to the sacrifice of redistribution in external holdings, should our rights to our bodies be seen as inviolable? This is an important question. We cannot in good faith dismiss the problem by characterising it as bizarre. While his example of eye-transplants sounded rather like a science-fiction story when *Anarchy State and Utopia* was published, recent advances in medical technology have meant that it is possible to talk sensibly of swapping such bodily parts.

One possible response to Nozick's challenge would be to claim that this should more properly be viewed as an issue of hard scarcity, rather than one of moderate scarcity. Goods such as hearts and brains are not produced in excess. Thus the redistributive principle would not apply to our bodily parts for the simple reason that we are dealing with issues of hard scarcity rather than moderate scarcity. However, this line of argumentation does not appear very promising. For while hearts and brains are scarce, other non-external basal holdings (such as eyes and hands) can be divided equally between persons. If one person has two eyes and another none, then it is possible to take one eye from the sighted person and give it to the blind man to achieve an equality of sorts. Thus, these bodily parts are to be found in conditions of moderate scarcity, rather than hard scarcity.[22]

However, Nozick's challenge here is not that difficult to meet.[23] Commitment to the sacrifice of redistribution 'across persons across interests' does not necessarily involve sacrifice across basal interests in ways which threaten the life and functioning of human beings as biological beings. We do not have to commit ourselves to an absolute thesis of self ownership such as Nozick's, in order to rule out eye transplants, for instance. Nozick claims that our horror at redistributive eye transplants demonstrates our belief in self-ownership of our bodies, and further, that if we accept such self-ownership, there is no reason that we should not accept the ownership of external holdings. However, while self-ownership is an appropriate notion to apply to our bodies, acceptance of the idea of self-ownership does not immediately generate absolute ownership beyond our bodies.[24] If we distinguish between *natural* and *social* basal goods, then it becomes apparent why this argument concerning self-ownership is not applicable to external holdings. Our natural basal assets, such as our eyes, hands and kidneys, are the natural parts of our bodies. These are goods which must be literally ripped out of a person in order to be redistributed.. On the other hand, our social basal goods includes all those goods which realise basal interests and which lie beyond our bodies. If we invoke this distinction, and argue in addition that redistribution across persons across interests applies only to the social basal goods, then it is possible to avoid the problems raised by Nozick's challenge.

Moreover, we can argue against such eye-transplants by focusing on the ideas of personhood and the principle of respect for persons as ends. Presumably having a fully functioning body is a basic condition of personhood and we do not do justice to the idea of respecting persons by creating personhood in one while degrading it in another. While individuals may voluntarily decide to transfer basal goods, and even to sacrifice their own lives, natural basal goods, e.g. bodily parts, cannot be redistributed by social institutions.[25] The very *grounds* of personhood are not up for redistributive sacrifice.

Of course, this prohibition against the redistributive sacrifice of natural basal resources would not rule out altruistic self sacrifice. For instance, a man might wish to donate a kidney to another brother whose kidneys have failed.[26] This, of course, would threaten his physical integrity, given that he is left with only one kidney, however, we should not prohibit the gift for the moral evaluation of such freely chosen noneconomic transaction actions lies beyond the scope of distributive justice.[27]

To recap, although the B.I.E. Principle involves maximising across persons or 'intrapersonal compensation' and thus involves redistributive sacrifice, it does not involve a form of sacrifice of basal interests which threatens the integrity of persons. Thus, even though the B.I.E. Principle is maximising—as most consequentialist theories will tend to be—it does not justify the sacrifice of whole human lives, nor would it provide justification for sacrificing the physical integrity of persons.

Two unwarranted forms of sacrifice

Thus far I have argued that although the sacrifice of whole human lives is unacceptable—as are forms of sacrifice which threaten the integrity of persons—it is nonetheless *in principle* acceptable to sacrifice across persons across interests. Given the priority accorded to basal interest satisfaction amongst the goals of distributive agencies, the rule of sacrificing across persons across interests might well entail the sacrifice of satisfaction of other categories of interests in order to ensure adequate basal interest satisfaction for all; the emphasis here being upon adequate basal interest satisfaction.[28] Two kinds of case concern directing resources towards: (i) the chronically physically disadvantaged and (ii) the prevention of harm.

We must recognise certain limitations upon the strategy of sacrificing across persons across interests which will arise in any society which does not have infinite resources. They are limitations which arise because of the insatiable nature of certain kinds of basal interests such that they would prevent us from attaining levels of adequacy for all, if we tried to satisfy them. This insatiability is such that if a society without infinite resources tried to satisfy these interests completely, then the attempt would deplete all of that society's resources. In such societies the attempt to satisfy these 'insatiable' basal interests adequately would in all cases lead to the sacrifice of *all other* possible interests which may be realised. I shall refer to such instances as 'Unwarranted Forms of Sacrifice'. They are unwarranted in the sense that they force us to acknowledge the absurdity of attempting to satisfy such interests completely and wholly. These cases differ from the Camp Concentratamento example because here the ideal of adequacy *cannot* be achieved, whereas in Camp Concentratamento, a decision is made to continue directing social resources solely towards basal interest satisfaction, long after levels of basal adequacy were achieved.

Let us consider some examples of these unwarranted kinds of sacrifice in order to gain a clearer picture of what is at stake. The first kind of unwarranted sacrifice concerns our basal interest in health; or more precisely, it concerns the problem of health care for the severely handicapped. Suppose that we wish to help a group of people who are severely impaired in some particular dimension of human skill or capacity. They may, for instance, be extremely mentally retarded, physically handicapped or chronically ill. In order to help such persons, resources might be poured into facilities, medical research and training, all of which will improve their lot to some extent. Yet their condition is such that, no matter how many resources are provided with the aim of improving their condition, they will never reach *adequate* levels of basal interest satisfaction. Of course, this is not to deny that these resources make minor improvements, but nonetheless these resources never enable those persons to achieve levels of basal interest satisfaction which would enable them to pursue other categories of interests fully.[29]

Now such a situation creates a minor dilemma for the B.I.E. Principle. If we attempt to implement it as our first principle of justice with the aim of ensuring that all persons acquire adequate levels of basal interest satisfaction, resources may well be drained to such an extent that few resources, if any, will be left over for other kinds of interest realisation. In such circumstances, we cannot satisfy the requirements of the B.I.E. Principle without excluding the possibility of realising other categories of interests. This is a dilemma which is derived essentially from the insatiable nature of some persons' health needs (given that we intend to attempt to bring them up to adequate levels of basal interest satisfaction).

The second kind of problematic case concerns the *prevention of injury* or *harm*. There will be certain kinds of harm-prevention which would require infinite resources in order that they be properly satisfied. Imagine, for instance, that a society decides that its citizens' basal interests in harm-prevention require that helicopters be available for injured bushwalkers. (I am assuming that in this context helicopters count as basal goods.) The question to be asked is how many helicopters would be required to ensure that all bushwalkers can be saved; how many helicopters would be required to satisfy the B.I.E. Principle adequately? Alternatively, it might well be argued that since we are all capable of falling off mountain tracks when bushwalking, that rails and safety nets should be placed alongside all mountain tracks.[30] Not only would this display an extreme lack of aesthetic sense, and in the process destroy a good which people seek in bushwalking (namely the confrontation with what the person takes to be untouched nature), it would also involve a tremendous drain upon social resources which could have otherwise been directed towards other social goals.

While such public policy dilemmas may appear ludicrous to some readers, they do in fact have some not insubstantial connection to contemporary social reality. Social institutions have certain responsibilities towards the prevention of significant unnecessary harm. For instance, it is generally thought (quite correctly I would add) that working conditions should be made as safe as is technically possible. Resources should also be directed towards the design of safer vehicles, towards research to develop vaccines against diseases and towards the prevention of mineral and vitamin deficiencies. But a question arises (as the above examples illustrate) as to what extent we must completely fulfil the conditions of harm-prevention. It would seem then that like certain health problems, the prevention of harm is capable of being 'insatiable' as it were, and hence, if we concern ourselves solely with its satisfaction, it is capable of preventing any further interest-realisation. In effect, implementing the B.I.E. Principle in such cases might very well lead to the sacrifice of all other possible forms of interest realisation.

These two kinds of sacrifice—which involve the sacrifice of other categories of interests in order to prevent harm and to satisfy the health requirements of the severely physically impaired—are unwarranted forms of sacrifice. How should they be dealt with? What is the appropriate response? The first point to make here is that a world in which there was only life-saving would not be totally devoid of 'non-basal' human goods. Presumably there would be non-distributive human goods such as companionship, love and friendship, even in societies which direct all of their distributive resources towards basal interest satisfaction. Even so, if we attempt to satisfy these insatiable basic demands, there would still be a lack of many important non-basal goods.

One possible line of response would be to argue that the problems associated with these unwarranted forms of sacrifice are irrelevant to distributive theory because they are so bizarre; distributive theory should concern itself solely with the actual. However, this response is not a very promising one for the very reason that our examples are not bizarre in any way which excludes them from the sensible world. With regard to the unwarranted forms of sacrifice discussed here, we are not dealing with Martians or some of the other strange beasts who inhabit the philosophers' counterfactual zoo, rather we are considering problems which arise in everyday life.

The treatment of the seriously ill, the ageing and the chronically deformed, for instance, can be very expensive. Distributive theory must confront issues such as these if it is to reflect the complexity of, and be relevant to, contemporary social life.

A second approach to this problem—and the one which I shall pursue—involves recognising that such unwarranted forms of sacrifice leave us with problems of practical reasoning.[31] At some point, before the possibility of other forms of interest realisation has been precluded (which I will not try to pinpoint), we must decide that sufficient resources have been allocated to these problematic cases. While we cannot abandon the needs of the severely impaired nor relinquish our duties towards harm prevention, we also cannot allocate all of our resources towards such cases. How far a society goes towards improving the situation of the chronically handicapped and in preventing harm, is a matter of practical judgement; it is an issue which societies themselves must resolve. At this specific level the B.I.E. Principle cannot provide *actual concrete detail* as to how far we should go toward satisfying these insatiable basal needs.

I should not be interpreted as claiming that such difficulties invalidate the B.I.E. Principle. It is not for principles of distributive justice to adjudicate in the minutiae of every distributive problem. Principles of distributive justice provide general rules for the deliberations of social institutions and arrangements and there is still a role for human deliberative reasoning in practical life. Moreover, if we think about philosophical principles in general, there are *paradigm cases* where such rules apply easily and without ambiguity. However, as one moves away from the paradigm cases, issues become more difficult; they become matters of practical reasoning which require individual human deliberation and this is exactly as it should be.

Hard basal scarcity

Thus far, my discussion of the distribution of basal goods has, on the whole, focused on conditions of moderate scarcity. The term 'moderate scarcity' refers to conditions in which goods are available in sufficient quantities for all to realise some of the relevant interests and yet in which goods are not so abundant that all possible interests may be realised. (I contrast moderate scarcity with hard scarcity, which concerns conditions in which resources are so scarce that they cannot be allocated to adequate levels to all persons). I have not as yet discussed how the B.I.E. Principle might function in conditions of hard scarcity. What about conditions of hard basal scarcity where basal goods are so scarce that they cannot be distributed universally? How is the principle of basal interest equality to be applied to situations where basal resources cannot be distributed equally?[32]

An instance of hard basal scarcity would be conditions in which there is a shortage of some life saving mechanism, such as for instance a kidney machines, to re-use an old chestnut. Suppose, for instance, that a hospital has only three kidney machines and that there are seven people who require them. It is almost certain that those who miss out on the use of these machines will die. What distributive principle should we apply in these circumstances? The B.I.E. Principle, as it stands, cannot do much work here because we have not stipulated how resources should be allocated in conditions of hard scarcity. No matter what principle of distribution is chosen, some persons' lives will be sacrificed.[33] How should we deal with this problem? The only possible guide that we have is our original abstract normative postulate, the principle of 'respect for persons as ends'. In determining which distributive principle or mechanism is to be chosen, we will ultimately have to rely upon this primitive normative postulate.

Two distributive principles can be eliminated at the outset. To start with, the principle of 'need' can be ruled out, since all need the machine equally. The principle of need provides no substantive mechanism for resolving the problem. The principle of equality can be eliminated, since by definition scarce resources are the sorts of goods which cannot be distributed equally. What principle(s) should we choose then?

One possible means of handling the problem would be to apply the utilitarian principle of maximising the good for the greatest number. On at least one version of utilitarianism, the utilitarian would resolve this problem of hard basal scarcity by either distributing scarce basal resources to those who are of most use to the society at large or alternatively to those who are most likely to derive the most use out of such resources.[34] Brain surgeons and computer specialists, for instance, might be allocated use of the machines, while unskilled old women, unspecialised factory workers and drunks would, in all likelihood, miss out. Alternatively, fit young twenty year olds might be allocated these scarce resources ahead of diseased sixty year olds. This, however, seems somehow intuitively repugnant and hardly in keeping with the idea of respecting persons as ends. It seems wrong to discriminate between persons on grounds of mere utility in what are ultimately matters of life and death. Moreover, given the general eschewing of utilitarian principles thus far, it would seem rather odd to adopt them when confronted by problematic situations. If utilitarianism is not adopted here more generally, then why should it be adopted when confronted by this problem of hard basal scarcity? Perhaps one might argue that calculations of utility should only be employed in situations where their use is the only reasonable way to minimise great evil. However, this line of reasoning seems rather weak.

Another possible way of dealing with hard basal scarcity might be to employ a meritocratic distributive principle. Where utilitarianism is essentially forward looking, meritocracy is concerned with the past, a meritocrat would assign merit to each person, according to some characteristic ascribable to them, derived from the past, and then decide, according to such assignations, to whom these scarce basal goods should be allocated. Of course, there are a number of possible interpretations of what would count as the grounds of desert. It might be grounded in effort or contribution. For instance, the allocation of concert tickets by queue would count as a meritocratic distributive method, in which merit is assigned in terms of effort.[35] However, I do not think that meritocracy is appropriate in this context. The State should not enforce meritocratic distributional patterns in conditions of hard basal scarcity. For example, while a queue (which I take to be a meritocratic distributive mechanism) might well be an acceptable mechanism for distributing concert tickets, it would be inappropriate for the allocation of scarce basal goods. We cannot decide meritocratically which persons deserve the very grounds of personhood. This rule holds universally and entails, *inter alia*, that we cannot choose on the grounds of merit between allocating scarce basal goods to a drunk and a Nobel Prize winning scientist. Discrimination in the basal sphere, on the grounds of merit, is morally abhorrent and not at all in keeping with the principle of respect for persons as ends.

With what then are we left? Principles of equality and of need have been ruled out *a priori* and meritocratic and utilitarian principles have been ruled out on the moral grounds that it is ethically improper in matters of life and death to discriminate between persons according to criteria of utility or merit. What principle for the allocation of scarce basal resources should we employ? We cannot avoid the problem, given that the kidney machines must be allocated to some persons and others must miss out.

At this point, a pessimistically-minded soul might be tempted to say that no acceptable moral principle for determining the allocation of resources can be formulated and, in a certain sense, this is the approach I adopt. In conditions of hard basal scarcity, the principle of respect for persons as ends would dictate that these resources should be allocated *randomly*, for the very reason that this is the only way of dealing with the problem which respects persons as ends. It is in fact the closest approximation to equality which can be achieved where basal goods are extremely scarce. For instance, if we consider the kidney machine example, which involves a case where decisions concerning the very grounds of personhood are being made, then the principle of respect for persons as ends would enjoin social institutions to distribute the kidney machines randomly. In acting in accordance with the dictates of this principle, the State might enter all relevant persons in a lottery and allocate the kidney machines according to the results of the lottery. This is the only just means of allocating these resources.

Thus, in conditions of hard basal scarcity the B.I.E. Principle should be interpreted as a principle of *random distribution* for the reason that randomness is the closest approximation to equality that can be achieved in these conditions.[36] Given that hard basal scarcity forces us to discriminate (effectively to choose who is to live and who is to die), the principle of random distribution is *indiscriminate discrimination*, so to speak. It is indiscriminate discrimination in a context in which discrimination is inappropriate and yet in which important resources cannot be distributed equally.

One might, of course, think that randomly distributing scarce basal goods is not the nearest thing to equality, but rather it is in fact equality. Given that these goods cannot be divided equally, then all that can be fairly distributed are chances, and so long as the procedure is not biased, then all persons would get that chance equally. According to this line of reasoning, distributing unequally would be to have unequal chances, such as when one uses a loaded dice. However, I think this is wrong. While it is the true that random allocation is equality if we focus at the level of chances, at the level of basal good allocation we must admit that such random allocation is ultimately not egalitarian because not all persons end up with equal holdings of basal goods.

It is also important to note that although my favoured solution to the problem of hard basal scarcity is in a sense procedural, such random distribution is not an example of Rawlsian 'pure proceduralism'.[37] This is not a situation in which the procedure by which an allocative decision is reached is the sole determinant of the justice of the allocation. The mere acceptance of procedural equality does not commit one to this particular Rawlsian doctrine. Rather than the justice of an outcome being dependent upon the procedure via which it was arrived at, random distribution of scarce basal resources derives its justice from being underwritten by a substantive conception of equality. Randomness in the case of scarce basal resources reflects not a concern with procedural justice, but rather a concern with equality.

A natural objection to such a system of allocation would be that it is not always practical. It is possible to imagine situations in which random distribution might appear counter-intuitive. For instance, in war one might be tempted to ensure that scarce basal resources are given to surgeons. This presumably would increase, to some extent at least, a nation's chance of winning the war and failing to do so would presumably lessen its chances.

However, this is a consideration of *utility* not of justice. It might be taken into account in the all-things-considered judgement, along with other reasons for action; however, it is not a consideration of justice. Thus any objection to the justice of random allocation using such examples concerning social necessity should be ruled out. Scarce basal resources are to be allocated randomly and issues of utility are irrelevant to the question of the justice of such distributions.

Finally, before leaving the issue of hard basal scarcity, it is important to note that the mere fact that the principle of respect for persons as ends would seem to require the random allocation of scarce basal resources by social institutions, does not rule out supererogatory acts of self-sacrifice. For instance, if we reconsider the kidney machine case, our first principle of justice does not rule out old people or the severely handicapped or priests, for example, sacrificing themselves in order that others may live. All that is ruled out by our principle is the practice of institutionally compelling such sacrifice on any grounds other than randomness. It is morally unacceptable for social institutions in charge of the allocation of these scarce resources to compel sacrifice on grounds of desert or utility. However, self-sacrifice is permissible. It might even be argued that the old and infirm have a *moral* duty to sacrifice themselves for those who have yet to have lived a life or those who could make more use of these life-giving resources.[38] On the other hand, it might be argued that self-sacrifice is merely a virtuous act, which is not morally required; that is, it would be, to use the old theological language, an act of supererogation; i.e. an act of doing more than is strictly required by moral law. Regardless of whether self sacrifice of the old and infirm is characterised as a duty or an extremely virtuous act, its resolution has no effect upon my claim concerning institutionally-compelled sacrifice.

The objection from harm

Some readers might think—in direct opposition to the B.I.E. principle—that the free provision of goods actually harms people. On this line of thought, people should develop the skills to provide for themselves and thus any provision of basal goods (or any other goods for that matter) is inimical to human welfare. According to this line of thinking, governments should provide opportunities rather than goods in themselves. Hence, the ultimately 'basal' good that government can provide is to keep out of the way of human productive activity.

I think that this objection involves a rather naive conception of what people are capable of, if they do not have access to basic material necessities. If persons do not have food, education and shelter, then, it is unlikely that they will be able to achieve very much at all. It takes more than sheer will-power to lead a full and rewarding life when one is born into a severely disadvantaged neighbourhood, such as the ghettoes of Calcutta. While it is true that the occasional individual, through either extreme ambition or good-luck, manages to fight their way out of such ghettoes, for the majority their lives are almost entirely consumed by the struggle to survive.

Secondly, one has to ask what is the nature of the harm that is perpetrated upon persons when they are provided with basal goods and services? Patently, the harm cannot be that they are fed, nor can it be that they are sheltered. Presumably, it is that people who receive welfare handouts become locked into a culture of dependence and thus lose their capacity to initiate projects for themselves.[39] However, this is a rather odd argument. In order for people to have the energy and foresight to be able to conceive of such projects it would seem to be more important that they have adequate food, shelter and clothing. While lack of such goods may spur a minority to initiate projects, such lack leaves the majority trapped in a state in which their only concern is ensuring that the next day's food is on the table. In fact, what the provision of basal goods and services may do is provide people with the resources not to take on servile and demeaning occupations, such as, to take another extreme example, shining the shoes of the rich. Given a choice between welfare payments and demeaning oneself, then, it is quite probable that many would choose the former. If this is the lack of initiative that motivates what we might call the 'Objection from Harm', then one has to wonder whether it is the harm done to welfare recipients with which its proponents are really concerned.

The Objection from Harm also seems to involve a rather cynical view of human nature. On this view, if people can get away with doing nothing, then, they will do so. This is a rather dubious claim however. While it is true that if people have a choice between servile occupations and welfare payments, they would probably choose the welfare option; it would also seem that most people would rather be gainfully employed than merely receiving welfare.

An internalist critique of Nozick

I have already suggested that the B.I.E. Principle would support, given appropriate empirical circumstances, redistributive taxation, patterned distributions, forced redistributive action and the existence of a welfare state.[40] The libertarian philosopher, Robert Nozick, would find such actions unacceptable for a number of reasons which I shall outline in detail in this section.[41] Given the influence of Nozick's work in political philosophy, it is important that his objections be dealt with. (I should repeat here that Nozick has resiled from the earlier more extreme views of *Anarchy, State and Utopia* in recent years).

Firstly, Nozick is committed to the thesis that patterns interfere with liberty. This claim is derived from his 'entitlement theory of justice'.[42] According to entitlement theory as Nozick outlines it, a person's rightful entitlement to his justly acquired holdings (which includes his property and services) entails that he be at liberty to give those holdings to whom he likes; that is, persons have rights of transfer over their justly acquired holdings. Additionally, if others choose to give holdings to him, then that is their right also. Here Nozick criticises what he calls 'patterned' theories of justice. Within reason, we should be able to do what we like with our property (e.g. my property rights in my knife allows me to leave it where I will, but not in your chest).[43] Theories of justice which attempt to impose a pattern (such as equality or merit) on the distribution of holdings across a society, must necessarily interfere with our freedom to do with our holdings as we like.[44] If the welfare state must interfere in order to ensure that the pattern of basal interest equality is realised, then Nozick would argue that this represents an unacceptable violation of liberty, and this is a reason for rejecting the actions of the welfare state. As Jonathan Wolff notes, Nozick has laid down a challenge to all non-entitlement theorists to demonstrate how their favoured pattern is compatible with a proper regard for liberty.[45] One charge which should be dealt with, then, is Nozick's claim that principles like the B.I.E. Principle violate liberty.

Secondly, Nozick argues that if redistributive taxation is forced, then it is morally illegitimate. He argues that such taxation forces those taxed to spend some of their working time working for others.[46] He suggests that such redistributive taxation is, in effect, a kind of forced labour. Hence, in defence of the B.I.E. Principle, we need to show either: i) that any redistributive taxation which arises out of the B.I.E. Principle is not coercive or; ii) if it is coercive, why this is not morally inappropriate. Nozick's work provides us with a challenge: why should any redistribution oriented toward the satisfaction of the basal needs not be regarded as a form of forced labour"

Thirdly, if the principle of basal interest equality favours forced redistribution, then, it must treat peoples' assets as collective in some sense. Nozick would argue that this fails to respect the separateness of persons and therefore it represents an illegitimate sacrifice of persons and their interests. (I make no claim that this list is exhaustive of the ways in which Nozick's work in *Anarchy, State and Utopia* might run counter to the B.I.E. Principle as outlined above. However it does, I think, cover the most conspicuous objections.)

I think that the most plausible way of defending the B.I.E. Principle against Nozick is: i) to examine Nozick's use of voluntary/coerced dichotomy and; (ii) to employ the internalist procedure outlined earlier in chapter two. It seems to me that it is still possible to attack Nozick's position and defend the B.I.E. Principle even if one accepts: i) that the entitlement theory is a coherent account of justice; ii) that Nozick does not need to outline how just acquisition of holdings comes about and; iii) that Nozick does not need to outline why it is that property rights not only involve rights of possession, but also rights of transfer. (The reader will recall that I am not defending the welfare state *per se* but rather the necessity of the welfare state in circumstances, all other things being equal, where persons' basal needs are not met). In responding to Nozick, there will be two foci of attack: firstly, Nozick's reliance upon the distinction between the voluntary and the coerced and; secondly, his naive theory concerning the separateness of persons in distributive theory.

Much of Nozick's work is premised on an acceptance of the moral distinction between the *voluntary* and the *coerced*. For Nozick, human volition is central to any account of political theory.[47] The state is not to coerce persons, except in cases where action is required to protect life and property. In Nozick's nightwatchman minimal state, the only acceptable state force is that undertaken by the army or police to protect life, liberty and property.[48] All other forms of state-coercion are impermissible. This helps explain Nozick's antagonism to such phenomena as redistributive taxation. For instance, in describing taxation for welfare purposes as forced labour, it is, in part, the coercion involved in forcing persons to work for others that renders it impermissible; similarly it is the coercion required to enforce contributions to the welfare state which he finds morally repugnant. To be sure, he is not opposed to persons voluntarily working for others nor to persons voluntarily contributing to the needs of others; it is merely the element of compulsion in cases of state-compelled charity, in the form of redistributive taxation, to which he objects. For Nozick, coercion or compulsion is the ultimate vice (although he does permit coercion in circumstances where the protection of property and life is required). The central point of his thesis about patterned theories of justice is that they do not respect the freely chosen actions of individual property owners.

Nozick appeals to the natural rights anarchist who believes that all action should be voluntary. His account of justice works with intuitions which many of us have about compulsion; intuitions which the natural rights anarchist turns into a whole philosophical system. However, I think that Nozick (and indeed the natural rights anarchist more generally) overstates the moral importance of the *voluntariness* of actions.[49] While it is important, broadly speaking, that action be voluntary, we should ask ourselves whether the voluntary consent of the subjects of state activity is the sole criterion for determining the moral status of social actions and policies? It is very unlikely that the voluntary/coerced distinction, defined in the absolute way that Nozick does, is plausible. Why should it be the case that either: i) all non-protective coerced actions are morally impermissible or; ii) the voluntary/coerced distinction should be thought of as the essential moral litmus test? With respect to the first claim, it seems clear that there are cases where non-protective compulsion is, in fact, morally legitimate. For instance, suppose that a young child is dying of a rare disease and urgently requires a highly specialised operation. Moreover, suppose there is only one doctor in the world who is capable of performing this difficult operation. Unfortunately, this doctor argues that he does not have to help the child if he does not want to. The doctor argues that he is the self-owner of his body and his services and thus believes that it is his right to refuse to provide his skills, if he so chooses. To add insult to injury, he lectures the child's parents on why compulsory charity is morally repugnant.

Nozick's argument here works with the intuition that most people would find forcing people to provide their services morally abhorrent. However, I think that we should challenge the *universality* of this intuition. In the example discussed immediately above, I think that many people would accept that the State should compel the doctor to help the child—by force if necessary—just as we consider it acceptable for doctors to be conscripted in times of war to save sick and dying soldiers. Entitlement theory, therefore, does not capture all of our intuitions about our rights to our own services; persons' rights to their own labour are not inviolable in all cases.

In response, the Nozick of *Anarchy, State and Utopia* might argue that my counter-example is excessively sentimental and that it perhaps has little to do with distributive theory. However, to the contrary, I believe that it demonstrates that the distinction between the voluntary and the coerced should not be thought of as being morally absolute. Grant that point and it also follows that his assertion that welfare state coercion is impermissible looks less convincing. Intuitively, this is not problematic – for as we noted, Nozick himself accepts coercive taxation for the purposes of funding the police and the army. A central aspect of a wide variety of cultures has been that people have worked and supported (and not necessarily voluntarily) those incapable of supporting themselves. Moreover, while Nozick finds compulsory charity repugnant, many others of us find it morally repugnant that people would be allowed to starve just so that no individual be coerced into some form of forced charity.

Secondly, the notion that the distinction between voluntary and coerced action should be the essential moral litmus test also has problems. Why should we accept that the voluntary/coerced distinction provides a fool-proof account of impermissible action? If we take the example of the little boy with the rare disease, it seems to be the case that we might well come to view positive assistance to save a person's life as being more important (in certain circumstances at least), than maintaining inviolate the voluntary nature of persons' actions. In terms of what we might call 'moral mattering', we assign far more weight to obligations to save lives than we do to any right of individuals for all their actions to be voluntary. The fact that Nozick places so much emphasis upon the voluntariness of action, seems to say something about Nozick's view of human nature, rather than telling us much at all about distributive justice. I shall say more about this later in the chapter.

Having challenged the universal applicability of Nozick's assumption that non-protective state coercion is always morally impermissible, I want now to apply an internalist critique to his work – particular attention will be given to his idea that maintaining respect for the separateness of persons is of utmost moral import. In a crucial passage of *Anarchy, State and Utopia* Nozick criticises theories which fail to respect the separateness of persons by treating them as means to some social end.[50] Nozick argues that using a person for the benefit of others, uses him and benefits others. It is only talk of an overall social good which covers this up. Nozick believes that to make use of a person in this way does not sufficiently respect nor take account of the fact that he is a separate person. To do so is, in effect, to sacrifice him.

However, I think we should reconsider Nozick's thesis in the light of the claim made in chapter two that the implementation of all distributive principles must involve sacrifice of some kind. Moreover, in that chapter I also argued that what kind of *sacrifice* a particular social theory permits or prohibits is determined to a large extent by the conception of human nature employed (either explicitly or implicitly) by the theory. (This, of course, was part of my defence of the internalist methodology.) In Nozick's case, the sacrifice which he permits may be uncovered by considering the fact that his theory would justify letting a child die in certain circumstances because of his reluctance to force persons to donate their services; or alternatively would justify allowing the impoverished to die or lead miserable lives of destitution because of the importance ascribed to liberty, over and above other values. Thus, the sacrifice which he permits is determined by his theory of the human good which values liberty and uncoerced action above other plausible values, such as the maintenance of human life or the material quality of human life. According to Nozick, what is of primary moral importance is that people should not be coerced, except in circumstances where persons' property or lives are actively threatened. While the State has an obligation to prevent persons being killed, it has no such obligation to provide goods which may prevent them from dying or which may improve their quality of life.

Where does this leave our argument? Is it enough merely to make the point that Nozick's theory involves a conception of the good? Some readers might concede that this is indeed true—Nozick's theory does involve an account of the good—but argue that this is no criticism because Nozick's conception is the correct one. Why should a conception of the good which invokes the moral importance of the basal interests be preferred to Nozick's conception? If I argue that my conception is preferable, then, isn't this just a matter of counter-assertion? What criteria do we possess for deciding between these various conceptions of the good?

In the end resolution of this dispute will rely upon our intuitions. One consequence of the implementation of Nozick's principles would be that the poor and weak of the society in question are sacrificed. Nozick, on the other hand, proclaims the liberty of persons to do what they like and to be free from coercion to be of utmost importance. Yet, as we have seen, if this commitment to uncoerced action leads to the sacrifice of some persons who are poor and weak, then, that is a sacrifice with which he is comfortable. However, we may contrast Nozick's theory with the B.I.E. Principle which, with its conception of persons as material beings who require basal interest satisfaction before they can realise other human interests, would prohibit such sacrifice.

Nozick, then, is willing to permit the sacrifice of the very *grounds of personhood*, for some persons. It is for this very reason that Nozick's theory should be rejected and the B.I.E. Principle accepted. There can be no respect for persons as ends-in-themselves, if the material grounds of personhood, i.e. the basal interests, are not satisfied when it is possible for them to be satisfied. William Galston says of Nozick's concern for persons as property-owners that it comes very close to self-refutation. "Many moral theories tell us that there are things that we must die for; very few, that we must die to maintain someone else inviolate in the possession of personal property."[51] The B.I.E. Principle should be accepted on the grounds that it puts the priority in the right place; it emphasises the importance of the basal interests. It acknowledges that basal interest satisfaction is necessary for persons to be persons; whereas Nozick's conception of persons is inadequate because it does not recognise the importance of the material grounds of personhood. It thus sanctions the sacrifice of the weak and impoverished and therefore should be rejected.[52] Nozick has a distorted moral hierarchy which places the priority first and foremost on liberty in holdings, and on entitlement, rather than where it should more properly be located, in the very grounds of personhood; namely, our basal interests.

Summary

In this chapter, then, I have outlined and defended the Principle of Basal Interest Equality which can be stated as follows:

> Distributive resources should be directed toward ensuring that all persons' basal interests are satisfied, at least to the level requisite for the pursuance of other human interests.

Moreover, I have argued that this principle is to be considered *conditionally prior* to all other plausible principles of distributive justice.

> *The Principle of Basal Interest Equality should be ascribed conditional priority. Hence it is to take precedence over all other possible principles of distributive justice until such time as the basal interest satisfaction of all has reached levels sufficient for all to pursue other human interests.*

I then considered some objections to the B.I.E. Principle. Against the Objection from Harm, according to which the provision of welfare is inimical to human well-being, I argued that such a claim involves a rather odd notion of what constitutes harm to human beings. Against Nozick's claim that such patterned principles violate liberty and entitlements, I argued that Nozick uses an inadequate conception of persons. In Nozick's case, instead of recognising the importance of material need in personhood, he focuses on entitlement and voluntariness. Such an emphasis is inadequate because it overlooks the fact that material need provides the very grounds of personhood.

Notes

1. I deal with the problem of hard basal scarcity—which arises in circumstances where material conditions are such that it is impossible to satisfy everyone's basal interests—later in the chapter.
2. A meritocratic distribution of basal interest satisfaction is not without precedent, as the following passages would seem to indicate: "A charitable organisation formed in Buffalo in 1877, devoted itself to organising charitable organisations 'scientifically', to prevent them from demoralising the

working class and encouraging laziness. It urged its constituent organisations to distinguish carefully between the worthy poor and the lazy and improvident, to distribute their assistance in such a way as to put people back to work as quickly as possible, and to consign tramps and other 'anti-social' elements to workhouses and prison rehabilitation.", Leiser. 1985, p.151.

3. Cf. Galston 1980, p.199. Galston claims that all individuals are equally entitled to the goods of existence and development.
4. It is possible to observe a formal analogy between the principles of justice outlined here and Rawls' lexical ordering of his two principles of justice.
5. Galston again makes a similar point in relation to 'needs', claiming that a rank-ordering of urgency exists among needs and thus in times of scarcity physical needs must be the first met. See op. cit., p.198.
6. The argument here is similar to that which Bernard Williams outlines in his article 'The Idea of Equality'. In this article Williams concludes not that people should receive an equal share of resources, but rather that vital goods should be allocated on the basis of need. See Williams, 1973, p.240.
7. Nagel, 1979, p.117.
8. It must be emphasised at this point that the B.I.E. Principle is not intended to be a principle of international justice, but rather applies merely to nation states. As was noted in the Introduction, it is assumed in this dissertation that when we speak of distributive justice, we are discussing a virtue of social institutions and arrangements; and thus in the current context international justice lies outside the scope of our inquiry. The principle is *universal* in that it is meant to apply to all nation states, but not universal in the sense that it is meant to apply *across* nation states, given the current context. Of course, this is not to deny that there are important issues of international justice, which concern the obligations of richer nations to poorer nations, particularly their obligations to needy members of poorer nations. Yet such problems stand outside our domain of inquiry. Much has been written on the subject of international justice in recent years. For a comprehensive study of the topic see Beitz, 1985.
9. Rawls, 1972, pp.243-45.
10. Ibid., p.43.
11. Ibid., p.43.
12. This example in all likelihood makes use of an implausible account of the relationship between human health and happiness. It is unlikely that people would be healthy if they were unhappy. However, for the purposes of argument at hand, let us assume that one can have all of one's basal interests satisfied and also be miserable.
13. Interestingly, in Rawls' general conception (as opposed to his special conception) of justice, he argues that there may be circumstances where it is permissible to sacrifice liberties for certain levels of material well-being: "...it may be reasonable to forego part of those freedoms when the long-run benefits are great enough to transform a less fortunate society into one where equal liberties can be fully enjoyed.", op. cit., p.247.
14. "Two quite different things are at issue here: 1. Sufficiency to live at a *minimal* level of subsistence... a level of bare survival, calling for a minima of food, shelter, clothing and medical attention...2. Sufficiency to live at a basic level of comfort..., a level for an adequate share of the good things of life.", Rescher, 1972, p.94.
15. Airaksinen, 1985, p.43.
16. We must also remember that what *resources* may be required for adequate basal interest satisfaction may vary from context to context. For instance, what level of sanitation is required for adequate levels of hygiene may be very different for a group of nomads than it is for a group of sedentary urban dwellers. This is not to say that their basal interests vary, but merely that the resources required to satisfy those interests may vary.
17. Cf. Galston, 1980, p.248.
18. This point is discussed briefly in chapter six. The idea that social resources are part of a collective pool is one of the assumptions of the dissertation.
19. Nozick, 1974, p.228.
20. Op. cit., p.72.
21. Op. cit., pp.206-7.

22. See chapter two for a discussion of the distinction between moderate scarcity and hard scarcity.
23. Ronald Dworkin has an alternative way around the problem which involves adopting endowment-insensitive/ambition-sensitive distributions of resources. See Dworkin, 1983, pp.38-39.
24. As G.A. Cohen notes in relation to Nozick's self-ownership debate: "There are ways of resisting compulsory eye transplanting without affirming (full) self-ownership, but they require more reflection than leftists usually spend on these matters. One way is to hold that non-contractual duties to others begin only once one's own basic needs are satisfied, and that having two eyes is a basic need.", Cohen, 1986, p.111.
25. The famous story concerning Maximillian Kolbe, who took another man's place and went to his death in a Nazi concentration camp, would be an example of such self-sacrifice.
26. An interesting question to ask at this point (though not one that I intend to examine in great detail) is whether acceptance of the voluntary sacrifice of persons' own bodily parts carries with it a commendation of the commodification of bodily parts. If we accept that it is morally acceptable for persons' to voluntarily donate their organs to others, on what grounds can we justify preventing persons selling their spare parts?
27. This mirrors Nozick's argument in 'On the Randian Argument', where he notes that while he objects to compelled welfare, he has no similar objections to philanthropy. See Nozick, 1971, pp.282-304.
28. This strategy of sacrificing across persons across interests will not resolve every problematic issue of distributive justice. It may be the case that some societies are so poor that there are no other categories of interests to sacrifice across. Even if we confiscate all of the goods and income of the rich, there may still not be enough resources to ensure that all are free from hunger.
29. David Gauthier's solution to this problem involves arguing that such handicapped persons are not party to the moral relationships grounded by contractarian theory and thus we are under no obligation to look after them. He is not concerned with transfers to the aged because they have paid for their benefits by earlier productive activity (although he does note that transfers to the aged have ominous redistributive potential). However, Gauthier's solution can have no place in this dissertation because of the emphasis which has been placed on treating all persons as ends and not as mere means. See Gauthier, 1986, p.18.
30. It is sometimes said of Marx that he wanted to turn the whole world into a giant work-house; if we followed the idea of harm-prevention to its ultimate conclusion, we may turn the world into a giant padded cell.
31. By the term 'practical reasoning' I simply mean the function of reason or thought in matters of voluntary decisions; and since voluntary actions and attitudes exhaust the ethical, it is frequently limited to the latter.
32. It is interesting to note that Rawls' difference principle provides no obvious way of dealing with scarce resources, especially scarce basal resources. In cases of hard scarcity, the worst off cannot be made better off. Of course, his principles of justice are meant only to apply in conditions of moderate abundance.
33. The idea of sacrifice which is operating here is one that is outlined in chapter two 'Distributive Justice and the Necessity of Sacrifice'.
34. This is just the sort of approach taken in the British National Health scheme, where people are allocated 'qalis', which measure how much use people are likely to derive from any particular operation (e.g. depending on their age and level of fitness), and which are used to determine who should receive various medical resources.
35. Furthermore, as well as the actual grounds of desert, any meritocratic theory must also address the issue of how weights are to assigned to different meritorious acts, or indeed if any weights are to be assigned at all; that is, they must address the issue of how much each meritorious act is worth in terms of reward.
36. It would, of course, need to be *genuinely* random; that is, it would need to be the case that the selection could not be rigged in any way. An essential condition of the principle of random distribution being the just way to distribute resources in cases of hard scarcity, is that the randomness be genuine
37. Rawls distinguishes between pure procedural justice and perfect and imperfect procedural justice. *Perfect Procedural Justice* refers to situations where mistakes cannot be made. For instance, an

omniscient being's judgement would be an example of perfect procedural justice. *Imperfect Procedural Justice* refers to situations where mistakes can be made. This is essentially the sort of thing that goes on in our law courts, where there is always the chance for a mistake to be made. What unites these two forms of justice is that there is an independent means of knowing what the outcome should be. However, in Rawls third category, *Pure Procedural Justice*, there is no independent means of determining the rightness or wrongness of a decision. It is like a case where a group draws straws to determine who should defuse a bomb; there is no independent way of knowing who should get the terrible job. Rawls characterises his theory of justice as an example of pure proceduralism. For a discussion of these ideas see Nelson, 1980, pp.502-11.

38. For a discussion of this issue see Battin, 1986, pp.317-40.
39. It seems to me that a more plausible candidate for the harm that is perpetrated by welfare provision would be the surveillance that such welfare agencies often impose on welfare recipients.
40. The establishment of a welfare state would be one way of ensuring that the basal interests of all are satisfied. Socialism, of course, might be another way. The principle of basal interest equality is not partisan toward any particular social form: all that it demands is that all persons' basal interests should be satisfied.
41. In discussing Nozick's ideas here I am solely concerned with those arguments put forward in *Anarchy, State and Utopia*. However, it does seem that in a later work, *The Examined Life*, he repudiates many of his earlier hard-line libertarian views. See Nozick, 1989.
42. Nozick defines his entitlement theory in the following manner: "If the world were wholly just, the following inductive definition would exhaustively cover the subject of justice in holdings. 1. A person who acquires a holding in accordance with the principle of justice in acquisition is entitled to that holding. 2. A person who acquires a holding in accordance with the principle of justice in transfer, from someone else entitled to the holding, is entitled to the holding. 3. No one is entitled to a holding except by (repeated) applications of 1 and 2.", op. cit., p.151.
43. Ibid, p.171.
44. Ibid, p.151.
45. See Wolff 1991 pp.79-90 for a useful discussion of the relationship between patterned theories of justice and liberty.
46. Nozick op. cit., pp.169-72.
47. See ibid., pp.ix and 169-72.
48. Ibid, pp.25-27.
49. We should also note that Nozick's account of the distinction between the voluntary and the forced is, in some respects, rather idiosyncratic. He writes: "Whether a person's action are voluntary depends on what it is that limits his alternatives. If facts of nature do so, the actions are voluntary....Other people's actions place limits on one's available opportunities. Whether this makes one's resulting action non-voluntary depends upon whether these others had the right to act as they did.", Nozick, 1974, p.262. Jonathan Wolff argues that Nozick's account has the consequence that a criminal rightfully imprisoned is not forced to remain in jail; or that miners, trapped underground by a rock-fall, are not forced to remain where they are until rescued. See op. cit., p.85.
50. Op. cit., pp.32-33.
51. Galston, op. cit., p.188.
52. This argument might be filled out—if one was so inclined—in the language of rights. It could be said that the right to food, shelter, clothing and medical needs is to take priority over rights to holdings and that to argue otherwise is to use an inadequate conception of persons.

8 The eudaimonian sphere

The principle of equal well-being and the eudaimonian sphere

The second sphere to which I shall apply the principle of equal well-being is the eudaimonian sphere. In this sphere application of my egalitarian regulative ideal is much less straightforward than was the case in the basal sphere, for in the eudaimonian sphere conditions of hard scarcity—by which I mean conditions in which the goods in question cannot be allocated universally—obtain as a matter of course. If eudaimonian goods are scarce in this manner, then applying this egalitarian general conception of justice becomes difficult. Hence, in the eudaimonian sphere principles cannot be generated simply by applying the general conception to the sphere, instead a principle of 'compensatory meritocracy' will be formulated – a principle which is underpinned by the principle of equal well-being.

Let us say a little more about what the eudaimonian spheres consists of. The term 'eudaimonian sphere' circumscribes those distributive goods which realise eudaimonian interests; distributive goods which enable us to engage in activity in which we may develop and employ subtle skills. There are two main sites where eudaimonian distributive goods are to be found. These are firstly the workplace and secondly, the 'organic social domain', i.e. the domain of non-institutional activity outside of the workplace. Additionally, there is a third site, the 'educational domain', which primarily provides the preconditions for eudaimonian interest realisation in the workplace and the organic social domain (although the educational domain is a workplace of course for teachers). I will have little to say about this domain of activity

By 'work', what is meant is simply occupation in the ordinary sense of the word.[1] The term refers to the kind of activity from which, amongst other things, one's means of subsistence are derived. The workplace is where one is employed to perform various socially-desired tasks, for which one is paid. The workplace is also a possible site of eudaimonian interest realisation, for some kinds of work are 'eudaimonian' or 'meaningful'. (I shall use the terms 'eudaimonian work' and 'meaningful work' interchangeably hereafter.) Meaningful work is any form of work, from architecture to beekeeping, in which a person is able to develop her capacity for autonomous and self-directed activity. [2] The main focus of the chapter will be the distribution of eudaimonian activity in the workplace.

Secondly, there is the 'organic social domain'. Activity in the organic social domain is activity which occurs outside of the workplace as defined above. It occurs outside the confines of paid employment and includes amongst other things, painting one's house, standing for election on the local council, participating in amateur sporting events, rearing children and various religious or spiritual activity. Equally, the organic social domain is also a site in which eudaimonian activity can occur. An example of eudaimonian activity in the organic social domain might be teaching oneself a second language or learning the bassoon. It is the kind of activity which the French social theorist Andre Gorz believes should become more central in our lives. In *Critique of Economic Reason,* Gorz argues that undue emphasis is placed upon paid employment.[3]

Finally, there is what I shall call the 'educational domain'. Education provides, amongst other things, the *grounds* of the eudaimonian; that is, it provides the basic conditions for people to realise such interests. It provides part of the necessary background for people to be able to realise eudaimonian well-being. While it may also be a site where eudaimonian interests are actually realised (such as in research work at a university), its primary importance is as the grounds of eudaimonian interest satisfaction. Moreover, it would be a mistake if education was conceived of too narrowly; there is 'eudaimonian education' in both formal institutional settings (such as at schools) and non-formal settings (such as in the home and playground). Whilst education may be primarily thought of as a precondition of the eudaimonian, the two major sites of *actual* eudaimonian interest realisation (as opposed to grounds) are at work and in the organic social domain.

While my main concern will be with meaningful work, that is, with eudaimonian activity in the workplace, it should be noted that there will be benefit to be obtained from certain kinds of work which does not involve eudaimonian self-realisation, which will encourage persons to pursue careers in these occupations. For instance, in choosing a career some people will be attracted to jobs which involve service to others, such as nursing the sick and elderly. They might choose such activities in preference to eudaimonian work because they believe that such work is important and thus they gain satisfaction from performing it.[4] However, despite these complexities, it is the eudaimonian benefit which will be my main concern. I shall assume that such benefit is the primary benefit to be obtained from work. Thus, I shall also assume that tedious non-eudaimonian work, which involves service to others, is to be thought of as a burden, even though some of the people who perform it find such service to others satisfying and would choose such work in preference to eudaimonian work. Moreover, in cases where eudaimonian benefit is not the only benefit to be had from work, I shall assume that the primary benefit is the eudaimonian benefit. Later in the chapter I shall argue that such an assumption is justifiable for the very reason that the eudaimonian benefit is the description of the benefit which we distribute, namely occupation.

Thus the primary method for determining the benefit to be obtained from work will be my notion of the 'eudaimonian'. Work is to be assessed in terms of whether it enables persons to develop eudaimonian skills. Hence, with regard to work, our two important theoretical categories will be *eudaimonian work* and *non-eudaimonian work*. These two terms, the eudaimonian and the non-eudaimonian, being a pair of contradictories, characterise all possible forms of work. All work is either eudaimonian or non-eudaimonian, i.e. it is either meaningful or non-meaningful.

It is also important to draw the distinction between the term 'non-meaningful' from demeaning work; that is, work which people find demeaning and which lowers their dignity. While non-meaningful work may in some circumstances be demeaning (such as the work of endlessly cleaning toilets), it is quite possible that there be eudaimonian work which some people, for reasons of social prejudice, find demeaning. All that is meant by the term non-meaningful is a lack of the eudaimonian. It may be work which is repetitive or which occurs in large scale operations or in which work is divided into minute parts.[5] All of these are ways in which work might be non-eudaimonian. This distinction between the meaningful and the non-meaningful provides a criterion for the evaluation of work which can be used by the state and other social institutions to determine the justice of various distributions of work.[6]

Interestingly, my distinction between eudaimonian and non-eudaimonian work bears some similarity to the Kantian distinction between *independent* and *servile* occupations. For Kant, independent occupations are those in which one sells or exchanges one's skills or the products of one's skills; whereas the servile occupations are those occupations in which other individuals direct the use of one's labour power.[7] In both the Kantian distinction and the eudaimonian/non-eudaimonian distinction the emphasis is upon self-direction. Furthermore, just as Kant finds servility ethically repugnant, so too it will be argued that the existence of non-meaningful work is, in the great scheme of things, undesirable. It is not just that the non-meaningful lacks benefit, it is also that it represents a burden imposed on persons for the very reason that it is activity which leaves us permanently scarred in a variety of ways. The performance of what I term 'non-meaningful work' is a burden which generates forms of perversion in human beings.

The distinction between the organic social domain and the domain of work is also central to my analysis of the eudaimonian sphere. Given this centrality, it is instructive to compare it with the Marxian dichotomy between the 'realm of necessity' and the 'realm of freedom'. Marx thought of the realm of necessity as requiring activity which is directed towards ends which are instrumental to achieving other ends, such as human survival. The realm of freedom, on the other hand, is one where the activities which are carried out are directed towards goals which are posited by the actors themselves. This is activity, which while not non-material, is not material production proper.[8] If it is assumed that eudaimonian interest-realisation in the workplace occurs within work that is directed by material need, whereas eudaimonian interest realisation external to the workplace is freed from such considerations, then Marx might possibly consider eudaimonian work to be part of material production proper (that is part of the realm of necessity) and the organic social domain to be part of the realm of freedom. In the organic social domain, people generally would act upon goals which were set by themselves, rather than by the contours of material necessity and production; whereas work would presumably be shaped by such necessity. It is the role of material necessity which links the distinction between work and the organic social domain with Marx's dichotomy. There are also some dissimilarities. Activity outside the workplace may be of an economic nature and directed toward instrumental economic needs. For instance, a person might paint in her spare time with the aim of eventually selling her paintings. This is in contrast to the realm of freedom in Marx's system, which is a realm of activity freed from economic considerations.

An ideal implementation of the principle of equal well-being

What would implementation of the principle of equal well-being in the eudaimonian sphere involve? At first sight, what it would seem to involve would be the creation of conditions under which all could realise eudaimonian interests in all three sites. It would require the provision of creative self-developmental activity for all. Bringing this about would not only require resource allocation, but also the *transformation* of those structures—particularly in the workplace—which impede the equal realisation of eudaimonian interests. I shall now attempt to lay out in greater detail what egalitarianism in the eudaimonian sphere might involve.

In the first place, implementation of the principle of equal well-being in the eudaimonian sphere would ideally involve *universal education*, designed to raise all citizens to the requisite standards for eudaimonian interest-realisation in other facets of social life. This is an important program because lack of education may be an impediment to any person realising eudaimonian interests in their work. Here, of course, a sceptic might ask what the actual level required would be, given that the level of education required in a feudal society would be different to that required in a modern one. In response, it is enough to say that the requisite standard is that which is required by the person's society in order for them to function in the various forms of meaningful work which occur in that society.

Secondly, implementation of the principle of equal well-being would also seem to involve the transformation of the working conditions under which people labour.

Workplaces would ideally be transformed in such a way that all work becomes meaningful; all non-meaningful work should be eliminated. Realising this particular ideal would require a transformation of the technical division of labour (which sees work divided into minute tasks), a breakdown of the mental/manual distinction (which finds persons directed toward the development of only one side of their being), an ending of the social division of labour (so that all perform a variety of tasks) and the implementation of democratic decision-making procedures. It would require the creation of a workplace in which all workers take part in decision making, in which workers produce whole products and in which they perform a wide variety of tasks.

Thirdly, implementation of the principle of equal well-being in the eudaimonian sphere would also involve transformation of the organic social domain via transformation of the cultural environment which human beings inhabit. It is our cultural environment which shapes, in part at least, our understanding of what role activity in the organic social domain has to play in our lives. Certain cultural environments discourage self-developmental activity outside of the workplace; or alternatively certain cultural environments encourage us to think of such non-institutional activity as trivial. However, it is important that people recognise that the organic social domain is an important site of self-developmental activity. Thus the requisite cultural environment is one in which people are encouraged to see activity outside of the workplace not simply as relaxation, but also as a possible site of self-realisation.[9]

Constraints upon the egalitarian distribution of eudaimonian work

Whilst the measures outlined above for the hypothetical application would, I believe, be egalitarian, they are unfortunately merely ideal. There are difficulties which arise when one attempts to implement the principle of equal well-being in the eudaimonian sphere. More specifically these difficulties relate to eudaimonian activity in the workplace or 'meaningful work'. While it is both possible and highly desirable to instantiate the general conception in the region of education and in the organic social domain, difficulties begin with eudaimonian activity in the workplace because of the hard scarcity associated with such meaningful work; hard scarcity which means that some persons *necessarily* miss out on this eudaimonian benefit. This hard scarcity is generated by two elements. Firstly, it is generated by the existence of a *natural distribution of occupation.* In any conceivable contemporary society (at least for the foreseeable future) there will be both eudaimonian and non-eudaimonian work. While there will be various eudaimonian professions, such as architecture, there will also be non-eudaimonian jobs, such as street sweeping and various forms of factory work, which must be undertaken. Theories of distributive justice must recognise the necessarily non-eudaimonian nature of some tasks which must be performed. No matter how they are organised, activities such as toilet cleaning, cannot be rendered eudaimonian, so to speak. Such occupational activities are constitutively non-eudaimonian. Moreover, the fact that there will be a continuing necessity of a technical division of labour means that other jobs, which are not intrinsically non-eudaimonian, will continue to be performed under non-eudaimonian conditions.[10] Additionally, a third point which must be factored into our calculations is that there is a limit to the availability of eudaimonian occupations. For instance, there will only be so many architects and bee-keepers required in any given society. Similarly, there will be limits to the numbers required in certain non-eudaimonian occupations. The number of sewer men required in any society would be relatively fixed, depending upon the level of technology available. This is not to say that in every society there will be exactly the same ratio of non-eudaimonian to eudaimonian work. In different societies the ratio may well vary, depending on government policy, social tastes and the level of economic development. A particular society, for instance, might value sculpture highly and thus provide funds for a large number of its citizens to work as sculptors, thus decreasing the ratio of non-meaningful work to meaningful work. The natural distribution is *determinable* rather than *determinate*; while there will necessarily be both eudaimonian and non-eudaimonian work, there is the possibility of great variance in the ratios of the two categories in any given society or set of societies.

However this, of itself, is not sufficient to preclude straight implementation of our principle of equal well-being. The existence of a natural distribution of occupation on its own will not be sufficient to generate conditions of hard scarcity. The existence of a technical division of labour does not prevent the overall sharing of meaningful and non-meaningful work; meaningful jobs may be rotated or shared, for instance. In order to demonstrate that hard scarcity exists in the eudaimonian sphere, we require a second claim and that is that the eudaimonian jobs cannot be feasibly divided in such a way as to ensure that all are able to share in them. This we may call the 'argument from indivisibility'. This argument is drawn in response to two possible egalitarian strategies: i) rotation and; ii) collectivism. Against these strategies, the argument from indivisibility involves the contention that the circumstances of justice—which include the continuing necessity of a technical division of labour, the continuing necessity of large scale productive units and the existence of constitutive size constraints upon eudaimonian interest realisation—are such that these strategies are implausible.

A policy of rotation would require that occupations be rotated so that every person, at some point or other, perform all of the various tasks in a productive process. Rotation would require the swapping of occupational positions in the technical division of labour and the performance by all of constitutively non-eudaimonian jobs, such as toilet cleaning. It is a policy which responds to the problem of the natural allocation of occupations, by swapping people between jobs, rather than fetishising the relation between persons and jobs. There are at least three problems with this rotational approach however, which arise because its implementation would seem to lead to occupations always being performed by novices. There are many occupations, necessary for the proper functioning of society, which demand that those performing the task have more than a brief acquaintance with the requirements of the particular profession. In the case of occupations such as medicine, years of familiarity with the job requirements might well be desirable; and while it is important that everybody should realise eudaimonian interests, it is also important that the various occupations be performed satisfactorily. The satisfactory performance of occupations requires that they be performed in ways such that the *telos* of the activity is fulfilled. In the case of bricklaying, that goal is that bricks be laid in such a way that they are part of proper functioning walls; in the case of doctoring, the proper goal of the activity is the healing of the sick.

Secondly, unless each individual performs each particular job for absurdly short periods of time, then, it must be the case that there is not enough time in human lives to ensure that each person shares equally in all of the benefits and the burdens of work. Moreover, if people only perform each occupation for a very short period of time, then this would prevent many occupations from being eudaimonian. Many eudaimonian occupations require more than a mere week's performance, for instance, for it to be possible for persons to realise any eudaimonian benefit from their performance.

Finally, there are occupations whose dangers and rigours are such that they *should not* be rotated. For example, high-altitude construction work and coal mining are the kinds of occupations in which initiating a policy of short periods of activity by novices could well be extremely dangerous. These are jobs which require familiarity in order for their rigours and dangers to be reduced. Soldiering is another example of an occupation for which the instigation of a policy of rotation might well be problematic. William Galston, discussing this very issue, notes that there seems to be strong evidence to suggest that the program of frequently rotating junior officers in the Vietnam War led to higher mortality rates for them and the men they commanded than might otherwise have been the case.[11]

The other egalitarian strategy mentioned—collectivism—would require some form of transformation of work in order to ensure that the natural distribution of occupation did not prevent all from sharing equally in work's eudaimonian benefits. There are a variety of possible collectivist strategies. One such collectivist strategy would involve the institution of a system of industrial democracy such that all workers would share in decisions concerning both the general structure and day-to-day organisation of work. Thus, while under the description of it as occupation work might not be eudaimonian, it might well be eudaimonian under the description of it as the activity of determining the direction of the group's work activity. Another possible collectivist strategy might involve the socialisation of ownership of the means of production. Presumably, the idea here would be that ownership and control of one's work enables work itself to be its own reward. In some sense such ownership would enable persons to realise eudaimonian benefits.

However, both of these collectivist strategies run foul of the continuing necessity of large scale productive units. For the foreseeable future at least, work will continue to need to be organised in large scale units so that we can generate the surplus requisite for human existence. If we connect this contingent claim about the nature of the world with the empirical claim that there are constitutive size constraints upon the possibility of eudaimonian interest realisation for individuals involved in collective acts, then we can discern the problematic nature of such collectivist strategies. Industrial democracies instigated within large-scale productive units might well be democratic, but such democratic decision-making will not realise eudaimonian benefit. Indeed, it is difficult to know how within any large group all individuals could have significant effects upon the collective decisions of these large groups, such that all could realise eudaimonian interests. It is a constitutive fact of what I have dubbed eudaimonian interest realisation that there be a size-constraint upon its realisation in collective units. Given these facts, the collectivist strategy comes to appear rather implausible. It seems absurd to argue that legal ownership of the means of production confers on the worker in a large factory anything more than nominal control. It certainly does not confer the sort of ownership and control that might enable such workers to realise eudaimonian benefit. We can conclude, then, that both the collectivist and the rotational strategies cannot, on their own, deliver egalitarian outcomes because eudaimonian tasks cannot be divided in such a way that all can share in them. Whilst not denying the value of such transformations of work—indeed we may well wish to incorporate them into the egalitarian project—the circumstances of justice are such that eudaimonian benefit in the workplace is indivisible and hence these strategies by themselves cannot give rise to significant egalitarian consequences.

It is the 'indivisibility of the eudaimonian' and the 'natural distribution of occupation' when combined which create the hard scarcity and it is this hard scarcity which prevents straight-forward egalitarian implementation of the principle of equal well-being in the eudaimonian sphere. There would be no hard scarcity if meaningful work is in fact divisible because the meaningful work which we do have at our disposal need only be divided amongst all the citizens of our society. Similarly, there would be no hard scarcity if there were no natural distribution of occupation, for again all that would need to be done would be to eliminate the non-meaningful work and to increase the amount of meaningful work. However, given that it does not seem feasible to rotate jobs, and given that there is a natural distribution of occupation, it follows that some persons will miss out on eudaimonian benefit at work. It is not that work should not be made universally meaningful, but rather that it *cannot*. Thus, while some work will be eudaimonian, it will necessarily be the case that some work will be non-eudaimonian. Accordingly, the holding of certain jobs will be a benefit, whilst holding others (the non-meaningful) will be a burden.[12] This scarcity of eudaimonian benefit is made all the more morally problematic for the reason that for the foreseeable future there will continue to be a realm of necessity. This means that rather than being freed from the workplace, an integral part of human existence will be the continuing necessity to work.[13] Thus, those framing theories of justice must acknowledge the facts of scarcity and the continuing necessity of work.

My conclusion here concerning the hard scarcity of eudaimonian benefit in the workplace would seem to inject an element of tragedy into my theory which runs counter to the general spirit of Aristotle's writings. Aristotle was essentially an optimist. He believed that there are no moral or political questions which we cannot resolve, provided that we are rational and persistent and so long as we adopt suitable epistemic standards.[14] My claim here is that the world is such that although egalitarianism is morally desirable, it cannot be straightforwardly implemented in the eudaimonian sphere. This is an essentially tragic claim.

Two conclusions can be drawn from the discussion thus far: i) eudaimonian work is a scarce good and ii) there are other socially necessary tasks which, regardless of efforts to change them, will remain intractably non-eudaimonian. This provides a serious challenge for egalitarians. The fact that some persons must undertake these tasks means that they are condemned to the non-meaningful, and hence, they are condemned to activity which fails to realise an essential part of the human *telos*. Non-meaningful work which involves, for instance, repetition might develop some part of us, such as the forearm, and leave the rest of our talents, both physical and mental, underdeveloped. The central problem in the eudaimonian sphere for the egalitarian, then, is how to reconcile the hard scarcity of eudaimonian benefit with the demands of the principle of equal well-being. We may redescribe the problem in Kantian terms. Grant it that meaningful work is a scarce resource, then any distribution of occupations in which some persons acquire meaningful occupations and others non-meaningful occupations, is a way of treating those performing the non-meaningful as mere means and not as ends in themselves. This distributive outcome would seem to fail the principle of respect for persons. Indeed, such a Kantian approach is adopted by Adina Schwartz in her article 'Meaningful Work'. Schwartz claims that work in which a technical division of labour is in place restricts the opportunities for persons to frame, pursue and adjust their own plans in a rational manner. Such work fails to allow them to act *autonomously*. In failing to consider the existence of these jobs to be a matter of moral concern—and indeed permitting such jobs to exist—we fail to treat all members of society as autonomous beings.[15] After noting that she takes meaningful work to be work in which persons are treated as ends, Schwartz then draws the further conclusion that the State is under an obligation to make work universally meaningful. For Schwartz, making work meaningful involves ending the technical division of labour.[16]

At this point we should note that it may not just be the lack of benefit which is problematic about being condemned to the non-meaningful, but also the imposition of a burden which may have deleterious effects upon our physical and emotional well-being. William Galston suggests that some productive activities may promote traits that are "more analogous to tumours or disfiguring marks than to overdeveloped organs."[17] Galston makes an important point here. A variety of pathological psychological effects can ensue from performing the non-eudaimonian. Indeed, Adina Schwartz, citing a number of psychological studies,[18] claims that persons who perform repetitive tasks for considerable periods of time tend to be less capable of, and less interested in, rationally framing pursuing and adjusting their own plans during the rest of their time outside of work. (Presumably, the thought which lies behind this claim is that the performance of non-meaningful work has a causal role to play in the non-working lives of those who perform it). On this account, the non-meaningful infects, so to speak, the lives of those who perform it outside of the workplace. This should not be surprising, given that a large part of our life is spent at work and this time must have some effect upon our individual character development.[19] To a great extent, our understanding of ourselves, the world and our role in that world are formed at work. It would appear then, that performance of the non-meaningful might not only be undesirable because of the lack of benefit, but because long periods of repetitive work may harm our capacity for autonomous action. Such evidence demonstrates the pathological nature of non-meaningful work. The point is not a trivial one, for as Albert Camus rather poetically notes: "without work, all life goes rotten, but when work is soulless, life stifles and dies."[20] In distributing the non-meaningful to some persons and not to others, we condemn those allocated such burdensome activity to lead diminished lives. Moreover, there would also seem to be some connections between autonomous self-developmental work and self-esteem; those who miss out on eudaimonian work suffer a loss in terms of self-esteem.

We should also note that there appears to be a connection between self-esteem and certain non-eudaimonian aspects of work. Social status, for instance, is a great generator of self-esteem and it is almost platitudinous to make the point that many jobs carry with them high social status. Yet equally, the relative social status of many occupations is not set in stone so to speak. In different societies and in different historical epochs, the status of various occupations has changed. For instance, in the former Soviet Union doctors did not enjoy great social status. This lowly status meant that such work is less likely to generate self-esteem. Yet such facts do not rule out the eudaimonian analysis of self-esteem; they merely force us to acknowledge that there are criteria other than what I have labelled 'the eudaimonian' which need to be factored in when examining the relationship between self-esteem and occupation.

We are left then with three questions which must be answered: i) how is eudaimonian work to be distributed?; ii) how is non-eudaimonian work to be distributed?; iii) what is to be done, if anything, about the fact that some persons must *necessarily* miss out on the eudaimonian work?[21] These questions need to be answered in a way that is, in some sense, in keeping with the principle of equal well-being.

Compensatory meritocracy and the scarce resource 'eudaimonian work'

Thus far, I have argued that eudaimonian work should be considered to be a scarce resource; that is, meaningful work exists in conditions of hard scarcity. This being true, the central problem becomes how an egalitarian should attempt to deal with such scarcity. What is the most faithful way of rendering the principle of equal well-being in relation to eudaimonian work?

The two most plausible principles for allocating meaningful work are random distribution and meritocracy. The former involves, as the name suggests, allocating eudaimonian work randomly—though not capriciously—while the latter involves assigning eudaimonian work to the best qualified candidate.[22] Before we discuss the relative merits of either of these approaches, it is important to emphasise at the outset that no matter whether we choose random or meritocratic allocation, some persons will still be condemned to the non-eudaimonian. Should we not be concerned with those who miss out on eudaimonian work? Are they not being treated as mere means? Why should they, by their own misfortune, be condemned to the non-meaningful? Furthermore, will it not be the case that those who miss out on such work might feel frustrated or have a diminished sense of self-esteem, as suggested earlier?[23]

However, I do not think that there is reason to become overly concerned here. The point to remember is that the aim of the principle of equal well-being in the eudaimonian sphere is to realise the eudaimonian interests of all. The mere fact that the eudaimonian interests of all cannot be realised at work, does not mean that the goal of fostering eudaimonian benefit should be abandoned for the very reason that these interests can also be realised in the organic social domain. Thus, instead of attempting to realise the eudaimonian interests of all in every facet of social life, the goal of public policy should be to achieve the overall realisation of the eudaimonian interests of all persons. This strategy requires *compartmentalising* distributive goods into different eudaimonian spheres where different distributive principles will hold. Social policy should aim to realise the eudaimonian interests of all by compartmentalising aspects of social life. I do not think that this approach should be thought contrary to the spirit of egalitarianism;

not every aspect of social life need embody the egalitarian ideal in order for the overall realisation of the eudaimonian interests of all to be brought about.[24] In place of an egalitarian distribution of meaningful work, a regime of compensatory justice should be instituted. Such a policy would involve ensuring that those who miss out on eudaimonian goods in the workplace are compensated in various other ways. Our goal is to ensure that those who miss out on eudaimonian benefit in the workplace are provided with opportunities for eudaimonian interest-realisation outside of work. Thus a *plurality* of distributive principles will be postulated in order to realise the egalitarian ideal overall.[25]

The main point of my discussion here is that both the meritocratic and random strategies for distributing eudaimonian work can be rendered egalitarian by the institution of a compensatory mechanism in the organic social domain which is designed with the aim of ensuring that all persons realise their eudaimonian interests. Grant it that this compensatory mechanism provides a plausible strategy, we must now attempt to choose between random and meritocratic distribution of eudaimonian benefit.

On the face of it, one might well be tempted to opt for the random distribution of eudaimonian work. While random allocation is not an egalitarian principle of distribution in the strict sense, it is procedurally egalitarian. Moreover, a precedent has already been set; in chapter seven I argued that scarce basal resources should be allocated randomly. Thus, it would be quite natural to suppose that consistency would dictate that randomness should be chosen in this instance as well. A third factor mitigating in favour of random allocation is that when one considers the meritocratic alternative, one might well be tempted to ask why those with natural talents should benefit from them. Many modern critics have rejected meritocratic accounts of justice because they believe that determining resource allocation according to level of skill or competence is rather morally arbitrary.[26] This is roughly Rawls' argument in *A Theory of Justice*. He suggests that no person deserves the advantages that his character or natural abilities make possible because no one deserves his character or abilities themselves. After all, it is a cosmic accident which determines whether one is born talented or strong-willed. How then might we justify the meritocratic distribution of this eudaimonian benefit?

However, despite initial appearances to the contrary, I think that the meritocratic allocation of eudaimonian work can be defended. Firstly, given the existence of our compensatory mechanism, random distribution is no more egalitarian than assignation according to merit. Secondly, the charge of moral arbitrariness against meritocracy does not do much for the cause of random allocation. Random allocation is also morally arbitrary. Rawls' objection to desert is its resemblance to a lottery. Yet we can hardly use this argument against desert to defend an *actual* lottery. Thirdly, there are problems with random allocation itself. Randomness may lead to a wastage of social resources. Random allocation might mean, for instance, that violin scholarships are awarded to students whose main interests lie in mathematics. Alternatively, jobs as doctors might be distributed to individuals who wish to pursue the study of ancient Greek history or who wish to be carpenters. I shall call this line of justification the 'argument from wastage'. Meritocratic allocation of eudaimonian work, on the other hand, does not (in principle at least) give rise to such problems of wastage. In distributing to the most capable, we are allocating resources, as far as we can tell, to those persons who are most likely to make good use of them.

Some readers might think that to rule out random allocation on grounds of wastage seems rather inconsistent, given the use of random allocation in conditions of hard basal scarcity in chapter seven. One might well wonder why the argument from wastage would hold in the eudaimonian and not in the basal sphere. If we cast our minds back to my discussion of the problem of hard basal scarcity, then why not argue that avoiding wastage of natural resources demands that the place in the lifeboat should be given to the budding twelve year old violinist in preference to the eighty year old drunk?

Nevertheless, I think that such objections can be circumvented without too much pain. The 'argument from wastage' which I defend is an argument from *individual* wastage, not an argument from *social* wastage. I am concerned with ensuring that all individuals maximise their eudaimonian interest potential. Yet, the argument from wastage presented in the context of hard basal scarcity would be an argument from *social* wastage. (Indeed, it could only be the latter because it does not make sense to compare individual wastage in situations where those who miss out on the distributive good in question lose their lives). My concern with individual wastage is a concern with the development of excellence. It is not underpinned by any utilitarian rationale. While there is no doubt that distributing benefits to the most able augments social utility, the rationale for being concerned with the rewarding of excellence should not be understood in such terms, rather it is that individual eudaimonian benefit will be maximised if we adopt this meritocratic strategy.[27]

Given the force of the argument from wastage, it would seem then that eudaimonian work should be distributed meritocratically; that is, it should be distributed to those persons most able to gain benefit from it. Eudaimonian work should be distributed much in a similar way that places to universities and scholarships to pursue artistic careers are currently allocated.[28] Accordingly, the distribution of the non-eudaimonian should also be determined meritocratically because those who miss out on the meritocratic distribution of the eudaimonian will be allocated non-eudaimonian occupations. Additionally, compensation should be provided for those who miss out on eudaimonian work. I shall call this overall strategy the '*egalitarian principle of compensatory meritocracy*'. It is a strategy which is compatible with the principle of equal well-being and involves a shift of focus from the demand for universal eudaimonian *work* to eudaimonian *activity* for all. Thus instead of state action being designed to promote meaningful work, it is designed to promote eudaimonian activity in general. In the following two sections I shall provide some concrete details of this pluralistic distributive policy.

Egalitarianism and the meritocratic allocation of meaningful work

Meaningful work, then, should be distributed meritocratically, provided that compensations are made in the organic social domain for those who perform non-meaningful work. This distributive pattern is a meritocratic one, in the sense that those who have the greatest level of relevant developed eudaimonian capacity will be the recipients of the good of meaningful work.[29] The recommended distributive mechanism, then is meritocratic in the sense that it is just that some miss out on this distributive good.[30] However, such a pattern of distribution is only contingently just; the justice of a meritocratic distribution in relation to meaningful work, being contingent upon the provision of compensation for those condemned to the non-meaningful.

Let us consider this meritocratic allocation of eudaimonian work in greater detail. In what sense is the theory I am advocating meritocratic? I shall respond to this question in the first instance by describing what kind of meritocratic theory it is not. Firstly, it is not an account of desert according to which being *more deserving* leads one to *deserve more*, as is the case in the Aristotelian theory of justice which advocates desert-for-effort; rather, it is a account of desert according to which a comparative level of skill qualifies one for selection for the scarce good of eudaimonian work. All that is assumed is that work should be allocated to the best qualified person.[31] On this account it is assumed that the person who will benefit most from receiving the job is the person who demonstrates the most ability. (Of course, on occasions this convergence of ability and likelihood of use can come apart, but on the whole it is justifiable to identify these two ideas). In focusing on the most able and, in particular, the most able to use the resource, the concern is with individual utility; i.e. with the development of individual self-realisation to the greatest possible extent.

Secondly, this meritocratic principle is not meritocratic in the sense that it is a prize which is won. At first sight, it might resemble a prize because the person who deserves a prize is that person who exhibits the highest degree of the quality or ability that the prize was established to recognise.[32] However, here such similarities end. For unlike a prize, which is essentially backward-looking and which one cannot be mistaken in distributing so long as the recipient actually legitimately won the prize, the principle outlined here is forward looking. As best as we can ascertain, the relevant authorities must decide that a certain person will benefit from it more than any other person. However, it is possible that we may be wrong. The person chosen might not make full use of his eudaimonian opportunities and in that case we have made a mistake in the distribution of our eudaimonian good. This problem of accurate prediction does not occur when desert is thought of as a prize.

We should distinguish the principle of meritocratic allocation from Sidgwick's 'principle of fitness' which is also forward looking. Sidgwick argued that the best relevantly qualified person should be allocated the job. He believed that this is the person who, as best as we can judge, will fulfil the requirements of the job most successfully.[33] He or she will contribute most to the productivity of the institution associated with the job—whether this is measured in economic terms or by using some other criteria—and thereby, in most cases, to the welfare of society. Thus, the final justification of Sidgwick's principle is utilitarian. However, the ultimate justification of the desert principle being outlined here is not social utility, but rather individual benefit. It is this very fact which distinguishes it from Sidgwick's theory.

Finally according to our principle there are a number of factors which are not relevant in the determination of desert. A person's race, sex, political affiliation or religion are not relevant in the allocation of eudaimonian work. These are all facts about candidates which are not relevant in determining whether they are the best qualified.[34] Just as eudaimonian work should not be distributed nepotistically, so too they should not be distributed with reference to other irrelevant personal facts.

From the foregoing discussion we may formalise the distributive principle being advocated here in the following way:

> Contingent upon the existence of compensatory mechanisms, eudaimonian work should be allocated to those willing candidates with the highest level of comparative relevant eudaimonian skills.

I shall call this the 'egalitarian principle of compensatory meritocracy'.

A related question which should be asked at this juncture is how much further desert should be extended, indeed if at all. Additional to eudaimonian work, meritocratic distributional patterns should be extended to those activities which are essential for human flourishing and which would lose their meaning if they were distributed in any manner other than meritocratically. Sporting activity, for instance, is one activity which is constitutive of the human good and yet which would not be the good that it is if it were not performed under conditions of competition and consequently whose prizes were not awarded meritocratically.[35] This meritocratic allocation is not inconsistent with a general egalitarianism, so long as the rewards of sport are not excessive (unlike the current situation with regard to high-profile sports such as tennis and golf). Here one is reminded of Thomas Nagel's comment that: "To try to sever the connection between talent and admiration would be wrong. But to sever the connection between talent and income, if it could be done, would be fine."[36]

Education and compensatory meritocracy

As noted earlier, education may be considered to be both: i) the grounds of eudaimonian interest realisation and; ii) a form of eudaimonian interest realisation in itself. The former aspect refers to the fact that some kind of education is necessary for persons to be able to realise eudaimonian interests in either the workplace or the organic social domain, while the latter aspect refers us to the fact that various careers in education can be eudaimonian. However, for our purposes it is the first aspect with which we should be concerned; that is, the focus of theoretical concern should be education as the grounds of eudaimonian interest realisation primarily because occupations in which education itself is a form of eudaimonian work, e.g. academic careers, are fairly marginal cases.

Now, given the goals of the principle of equal well-being and the fact that education is to be thought of primarily as a *precondition* of eudaimonian benefit, what should be the aim of social policy with regard to education? Obviously, given the egalitarian nature of the principle, the goal should the realisation of the capacities of all to adequate levels. The level of eudaimonian capacity which should be aimed for is that which is requisite for eudaimonian interest-realisation in the workplace and for developing eudaimonian projects outside the workplace.

However, this policy does not necessarily involve all developing the same level of skills in every facet of human activity. Rather it involves the provision of equal opportunities for all persons to develop their talents to the full. The policy recognises the diversity of talents and skills which people have and thus only recommends that all be placed in a position where they may develop eudaimonian skills. Here one is reminded of R.H. Tawney's claim that "What a wise parent would desire for his own children, that a nation, in so far as it is wise, must desire for all children."[37] Tawney believes that educational equality is to be achieved at school, as it is achieved in the home, by recognising that there are diversities of gifts which require diversities of treatment for their development. The aim, according to Tawney, should be to do justice to all by providing facilities which are at once various in type and equal in quality. Following on from Tawney we may say that resources should be provided to encourage all to develop their capacities in what ever is their chosen eudaimonian field.

Additionally, various contingencies must be taken into account to ensure that all persons reach the requisite educational levels. For example, if children from non-professional backgrounds are educationally disadvantaged in comparison with those from professional backgrounds, then these children might well require additional social resources to ensure that they are compensated for handicaps which arise from their home backgrounds.

Compensation for the performance of non-eudaimonian work

I have argued that meaningful work should be distributed meritocratically and that this meritocratic allocation is consistent with the principle of equal well-being. It is possible to make this latter claim concerning the distribution of meaningful work to the most talented; i) because of the compensatory mechanism and; ii) because of the existence of a region of eudaimonian activity, outside of the workplace. It is now time to examine the issue of compensation in some greater detail.

What should be done, then, to compensate those condemned to the non-meaningful for their loss? Given that my overall aim is the realisation of the eudaimonian interests of all, the focus must obviously be upon eudaimonian activity outside the workplace. We can justify this compensation in two different ways: i) because the person who is condemned to the non-meaningful is not being treated as an end or; ii) because compensation for the non-meaningful ensures that persons are treated as ends when they perform the non-meaningful, i.e. it being the performance of the non-meaningful in the context of compensation which prevents it from being a case of treating people as mere means. While the former option has its attractions (as we shall see), it is the latter one which I believe should be adopted.

However, before examining the concrete details of this compensatory mechanism, I shall briefly consider what compensation consists of and secondly consider in what sense compensation is part of an egalitarian strategy. In recent years there has been much philosophical discussion of 'compensatory justice'; in fact, in some quarters it has even overtaken issues of distributive justice as the central topic of political philosophy. Compensatory justice, in the sense in which the term has been used in such recent debates, is concerned with restoring the balance of justice after an injustice has been committed to some persons or group of persons. It demands that counter-balancing benefits be provided to those individuals who have been wrongfully injured in the past. Much of this debate has been concerned with rectifying the wrongs done to groups such as indigenous peoples who have been the victims of invasion and subsequent oppression or with wrongs perpetrated upon minority and oppressed groups such as Negroes in the United States.[38] While these issues have dominated much of the political agenda, the philosophical debate has been concerned on the whole with the problem of whether such compensation should be understood as a fundamentally rights-based or egalitarian policy.

There are a number of features such theories of compensatory justice usually exhibit. Firstly, such theories assume the existence of harm or injury.[39] Secondly, this harm is typically construed in such a way that those who suffer the harm are thought of as victims of unjustifiable harm. Thirdly, there is also assumed to be wrongdoing; the perpetrators of the wrongdoing being groups of people or institutions. The perpetrators of this wrongdoing, such as the white settlers of Australia, are thought (quite rightly I might add) to have acted in morally reprehensible ways and are thus held liable for the plight of the victim or victims. Furthermore, such discussions of compensatory justice, in general, involve a degree of moral outrage. Fourthly, such debate is usually historical in nature for the reason that it is a response to past improprieties and thus can be said to be backward, rather than forward looking; that is, these debates are primarily concerned with the past. Finally, such theories of compensatory justice assume violation of some basic principle. In most contemporary literature the basic principles violated are taken to be human rights.[40] Compensatory justice, then, in the context of this debate is a retrospective response to wrongdoing, as well as to harm suffered.[41] In this sense, compensatory justice is a second-level principle of justice, in so far as it operates on more basic principles, i.e., it is parasitic upon more basic conceptions of justice. Hence it is an example of what Rawls refers to as 'non-ideal' theory because it relies upon a prior claim of an unjust distribution of resources.[42]

However, it is not this sense of compensatory justice with which I am concerned. While I believe such questions are very important, my concern is simply with compensation in relation to the scarcity of eudaimonian benefit in the workplace. This concern is markedly different from the standard debate in a number of respects. Firstly, while performing the non-eudaimonian involves harm, at least as I employ the principle of compensation, there is no sense of wrongdoing involved. Compensation arises not because of the morally reprehensible actions of past persons, but because of certain structural features of modern society – namely our incapacity to ensure that all are able to obtain meaningful work. This idea of systemic wrongdoing is not without precedent. For example, it is sometimes argued that the unemployed deserve some form of compensation, even though there may be no person to blame for their situation. It should not be thought to follow that because loss occurs that there must automatically be some person or institution who is liable. As Joel Feinberg notes "When a person suffers a loss, it may be the fault of another person or it may be no one's fault; and, as we have seen, the nature of desert differs in the two cases."[43] In the case of those condemned to the non-eudaimonian it is quite proper to talk of them deserving compensatory bonuses without any person being held to blame. Secondly, the principle of compensation, as it is used here, is not an historical concept. Compensation in this context is a response to the fact that harm will continue. It is not merely reparation, but a response to harm which will in all likelihood occur in the future. The tragic fact that there will continue to be those who must perform the non-eudaimonian means that there will continue to be violations. Underpinning my principle of compensation is the belief that reward should be determined by the costs incurred in a work activity.[44] Those who perform non-meaningful work should receive compensatory bonuses.

It should be noted that when Feinberg discusses compensation he does so in meritocratic terms. However, although Feinberg provides a meritocratic account, compensation can in fact be interpreted in a variety of ways. David Miller notes two of these interpretations: i) where costs are taken as deserving facts and; ii) where costs are taken as factors to be redressed. Miller argues that on one interpretation we might regard costs as facts about an individual's activity which serve as a basis for his desert in the same way as, say, the skill he displays. "But we might also understand such costs not as the basis for desert, but rather as a reduction in the benefit which a person is receiving, so that he should be given extra economic benefits to make good the loss."[45] The first interpretation Miller takes to be desert-based; persons' deserts are different because of the different costs they incur in their work, and thus rewards should be proportional to desert. However, the second interpretation Miller takes to be an egalitarian principle. Persons should receive equal rewards but, in so far as one person's work is more costly than another's, the loss should be made good by increased monetary income.[46]

To be sure, compensatory goods should not be limited to monetary income. The central point here is that one interpretation of the principle of compensation may be considered to be egalitarian. In a similar vein Joel Feinberg argues that "the principle that unpleasant, onerous, and hazardous jobs deserve economic compensation, unlike the claim that superior ability deserves economic reward, is an egalitarian one, for it says only that deprivations for which there is no good reason should be compensated to the point where the deprived one is again brought back to a position of equality with his fellows."[47] Feinberg suggests that it is not that any compensation awarded gives the person in question more than other comparable persons, all things considered, but simply that it allows him to catch up. It is the fact that the principle of compensation might be interpreted as a means of catching up which qualifies it to be treated as an egalitarian principle.[48]

How might we compensate those condemned to non-meaningful work? What policies should be implemented in this context? I make the following recommendations. Persons condemned to non-meaningful work should receive the following compensations: i). extra time; ii). extra monetary recompense; iii) access to the education system. The extent to which these compensations are implemented is contingent upon the particular determinate amount of eudaimonian jobs governments encourage. Time-compensation would involve ensuring that those engaged in non-meaningful occupations work less than those engaged in meaningful work. As opposed to a five day week—which may be necessary for those engaged in meaningful work—those engaged in non-meaningful work might only be required to work one to two days a week. This strategy is intended to ensure that those engaged in non-eudaimonian work have time to develop eudaimonian interests outside the workplace. Moreover, the fact that those who hold non-meaningful jobs only work a small number of days per week limits the extent to which relations of domination (which often operate in the workplace) have serious psychological effects upon them.

On my account, while the amount of work expected of those engaged in non-eudaimonian tasks is less than that expected of those engaged in eudaimonian work, if those engaged in non-meaningful tasks wish to work longer hours, then they should be granted further dispensations. This is a concession to the fact that some persons may wish to work non-meaningfully in order to gain extra wages.[49] Another element of flexibility in the policy is that, if persons wish to do so, then they may perform all of their non-meaningful work in a set period of time; hence, providing those concerned with an extended uninterrupted period of time outside the workplace. Thus, for instance, a factory worker may work full-time for six months and then enjoy six months of activity outside of the workplace. It is important to remember here that the goal of compensation is to encourage the possibility of eudaimonian interest realisation and thus such flexibility is in keeping with the overall aim. Secondly, extra wages should be awarded to those engaged in non-meaningful tasks, in order to provide funds for being able to pursue eudaimonian activities. Finally, those engaged in non-meaningful activity are to be provided with access to educational resources which are designed to encourage the development of their eudaimonian interests.

Some readers might well be sceptical of the possibility of assessing cost in this context and here they would be in good company. David Miller, for one, believes it to be unlikely that costs for compensation could be assessed.[50] Indeed, the fact that the sacrifice involved in performing the non-meaningful is not financial, makes it difficult to determine the appropriate level of compensation.[51] However, we should not think it wholly indeterminate. Determining the actual levels of compensation is not impossible, but rather it is a matter of practical judgement.

In summary then, the compensatory program upon which the justice of the meritocratic allocation of eudaimonian work is contingent includes the provision of free time, training and extra remuneration for those engaged in the non-eudaimonian. These compensatory mechanisms are designed with the aim of encouraging the realisation of eudaimonian interests by those engaged in non-eudaimonian work. This compensation should occur regardless of whether the person chooses the non-meaningful work or not. Furthermore the notion of compensation employed here should not be confused with arguments to the effect that various forms of financial assistance are a means of compensating persons for loss that has arisen out of past injustice. My compensatory principle is not a principle of historical rectification, rather it is an egalitarian principle, concerned with the present and the future.[52]

Compensation for other burdensome aspects of work

Whilst not directly related to the eudaimonian sphere, there are other criteria which must be taken into account when determining just compensation for burdensome work. These include the following (the list is not intended to be exhaustive): i) dangerous work; ii) degrading work; iii) arduous work; iv) work which requires persons to be on call; v) work of long duration. Being non-meaningful is not the only cost incurred in work. Work may be dangerous, as is the case with construction work or mining. It may be degrading, as was the case with the work of night-man, whose job it was to collect other people's faeces. In such cases extra compensation, in the form of higher rates of pay, may also actually change social attitudes towards these occupations. Collecting garbage, for instance, if relatively well-paid, might lose some of the stigma associated with it. Some jobs are also exhausting. Shearing, for instance, would be an example of an occupation which may require extra reward because it demands so much physical exertion. Another form of work which can require further compensation, is work which requires the person to be on call; doctors or ambulance drivers could well require such compensation. Having the threat of being called out hanging over one's periods of rest and recreation, is a burden which should be compensated. Finally, duration of work should also be taken into account. If all other factors are equal, then, those who work longer should receive more pay.[53]

Compensation for these factors is consistent with the principles of justice outlined thus far. The principle of compensation essentially involves the claim that a person's reward should depend upon the costs incurred in work activity, and this is ultimately an egalitarian concern. Moreover, as we have seen, being non-meaningful is not the only cost incurred in work. As David Miller argues, work is costly when it is, for example, unpleasant (a dustman's job and a surgeon's, in different ways) or dangerous (a steeplejack's job). Miller argues that in each case the cost should be repaid through increased remuneration, and what we call 'reward' is really compensation for the loss incurred while the person is at work (in the case of dangerous work, it may be seen as an insurance against the possibility of future loss).[54] All of the examples outlined by Miller are cases where compensation is required for costs which are in fact incurred at work. Commitment to an egalitarian theory of justice would seem to require that compensation be paid for costs other than the non-meaningful. The fact that some persons may have taken up jobs as steeplejacks or garbage collectors, through bad luck, lack of skill or want of opportunity is no justification for their lives being utterly miserable. Nor should the fact that some people may actually choose their dangerous or arduous profession for 'vocational' reasons, rule them out of compensation for the special rigours of their occupation. For instance, the fact that a person becomes a coalminer because his father, grandfather and great grandfather were coalminers before him, should not prevent him from being a candidate for compensation if the work is especially dangerous. In such cases, those engaged in such jobs should receive more money or extra free time, not as inducements to encourage them to do jobs that no one else would do—for that would be a utilitarian justification—but rather to recompense them for their unpleasant circumstances.

I make no pretence that these compensatory mechanisms are the last word on the matter of cost. Even with compensatory mechanisms in place, harm incurred during productive activity is undesirable because of the imperfection of compensation. Remuneration does not take away the tiredness or danger, for example, associated with shearing or coalmining, nor will it take away the misery of an asbestos miner suffering from asbestosis or alternatively the incapacity of an industrial worker who has lost a limb. If these harms can be avoided via the development of better technology or medical services, then such changes are preferable *ceteris paribus* to compensatory mechanisms.[55] If coalmining can be made safer, then it should be and furthermore, if technology could be developed which eliminates the need for human labour in jobs such as coalmining, then, again it should be used.[56] If dangerous activities, such as coalmining, can be avoided, then, the demands of safety should take precedence over the appeals of vocationalism as a reason for action.

The objection from subjectivity

The category of eudaimonian activity provides us with a criterion for assessing the 'meaningfulness' of various occupations within a specific social structure which might be used by the state to assess the justice of social institutions and arrangements. It enables us to determine which occupations are to count as meaningful and which as non-meaningful, and thus which are to have compensations attached. Such a criterion is not, however, uncontroversial. One might argue that the eudaimonian criterion is in fact unjustifiably selective. If we examine the activities which people may commonly refer to as meaningful, many of them are not eudaimonian. Why select the eudaimonian out of this collection?[57]

Moreover, the subjective and diverse character of the forms of work which are commonly referred to as meaningful are such that it might be argued that we could not unify them into a single coherent account of meaningful work. Thus, on this line of thinking, not only is the eudaimonian definition arbitrarily selective, but it cannot be replaced with any alternative conception of meaningful work which would capture all of the different senses for which the term is used. This second argument requires further elaboration.

The subjective character of meaningful work refers to the fact that certain internal psychological factors are pivotal in making some work meaningful or fulfilling. For instance, while you or I may not find tending the wounds of soldiers in Central Africa particularly satisfying, there are people, such as those who work for the Red Cross, whose attitudes are such that they find this work meaningful. Clearly, in such cases it is the specific nature of their psychological states, rather than the nature of the work in itself, which makes work meaningful for them. According to this story, whether or not work is meaningful is reliant upon internal psychological factors. If this is true, then, it would seem to follow that any work at all could be considered to be meaningful, so long as one has the right attitude toward it. Pushing a rock up a hill, day after day for twenty years only to watch it roll down again might well be meaningful if one has the right attitude towards one's work. What this also seems to imply is that it is meaningless to distinguish between meaningful jobs and non-meaningful ones. There can be no such distinction, according to this argument from meaninglessness because what matters is not the social provision of meaningful work, but rather our subjective attitudes toward it. Hence, the issue of meaningful work is no longer an issue of justice, but becomes merely a matter of the phenomenological states of individuals.

Opponents of the idea that we could provide a philosophical criterion of meaningful work to be used by the State might also draw our attention to the diverse range of activities which people may refer to as forms of meaningful work. For example, Richard Arneson, in considering the sorts of goods which people might obtain from their work and which may cause them to regard their work as meaningful, suggests that there exists a "great variety of goods that people have obtained and might want to obtain from their work".[58] Arneson then proceeds to list seventeen such goods. They include, amongst other things, wages to be exchanged for consumer goods now or in future, pleasant companionship with work colleagues or customers, the knowledge that in producing particular goods and services one is being humanly useful to others or even contributing to the fulfilment of their vital needs, interesting and challenging work that calls for discrimination, skill and intelligence and responsible work that requires for its successful execution the display of prized virtues.[59] This list—which Arneson claims is only a partial list—provides a survey of the wide range of activities which may be called meaningful work.

Critics of my criterion of meaningful work might argue that the list provided above is so diverse that it is unlikely that one could formulate a set of necessary and jointly sufficient conditions of what is to count as meaningful work. Thus it may be claimed not only that the eudaimonian definition of meaningful work is highly selective, but that it cannot be replaced with a definition that is any less selective.

The above line of argumentation provides quite a powerful criticism. However, it does not provide a knock-down refutation of the idea of a state-mandated criterion of meaningful work. In response, I simply wish to make the point that I think that the eudaimonian account of 'meaningful work' is appropriate because it is the description of the meaningfulness of work activity which is also the description of the activity which we distribute, namely occupation. We should remember that my concern is with the allocation of distributive goods, not how time with friends should be spent. The eudaimonian account of meaningfulness provides us with a description of meaningful activity under the activity description of the activity which we distribute. Thus, it is the appropriate description: it is not arbitrarily selective. This, of course, is not to deny the meaningfulness of other possible descriptions of work's meaningfulness, it is merely to deny their direct relevance to the problem of distributive justice.

The objection from professional incomes

Some readers might want to argue that the egalitarian principle of compensatory meritocracy is wrong-headed, for the very reason that compensation—especially of income—is being allocated to the wrong recipients. What we are calling 'eudaimonian jobs' are, on the whole, professional occupations; and it might well be argued that those in professional jobs, such as doctors and lawyers, should receive higher wages than those in less skilled occupations for one of the following reasons: i) they deserve reward for skill or; ii) they deserve compensation for the years of training required to perform their tasks or; iii) they deserve compensation for the responsibility that their jobs entails.

Let us firstly consider the 'argument from skill'. This is essentially the claim that the superior skills of some persons entitles them to financial rewards over and above those enjoyed by people who have not undertaken such difficult training. According to this argument, a doctor, for instance, deserves to receive higher levels of income than, say, a garbage collector because of the level of skill involved in his or her occupation. It is her skill level which entitles her to a higher level of income. However, surely the appropriate reward for someone who is highly skilled in a particular field is work in that field. Just as the appropriate reward, for someone who is a highly skilled sculptor, is work as a sculptor, then similarly, one appropriate reward for a person who is academically gifted is work as a doctor. As Thomas Nagel notes "it does not reflect a social judgement that smart people *deserve* the opportunity to make more money than dumb people."[60] Nagel argues that they might well deserve better educational opportunities, but they do not therefore deserve the material wealth which accompanies it. Similarly, there seems to be little reason why those with high-skill levels, be they academic or otherwise, deserve to make more money than the less talented.

Another related line of argumentation is that the more talented should be paid more because this ensures that the best people undertake these important jobs. This is not a desert based argument; it is an argument from social utility. It is not that the more skilled deserve higher incomes, but rather that society will be better off if those in professional occupations are paid more because it will attract the more talented.

I think that there are good reasons for rejecting these two compensation arguments.[61] If we closely examine the argument that professionals should be compensated for their years of training, we find it to be sorely lacking; for the fact is that during their years of training professionals are being provided with social resources which enable them to develop their eudaimonian capacities. Professionals often try to construe their years of training as a burden: this, however, is correct, only in the narrowest of economic senses. It is more broadly speaking a benefit—rather than a burden—because eudaimonian skills are developed during training. Even if it is true that their years of lowly paid training leave them financially worse off than other persons who did not undertake extensive training and are employed during the same years in a non-eudaimonian occupation, this should not be construed as disadvantage. The professional has the benefit of eudaimonian training, as well as years of eudaimonian work. The 'argument from responsibility' is similarly unfounded. The claim that the extra responsibility, which professional jobs entail, means that people who hold these jobs deserve extra income ignores the fact that responsibility is also a eudaimonian good.

Furthermore, both compensation arguments, i.e the argument from training and the argument from responsibility, overlook the fact that professional jobs carry with them a large amount of status. On the whole responsibility and the years of training are both more than compensated by the status which holders of these jobs receive. Professional jobs provide opportunities for those who occupy these positions to realise their interests in subjectivity.

Finally, one might argue that those who end up in non-meaningful occupations are simply lazy; that is, that they deserve non-meaningful occupations because they have made little effort to improve themselves. This is a particularly dubious thesis. Given that some people must necessarily occupy the non-meaningful, it is hard to fathom in what sense those who receive the non-eudaimonian are deserving of this burden. However, even if it is true that such persons do not qualify for eudaimonian occupations because they are lazy—and it must be said that I am highly sceptical of such claims—it does not follow from this fact that those performing the non-eudaimonian deserve a life of uncompensated boredom, or equally uncompensated danger. S.I. Benn and R.S. Peters argue that although it is true that some men lack the job-getting qualities, and are forced to take the jobs that no one else wants, nonetheless a "lack of skill or personal charm may not be good enough reasons why a man should suffer the hazards of silicosis or a broken neck."[62] Accordingly, they suggest that if such jobs are to be done, they should carry with them compensations. This is the counterpoint of my earlier claim that no one deserves to be rewarded for superior skill or charm.[63]

The incentive objection

Closely associated with the argument from professional incomes is what might be called 'the incentive objection'. Here meritocratic considerations are replaced by utilitarian ones. The argument from incentive essentially consists in the claim that persons engaged in professional occupations should receive higher wages and other benefits, as an incentive to ensure either (i) that the job is actually performed or (ii) that it is undertaken by the best possible persons. It is assumed that without extra remuneration these important jobs will not be performed satisfactorily or even undertaken at all. Therefore, in order to achieve maximum utility, we must provide incentives for eudaimonian professions.

It might be argued that my theory of compensatory meritocracy would lead to important jobs not being performed or not being performed by the best persons. Let us say a little more about this objection. Given certain facts about human nature—namely that people may require incentives to perform eudaimonian jobs—and given the necessity of certain tasks either being performed or performed well, society as a whole requires that incentives be provided for such work. Furthermore, any theory of justice which rules out such payments would, if implemented, have disastrous consequences; the putative conflict here is between ensuring that jobs get done and distributing benefit justly.

Clearly, such arguments run counter to the egalitarian principle of compensatory meritocracy. What should the proper reaction to this objection be? One response might be to question the empirical truth of the claim that people will only perform occupations which require the development of skills or that the best people will perform these jobs, only if they are given extra financial rewards. Experience would seem to suggest otherwise. There are many occupations which require the development of skill which highly talented people undertake with little expectation of great financial reward. In the arts, for example, many people have pursued careers as musicians, actors or painters and have developed their skills to high levels, even though they have little prospect of significant financial reward; and if we look beyond the arts, there is every reason to believe that there would be no shortage of people who would perform eudaimonian jobs without extra financial reward simply because they recognise it to be intrinsically valuable and because such work requires that they use skills which they enjoy using. As Richard Norman notes, there is no convincing reason for supposing that competition for highly unequal material rewards is a necessary feature of an efficiently working society.[64]

Moreover, there are questions to consider concerning the causal role that hierarchical societies—which systems of differential incentives would inevitably create—play in diminishing the self-esteem of some members of that society. If some persons receive enormous amounts of money for the work they do and others little, this must surely affect the poorly-paid person's self-identity and self-esteem. A system of incentives which differentially rewards those who already enjoy high social status by virtue of the fact that they perform eudaimonian activities, is likely to have a demoralising effect on the rest of society.

However, let us assume for argument's sake that most people will not perform these necessary professional tasks without special remuneration all other things being equal. Our next move should be to question whether such claims are *contingently* or *necessarily* true. Is it necessarily true that people will always act in this way or is it merely a particular empirical observation about particular groups of people? For instance, if people were educated to value eudaimonian benefit above financial reward, would people still make such choices? If our education system valued eudaimonian activity would it still be the case that people made such choices? I think that, in fact, it would only be lack of acquaintance with the eudaimonian which would prevent people from choosing such meaningful work. If one lived in a culture which valued the eudaimonian and in which one was acquainted with eudaimonian activity at school, then, all would prefer occupations which enabled them to develop their skills and capacities. My argument is very similar *mutatis mutandis* to J.S. Mill's claim about our preference for what he called the higher pleasures.[65] Mill not only argued that some pleasures were 'higher' than others, e.g. poetry was better than pushpin, but also that once people had tasted the higher pleasures, so to speak, they would prefer them to the lower ones. Mill believed that people would prefer poetry to pushpin, once they came into genuine contact with the pleasures of poetry. Similarly, I would argue that it is mere lack of acquaintance with the eudaimonian which will in most instances make people prefer non-eudaimonian occupations to the eudaimonian solely in order to obtain financial rewards. We should not take peoples current choices as being *brute* facts.

Of course it is possible that people might prefer non-eudaimonian occupations because of specific non-monetary aspects of some occupations. As I have already noted, a coalminer might prefer the non-eudaimonian work of coalmining because of the importance he attaches to that way of life. This simply means that there are legitimate reasons for action and choice, other than the desire to avoid the non-meaningful. The existence of such reasons for action does not lessen the strength of the claim that the eudaimonian—once people are properly acquainted with it—is a powerful reason for action; a reason with sufficient weight to ensure that important eudaimonian activities are performed, even if they are not handsomely rewarded.

Some market-based objections

Another class of objections to my principle of compensatory meritocracy would arise out of concerns about the relationship between market-based outcomes and the justice-derived wage outcomes of the egalitarian principle of compensatory meritocracy. The most radical of such criticisms would involve the claim that issues of justice have no place in the determination of wages. According to such lines of thinking, justice is not a virtue of social institution, but rather a vice. Social institutions are only virtuous when they keep out of the way of the proper functioning of the market. Therefore incomes should only be determined by the market. If the market rewards those who perform the non-meaningful, then well and good; if it does not, then that is too bad. In either case there should be no state interference.

This criticism, however, would apply not only to the principle of compensatory meritocracy, but to the discipline of distributive justice *per se* and as such it is beyond the scope of discussion. It is a central assumption of this dissertation that justice is a virtue of social institutions.

However, there are also less radical market-based approaches which accept the importance of issues of justice and attempt to make some connection between markets and justice via preference; that is, they try to demonstrate that market-based outcomes are, in some important sense, just. According to this kind of view, markets should be allowed to determine outcomes (in this particular context wage outcomes) because markets are determined ultimately by people's preferences. Accordingly, respecting market-determined outcomes is a way of respecting people's preferences.

In what sense does the principle of compensatory meritocracy violate preferences? We might argue—somewhat facetiously—that if we consider the allocation of meaningful work, there seems to be no violation of preferences. Some people choose to develop certain talents and if they are lucky, they will obtain jobs which allow them to develop those talents further. If they choose not to develop those skills, then inevitably they will find employment in non-meaningful occupations. How could the principle be any more respecting of preferences?

Pursuing this rhetorical line of argumentation however would be to miss the main point of these market-based objections. It is the determination of the relative weight of incomes according to its component of meaningfulness which preference-respecting market-based theorists would find objectionable. Preference theorists would argue that the level of income should be set by what people are willing to pay for that particular job. In determining wage outcomes, then, the principle of compensatory meritocracy would seem to violate preferences.

This again is quite a powerful criticism. However, it is not unassailable. Firstly, preferences are not *brute*; they occur within specific social contexts. Thus we might well question the strength we wish to assign them in the determination of issues of justice. Secondly, we should question the relationship between markets and preference. Is it really the case that market outcomes represent the overall collective preferences of groups of people? Are there not other social factors at work? Take, for example, the current system where certain professionals (such as doctors and architects) can command large fees for their services. This is often cited as an example of a market-based determination of income. However, imagine that a government decides to pour enormous resources into the training of doctors and architects, resulting in a ten-fold increase in the number of doctors and architects. With ten times as many doctors and architects available, would such professionals still be able to command high salaries on the open market? The point here is that government policies and government funding in part determine how the market operates and government policies in some sense seem ineradicable. However, even if we had a pure free market, it is hard to know what the outcome would be. In all likelihood, wage levels would be quite different to those currently in place, even if they were not just in my sense of the term.

Summary

The 'eudaimonian' provides a criterion for the evaluation and allocation of work and of related issues of wages, working hours and working conditions. If work is eudaimonian, then it should be allocated meritocratically; that is, it should be distributed to the person (or persons) who has developed the relevant eudaimonian talents to the greatest degree and thus who is most likely to make use of the resource. Accordingly, this means that the non-meaningful will be allocated to those who miss out on the meaningful. Given that this imposes certain morally important burdens upon the person who must perform the non-meaningful, a variety of compensations are awarded to such persons to provide the opportunities for them to develop their eudaimonian talents outside the workplace, as well as to compensate them for the brutality of non-meaningful work. I have defined the egalitarian principle of compensatory meritocracy in the following manner:

> Contingent upon the existence of compensatory mechanisms (which provide compensation in the form of free time, training and remuneration for the performance of the non-eudaimonian), eudaimonian work should be allocated to those willing candidates with the highest level of relevant comparative eudaimonian skill.

Such a policy for the allocation of both work and the eudaimonian is flexible enough to be compatible with the continuing existence of the good of career choice; a good which has an important role to play in the lives of flourishing human beings.

Notes

1. Andre Gorz argues that work, as we understand it, is a thoroughly modern invention and that it is fundamentally different from work in previous epochs. See Gorz, 1989, pp.13-16.
2. This may appear to some a rather idiosyncratic definition of meaningful work; for many theorists the term refers to work in which the technical division of labour is abolished. (For an example of this interpretation of the term see Arneson, 1987. However, it is possible to think of examples of work where a technical division of labour is not in existence, and yet which we would be loath to call meaningful. For instance, breaking rocks might be an occupation in which there is no technical division of labour, and yet which very few would want to characterise as meaningful. Here the absence of a technical division of labour does not preclude meaningless work. Alternatively, the presence of a technical division does not necessarily exclude meaningful work. For instance, a brain surgeon may operate in a team of other surgeons, and perform highly specialised tasks and yet find the work meaningful
3. Op. cit., p.100.
4. To complicate matters further, there may also be occupations which employ subtle skills and which have other benefits, such as a service component. For example, medicine may be an example of an occupation in which there may simultaneously be a number of benefits; a doctor may enjoy the employment of subtle skills, as well as gaining satisfaction from serving the sick and elderly. In such occupations there are a number of benefits to be had.
5. Cf. Marx, 1975, p.490.
6. Richard Arneson objects to this idea of a state-mandated criterion of meaningful work. He finds it immoral. See op. cit., p.523.
7. Reiss, 1970, p.78. Cf. Galston, 1980, p.266.
8. Marx, 1981, p.958
9. Cf. Marcuse, 1968, pp.159-200.
10. As I noted in chapter six, for the foreseeable future there will be a continuing necessity for a technical division of labour. The relative material abundance which we do enjoy, is made possible by this technical division; overcoming it, would cause more disruption and seriously threaten peoples' basal interest satisfaction.
11. Cf. Galston, 1980, p.237.
12. Contrast this with the ideas of Joel Feinberg, for whom professional jobs are a burden because of the responsibility which they carry with them. For a useful discussion of Feinberg's work see Miller, 1976, p.113.
13. Of course not all political theorists would agree with this claim. It is a claim that would be contested, for instance, by the French social theorist Andre Gorz. Gorz argues that the development of technology is such that in the near future work itself will come to an end. In his books *Farewell to the Working Class* and *Critique of Economic Reason* Gorz argues that we should focus our attention on the sphere outside of work, because rather than being meaningful work which is scarce, it is work per se. Gorz is antagonistic to forms of socialism which attempt to locate emancipation and liberation in the sphere of work. This however seems a very 'Eurocentric' view of world history. For the large part of the world's population continues to need to work to sustain itself. Moreover many ecologists claim that there are ecological constraints upon the extent to which the forces of production can be developed; that is they might argue that the forces of production cannot be developed to the extent that material abundance is achieved, without destroying the ecological fabric.
14. Aristotle allows for misfortune, but not tragedy. Aristotle, 1969, Bk.I ch.11 [1101a10-35].
15. Schwartz, 1982, p.635.
16. It is worth noting that the continuation of a technical division of labour is not just problematic in terms of its role in making work non-meaningful or in the treating of people as mere means; it is also important as a conduit to relations of domination between people. Thus another thing which must be remembered when accepting the continuing existence of a technical division of labour is its role in maintaining relations of domination.
17. Op. cit., p.236.

18. See Kohn and Schooler, 1978, pp.24-52.
19. Adam Smith while enthusiastic about industrialisation was concerned about such psychological effects. See Smith, 1976, 2:302-3.
20. Cited in Schumacher, 1979, p.4.
21. I assume herein that our method of distributing the meaningful will provide a *de facto* procedure for distributing the non-meaningful.
22. In the ensuing discussions I treat 'merit' and 'desert' as synonyms.
23. Cf. Care, 1984, p.288.
24. To argue that all parts of the social whole must be organised according to egalitarian principles for overall equality to be achieved would be to commit the semi-formal fallacy of division.
25. We should not think of this option of realising eudaimonian interests in the organic social domain as merely an *ad hoc* solution conjured up after the realisation that it was impossible for all to realise their eudaimonian interests in the workplace. The idea of focusing political attention on the sphere outside of work is one which appeals to many political thinkers; predominant amongst these being the French social theorist Andre Gorz. Gorz believes that the ideal of self-realisation through work is no longer viable and thus we should shift our attention to what I have called the organic social domain. Gorz believes that the historical process is actually gradually making work obsolescent and thus we must aim at self-realisation outside of work. Citizens must not identify themselves with their work, but rather become more detached from it. They must develop other interests and situate their paid work, their occupation within a multi-dimensional version of their existence in society. Gorz believes that activities performed for economic ends are to constitute only one dimension of existence and to become less and less important. (op. cit., p.100) While not necessarily in accord with all that Gorz has to say, especially in relation to vocationalism, I think that Gorz's work demonstrates that some thinkers believe that self-realisation in the organic social domain is a desirable political goal.
26. Cf. Rawls, 1972, pp.15, 104, 175-6, 310-15. A good discussion of Rawls' critique of desert is to be found Sher, 1987, pp.22-36.
27. Cf. Feinberg, 1970, pp.80-81.
28. Cf. Miller, 1992, p.180.
29. We must acknowledge that in reality the assignation of work occurs at the level of training in many cases. It is when career training is allocated that we determine who is to gain this eudaimonian kind of work. However, for the sake of simplicity let us assume that job assignation occurs at the moment of employment.
30. It is sometimes said that a good litmus test of whether or not a theory is meritocratic is whether or not the theory claims it to be just that some persons may miss out on distributive goods.
31. Alan Wertheimer refers to this principle that the best qualified person should be hired as 'HBQ' (i.e. hire the best qualified). Wertheimer, 1983, pp.99-112.
32. David Miller makes this very point. Miller's aim is to show that his desert principle is not incompatible with positive discrimination programs. See Miller, 1992, pp.161-81.
33. Sidgwick, 1967, ch.5. For a particularly useful discussion of Sidgwick's principle see Miller, 1992, pp.164-65.
34. Ibid., p.161.
35. Cf. Norman, 1987, p.88.
36. Nagel, 1991, p.113.
37. Tawney, 1964, p.146.
38. Cf. O'Neill, 1987-88, p.73.
39. It is not true in all cases that demands for compensatory justice are in response to harms inflicted. For instance, Robert Nozick wants compensation not only for wrongdoing which leads to harm, but also in certain circumstances for wrongdoing itself; that is, for action which violates rights.
40. Onora O'Neill argues that those who construe justice in terms of a theory of rights, as many liberals of both persuasions do, hold that only damage arising from violations of rights constitutes *injury*, and that only injury provides the basis for a *right* to compensation. ibid., p.74.
41. There are, of course, many problems with such theories of compensation. For instance, how far back in time should we go to ascertain harms inflicted? Moreover, how responsible are the descendants of conquering groups for the harms that their ancestors inflicted? In the more recent

cases of colonisation, such as the European invasions of the Americas and Australia, such questions are more easily answered. But what about the descendants of William the Conqueror, for instance? Alternatively, do all persons of Irish descent in the Irish diaspora deserve compensation for the harms inflicted by the English invaders of Ireland from Cromwell onwards? Such questions raise difficulties for theories of compensatory justice.

42. Op. cit., p.246.
43. Op. cit., p.75.
44. Cf. Miller, 1976, p.110.
45. Ibid., p.111.
46. Ibid., p.111.
47. Op. cit., p.93.
48. In *Social Justice* Miller makes the further claim that ultimately the principle of compensation is not really a desert principle at all; he argues that the first interpretation of the principle does not actually work. It is, he claims, an indication of additional factors which need to be taken into account when rewards are calculated. It is either used in conjunction with the principles of contribution or effort or on its own as an egalitarian principle. (Miller, 1976, pp.112-13). Whether or not this is indeed the case and the egalitarian interpretation is the only plausible account of the principle of compensation, is however peripheral to the issue at hand, which is primarily that there is at the very least, an egalitarian interpretation.
49. This is the sort of option which Arneson is adamant must be maintained. op. cit., pp.517-45.
50. Miller 1976, p.113.
51. Cf. Galston 1980, p.202.
52. It is different, for example, from Nozick's principle of rectification, which is concerned with rectifying any acquisitions which have not been gained justly. See Nozick, 1974, pp.152-53.
53. Galston, 1980, p.203.
54. Miller, 1976, pp.110-11.
55. Cf. ibid., p.240.
56. For philosophical discussion of the issue of vocationalism, see Hardy, 1990.
57. I consider this objection in greater detail in 'Meaningful Work as a Distributive Good'. See Walsh, 1994.
58. Op. cit., p.528.
59. Ibid., pp.528-29.
60. Nagel, 1972-3, p.357.
61. Joel Feinberg argues for both of these compensation arguments. "Here is the real basis for the claim that the executive and the physician *deserve* higher incomes: not that their superior abilities deserve rewards, but rather that their heavier loads of responsibility and worry and (for doctors) their long periods of impoverished apprenticeship *deserve compensation*.", Feinberg 1970, p.93.
62. Benn and Peters, 1968, p.140.
63. Cf. Feinberg, 1970, pp.92-93.
64. Cf. Norman, 1987, p.88.
65. Mill, 1972, pp.8-9.

9 The sphere of subjectivity

Introduction

In this final chapter, I shall apply the principle of equal well-being to the sphere of subjectivity to generate the 'principle of equality of subjectivity'. As we shall see, implementation of this principle is particularly difficult in this sphere because of various constraints; these being primarily constraints upon the ability of social institutions to determinably shape final outcomes. Hence, rather than being concerned so much with *procuring* certain patterns of distribution, the emphasis will be more upon *facilitation.*[1] (In a sense, in considering the sphere of subjectivity, we are drifting to the outer edges of the domain of distributive theory). For the reason that goods of subjectivity cannot be directly allocated by the State, we must concentrate on providing the pre-conditions for attainment of these goods. Accordingly, the focus will be upon measures designed to bring such universal procurement, rather than actual distributive procedures.

I shall divide the goods of subjectivity into two main categories: those which it is possible for all to enjoy simultaneously, i.e. self-respect and non-competitive self-esteem, and secondly those which it is impossible for all to enjoy at the same time, i.e. competitive self-esteem. Those in the former category will be subject to measures which are designed to achieve straightforward egalitarian outcomes. In the second category, however, implementation of the egalitarian ideal is more problematic because, as we shall see, competitive goods of self-esteem must be allocated in a broadly meritocratic manner, if they are to be allocated at all. In response to this problem I shall recommend a strategy aimed at achieving 'equality of areas'. It is my hope that if the allocation of various goods connected to competitive self-esteem extends over a wide range, then such a meritocratic distributive pattern will not be problematic because the overall effect will be the universal realisation of competitive self-esteem.

Goods of subjectivity

I use the term 'sphere of subjectivity' to circumscribe those distributive goods which are instrumental in the realisation of our interests in subjectivity. In chapter four I argued that human beings are self-reflective beings who form conceptions of themselves which play a central role in their lives. It is this self-reflective aspect of our nature to which the term 'interests in subjectivity' refers; accordingly, the sphere of subjectivity is that sphere comprised of goods which are instrumental in the realisation of interests in subjectivity. The goods in the sphere of subjectivity are goods which generate, or are the pre-conditions of, self-esteem and self-respect, and include such items as sporting prizes, citizenship, state honours and political rights.

Let us recall the distinction drawn in chapter four between self-respect and self-esteem. You will recall that these two terms were distinguished from one another by the kinds of attitudes they embodied on the part of the subject. Self-respect is respect for one's own intrinsic worth and importance as a person. It involves the belief that one has projects and goals which are worthwhile, simply for the reason that they are one's own. Self-respect is conceptually-independent of one's capacities, achievements, attributes or moral status. Self-respect, we may say, is respect due because of one's status *as* a person, rather than because of the person that one is; or to put it another way, it is because I am a person that I am worthy of respect, not because I am the person I am.

Full human flourishing requires that persons are self-respecting. In order for any individual to live the best life, it is important that they have self-respect. Indeed, without self-respect there are many important interests that people are unlikely to realise. In considering the relationship between the good life and self-respect, it is well worth recalling Rawls' work on the topic.[2] Under self-respect Rawls includes a person's sense of his own value, his secure conviction that his conception of the good, his plan of life is worth carrying out[3] as well as a confidence in one's ability, so far as it is within one's power to fulfil one's intentions.[4] Rawls takes self-respect to be a primary good; it is something which is required no matter what one's plan of life. We can thus make a second point about self-respect; self-respect matters as a means to our fulfilling and realising our projects. It is instrumentally necessary if we are to flourish.

Self-esteem, as I noted in chapter four, concerns not just a belief in one's own worth, but rather a belief in one's worth in relation to personal or community standards of achievement or capacity and personal ideals. It is recognition of one's status as a person with regard to various capacities, skills, attributes and moral standing. It is self-assessment of oneself in relation to the kind of person that one is. Self-esteem is essentially a comparative notion. There are a wide variety of capacities, attributes, or activities which may be objects of esteeming. One's self-esteem can be derived from one's sporting ability, mathematical prowess, beauty, social skills or artistic or mechanical skills. Alternatively it can be derived from the completion of tasks that one has set oneself. Self-esteem, then, can be distinguished from self-respect, simply by noting the role that one's status *as* a person plays in its realisation.

Goods of self-esteem include such things as prizes, honours and status goods. The goods of self-respect will include in their number such things as legal rights, political rights and citizenship. Substantive realisation of the general conception of justice will require that equality is instantiated in some sense with regard to both goods of self-respect and goods of self-esteem.

At this point, a further distinction can be drawn between those forms of self-esteem which involve comparison of one's worth with reference to the achievements, capacities or attributes of others and those which do not involve such interpersonal comparison. Some forms of self-esteem which do not require interpersonal comparison. For example, one may make a resolution to run five miles every morning and feel good about oneself if one lives up to this ideal or have low self-esteem if one fails to live up to it. Here self-esteem need not refer to the activities of other persons. This kind of self-esteem we may refer to as 'non-competitive self-esteem'. Alternatively, self-esteem may be founded upon competitive comparison with others. For instance, a person might well gain self-esteem by winning an athletics competition. In this case, it is the fact that her activity is superior to that of others with respect to the relevant criteria which provides her with high self-esteem. This mode of self-regard I shall call 'competitive self-esteem'. It involves the pursuit of goods, capacities, attributes and skills which enable one to compare oneself favourably with others.

The principle of equality of subjectivity

Having reminded the reader of the conceptual terrain, I shall now apply the principle of equality of well-being to the sphere of subjectivity. When so applied the principle of equal well-being generates the 'principle of equality of subjectivity'. This principle commands that goods of subjectivity be allocated in such a way as to realise the interests in subjectivity of all citizens. The focus of state activity in this area when allocating goods which either realise interests in subjectivity or which are the preconditions of such interest-realisation should be upon the provision of a social context in which all persons may flourish with regard to the interests in subjectivity. The primary aim of state action then should be to facilitate self-respect and self-esteem rather than to procure these aspects of human subjectivity.

However, as we shall see, the peculiar nature of many of the goods of subjectivity is such that there are various constraints upon the extent to which we can implement our egalitarian ideal; accordingly, we must forge principles which recognise these constraints. The principle of equality of subjectivity will thus be divided into two component parts: (i) those which concern self-respect and non-competitive self-esteem and (ii) those which concern competitive self-esteem.

Constraints upon egalitarianism in the sphere of subjectivity

Before examining the substantive ways in which social institutions and arrangements can implement the principle of equality of subjectivity, it is important to note several impediments upon such implementation. Firstly, there are what might be called general constraints upon the extent to which any ideal may be concretely instantiated in the sphere of subjectivity. These are constraints not just upon the implementation of egalitarian ideals, but upon state activity in general in the sphere of subjectivity. (In a sense these constraints concern the extent to which we may claim that goods of subjectivity are distributive goods). Secondly, there are logical constraints upon distributing goods connected to competitive self-esteem; that is, goods of competitive self-esteem are so constructed as to make it logically impossible that they be distributed equally. These we may refer to as specific constraints.

Let us firstly consider some conspicuous general constraints upon egalitarianism in the sphere of subjectivity. Two kinds of constraints spring immediately to mind: firstly, what may be called 'social' factors, and secondly, what we may refer to as individual psychological factors. The first general constraint concerns what might be termed 'organic social life'; i.e. it concerns the sphere of human activity not directly regulated and controlled by social institutions such as the state.[5] The determination of persons' subjectivity, and particularly their self-respect, is, to a significant extent, the province of organic social life. It is the product of the actions of the groups of people with whom they interact at work and outside the economic sphere. Rawls stresses in *A Theory of Justice* that the opinions of others have an important role to play in our self-understanding. He suggests that unless our activities are appreciated by our peers, it is impossible for us to maintain the sense that they are worthwhile; and consequently it is difficult to maintain our own sense of worth.[6] Similarly, if we are reviled by our peers, then again it is difficult, although not impossible, to maintain any sense of worth. Our subjectivity is partially socially determined by non-institutional social groupings. These non-institutionalised interactions between people—which in part determine our conception of self—are aspects of organic social life, and cannot be completely controlled by state and corporate bodies.

Consider the good of public honour. Public honour is a means of gaining self-esteem; and inasmuch as people mistakenly link self-esteem and self-respect, it is also a means of gaining self-respect. Moreover, public honour is bestowed upon persons by social groups; some of whom are state and corporate bodies. While there is often a close connection between government decisions concerning the allocation of public honours and a person being honoured by the community at large, equally it is true that mere government decree cannot ensure that a person is publicly honoured in the broader community at large. To a certain degree, public honouring by the community cannot be wholly determined by governments. This means that in distributing the goods of subjectivity there is a limit upon distributive justice (and a limit upon the principle of equal self-respect) because distributive justice is implemented by social institutions such as the State. To put it more simply, social recognition is not the sole province of the state. In order to illustrate this point, think of the phenomenon of 'Stakhanovism' discussed in chapter six. In this case, the mere fact that Stakhanovite prizes were awarded by the State did not ensure that the recipients of these prizes were respected by their workmates. In fact, anecdotal evidence has it that the Stakhanovites were harassed at work and ostracised.[7] Social recognition did not come from the mere distribution of government honours. On the other hand, some institutionally determined prizes do, of course, bring about social recognition; one need only think of educational scholarships or prestigious awards such as knighthoods or the Nobel prize. I limit myself then to the claim that there is no necessary connection between the institutional distribution of public honours and social recognition.[8]

These examples—which concern the relationship between honour (or public recognition) and the institutional determination of public honours—illustrate the general relationship between organic social life and the institutional distribution of goods of subjectivity. It is illustrative of the role that organic social life has to play in the allocation of goods of subjectivity, such as honour and respect. Given that our subjectivity is in part socially-determined and that this determination is not wholly the product of institutional action, it is possible to see why there would be a limit to the extent to which the principle of equality of subjectivity can be substantively realised.

Of course, you might argue that the examples which I have chosen concern self-esteem, rather than self-respect. Public honour is a good of self-esteem because its main purpose is to single out individuals for admiration and emulation. However, I think that the sort of point made with regard to the 'self-esteem good' of public recognition—which concerns the role that organic social life plays—also applies to goods of self-respect. It is a general point that applies to all goods of subjectivity. For instance, if a person who lives in an small isolated community is reviled by the members of that community, it is very unlikely that they will enjoy the good of self-respect. Regardless of whether government programs attempt to outlaw social harassment, such government decree is unlikely to make that person feel any more a part of the community, nor to generate self-respect immediately. This is not to rule such measures out. Important gains have been made via government decree in relation to the treatment of the Untouchables in India and the Aboriginal populations of Australia. Yet such measures, while commendable, are of limited value if they are not accompanied by a change in the attitude of the members of the general community.

The second general constraint upon the implementation of our egalitarian ideal in the sphere of subjectivity derives from the fact that a person's relationship to her self is also self-determined, so to speak. The sphere of subjectivity circumscribes those goods which involve the development and flourishing of our self-reflective nature. The development of our interests in subjectivity is partially reliant, then, upon internal subjective psychological processes which lie outside the complete control of social institutions and arrangements. Thus, there is a limit to the extent to which social policy can procure the self-respect and self-esteem of all citizens. To illustrate this point think of the person who systematically dismisses as worthless every achievement that she attains and in so doing believes herself to be worthless. No matter what social policy is implemented, it is unlikely that she will become self-respecting.

These constraints are limits not simply upon equality, but upon state activity in the sphere of subjectivity in general. If we take distributive justice to be a virtue of social institutions and arrangements, then the existence of various constraints upon state policy is theoretically significant. However, one should not overemphasise this indeterminacy. As we shall see, there are a number of policies—some of which have already been outlined in earlier chapters—which will increase the likelihood of achieving equality of self-respect. For instance, if implemented the principles of basal interest equality and compensatory meritocracy in the eudaimonian sphere would increase the likelihood of all realising interests in subjectivity.

I turn now to consider some specific constraints upon implementation of the principle of equality of subjectivity which concern those goods connected to competitive self-esteem. In an earlier discussion I suggested that self-esteem is an estimate of one's worth. It is something which persons believe about themselves in relation to other persons, personal standards and personal ideals. Moreover, I claimed that it is possible to distinguish between competitive self-esteem and non-competitive self-esteem. If we think carefully about the competitive aspect of self-esteem we find that those goods which are the preconditions of this interest in subjectivity are necessarily non-universal, for they cannot be enjoyed by all simultaneously. They are goods which would not be the sorts of goods they are unless distributed according to meritocratic ideals. For instance, if we think of various competitive goods of self-esteem which the state is associated with—namely prizes and honours—we find that they are not prizes and honours unless distributed according to ideals of desert. Thus it is difficult to see how the preconditions of this kind of self-esteem could be distributed universally or equally. If, for instance, members of a community think sporting ability is a measure of one's worth, and each person compares his or her sporting ability to that of his or her peers, then in all likelihood some members of that community will have more self-esteem than others. Of course, it is possible that members of the community are capable of self-deception; and those with lesser ability believe themselves to be more talented than they are. This would mean that all acquired equal levels of self-esteem. However, while self-deception is quite common, it would be implausible to suggest that a whole society could be self-deceiving in the way required by this line of thought.

The thrust of my argument is that given the link between competitive self-esteem and meritocracy, in all likelihood, particular goods of self-esteem cannot be equally obtained by all. This would seem to create difficulties for our regulative ideal. Therefore, I shall deal with the competitive goods of self-esteem in isolation from the goods of self-respect and non-competitive self-esteem.

The implementation of the principle of equality of subjectivity

Self-respect

In attempting to realise the general conception in the sphere of subjectivity, my first concern shall be with self-respect; or more precisely my concern shall be with those goods which are the preconditions of self-respect. Unlike goods of competitive self-esteem (e.g. prizes and honours), these goods are capable of being distributed equally. While there are limits upon the State's capacity to affect the overall allocation of self-respect, there would seem to be no constitutive constraints upon its universal realisation. Self-respect involves our beliefs about our own worth, not our beliefs about our comparative value. Rawls makes the point in *A Theory of Justice* that self-respect can be a universal virtue.[9] It can be enjoyed by all.

Let us begin with various 'psychological' methods for realising universal self-respect. One such route would involve the allocation of resources to fund programs of moral instruction designed to make people aware of their worth, independent of their skills, capacities and attributes. However, the idea that people will come to recognise, via instruction, their own intrinsic worth is a rather dubious one.

Another possible route would be to enshrine the value of persons, independently of contingent facts about themselves, in various forms of institutional frameworks such as the law and political constitutions. These measures would involve recognition by the State that one has certain rights merely by virtue of one's status as a person, not by virtue of the sort of person that one is. Such measures would be designed to help generate universal self-respect. This kind of route was favoured by Rawls in *A Theory of Justice*. Rawls argues that the basis of self-esteem in a just society is "the publicly affirmed distribution of fundamental rights and liberties. And this distribution being equal, everyone has a similar and secure status when they meet to conduct the common affairs of the wider society."[10] Rawls considers the establishment of the priority of liberty to be an effective social basis for the equal distribution of self-respect.

A third route would involve use of the psychological connection between self-respect and self-esteem. Many people come to believe that they are worthy as persons when they become the sorts of people that they aspire to be. Thus even though self-esteem and self-respect are conceptually independent of one another, it is possible to generate self-respect via the generation of non-competitive self-esteem. By increasing one's self-esteem through the principle of compensatory meritocracy in the eudaimonian sphere, one increases the chances of generating self-respect. The danger of such programs, which use a mistaken conception of moral psychology, i.e. of a connection between self-respect and self-esteem, is that they leave open the possibility that those who cannot improve their self-esteem will not gain self-respect..

I conclude, then, that given the implausibility of moral instruction as a means of generating universal self-respect, the proper approach would be: i) to ensure that certain state institutions enshrine the non-contingent value of persons in themselves and; ii) to introduce programs for the encouragement of universal non-competitive self-esteem.

One necessary legislative measure for encouraging universality of self-respect is the granting of citizenship to all members of a community. By citizenship, I mean membership of the community in such a way as to provide access to all the rights and privileges of that community. These rights and privileges would include such items as the opportunity to vote in whatever elections are relevant, access to the same work conditions as others, access to welfare provision, protection by the State from aggressive acts by other states, protection from other members of the community and protection from illegal acts of force by the state itself.[11] Citizenship thus becomes the institutional recognition of membership of a community or nation. It is public affirmation of a person's right to take their place in the community in which they live.

Citizenship is connected to self-respect in a pragmatic way in that members of a community who are not citizens are less likely to be treated respectfully, and subsequently less likely to be self-respecting. Therefore, it is an essential base of self-respect. Rawls also focuses on citizenship as a means of securing the grounds of self-respect for all. For Rawls, it is the primary means of achieving self-respect.[12] Given the central role which citizenship has to play in the formation of self-respect, if we wish to ensure that all have self-respect, then all persons in a community must be equally recognised as citizens of that community. The political rights of citizenship must be open to all members of the community; and in so doing we encourage equality of self-respect.

However, we should not overstate the role of formal citizenship in securing self-respect. Rawls, for instance, claims that in a well-ordered society self-respect is secured by the public affirmation of the status of equal citizenship for all.[13] He argues that in such a society it is unlikely that people will gain their self-respect from the acquisition of material goods; instead citizenship will secure the bases of self-respect on its own. This seems a rather implausible claim. It is hard to believe that merely conferring rights of equal citizenship will negate, even in a well-ordered society, low forms of self-regard based on one's access to material and positional goods. Moreover, the Rawlsian claim seems to ignore the role that work has to play in the construction of our subjectivity. One need only think of general community attitudes towards night-men or prostitutes on the one hand and brain surgeons on the other to recognise the role that work plays in the securing of self-respect. Nor should we think that a stateless person must lack self-respect. Citizenship is but one way of gaining self-respect. Equality of self-respect, then, also requires that egalitarian policies (such as the egalitarian principle of compensatory meritocracy) be implemented in the workplace.

A third measure for the facilitation of self-respect would be the implementation and maintenance of conditions of political equality. The recognition of political rights previously denied to persons, such as the right to vote, is also an important way in which self-respect can be encouraged. Rawls, for instance, argues that involvement in democratic processes requires that one have a sense of self-worth and thus the practice of exercising one's democratic rights helps bring about that sense of worth.[14] The plausibility of this claim becomes more apparent if one considers the conditions which obtain in the absence of political equality. For instance, the property qualification for voting—such as existed in Australia in the nineteenth century—would, in all likelihood, have a deleterious effect on the self-respect of those without property. According them the status of second class citizens would inevitably cause them to have lower self-respect than would otherwise be the case. In conclusion, then, universal suffrage is another measure which should be implemented, in order to attempt to secure the self-respect of all.

There are other measures which if implemented would assist in the procuring of universal self-respect. In chapters seven and eight I outlined the principle of basal interest equality and the egalitarian principle of compensatory meritocracy. Given that egalitarian policies in the basal and eudaimonian spheres will, in all likelihood, increase the levels of self-respect in a community, egalitarian policies in these spheres increase the likelihood that the relevant goods of subjectivity will be distributed to all. Let us examine this claim in greater detail.

Firstly, consider the basal goods. If it is true that persons' basal interests are satisfied up to levels appropriate for the pursuit of other interests (as the principle of basal interest equality specifies), then it is much more likely that they will be 'self-respecting'. Alternatively, the person whose basal interests are not adequately satisfied, is less likely to believe that he is a worthwhile person, or to have the confidence that his projects are worth pursuing. The person who begs on the street, or the person who is forced to go through rubbish bins in order to find food, is unlikely to enjoy the bases of self-respect.

We can deduce the presence of some sort of causal nexus here. Those persons whose basal interests are not being satisfied are less likely to be self-respecting, whereas those whose basal interests are satisfied are more likely to be self-respecting. Clearly, distributive policy which is directed toward the implementation of the principle of basal interest equality is causally efficacious in increasing the likelihood that all members of that society will be self-respecting.

Let us now consider the role that implementation of the egalitarian principle of compensatory meritocracy in the eudaimonian sphere would have to play in the facilitation of universal self-respect. If we assume that eudaimonian goods constitute a form of activity enabling goods of non-competitive self-esteem to be realised, then it follows that the provision of eudaimonian goods for all persons will, in all likelihood, increase the self-esteem of all. If we also assume that an increase in the self-esteem of all will increase the possibility that all will be self-respecting, then it follows that the implementation of the principle of compensatory meritocracy could have a role to play in bringing about universal self-respect. This, then, is our fourth measure for generating universal self-respect. So long as a causal relationship exists between the satisfaction of eudaimonian interests and the incidence of self-respect, then the principle of compensatory meritocracy, if implemented, provides a further possible mechanism for the generation of universal self-respect.

However, there is something slightly perplexing about this last claim. Why should it be that increasing a person's skills and capacities should increase her self-esteem and hence her self-respect? I think that part of the answer to this lies in certain facts about the moral psychology of human beings; namely, that human beings tend to feel better about themselves when the activities in which they are engaged require personal input i.e. when the activities they perform are in my terms 'eudaimonian'. Rawls makes a similar point, when he notes the connection between self-esteem and his 'Aristotelian principle' (which is the idea that other things being equal, human beings enjoy the exercise of their realised capacities, and this enjoyment increases the more the capacity is realised, or the greater its complexity). Rawls argues that when activities fail to satisfy the Aristotelian Principle, they are likely to seem dull and flat, and to give us no feeling of competence or a sense that they are worth doing. Rawls believes that a person tends to be more confident of his value when his abilities are both fully realised and organised in ways of suitable complexity and refinement.[15] Rawls' emphasis here is upon the connection between self-respect and developmental activity. Alternatively, we may say that when a person's activity is dull and repetitive, this has an effect upon her self-esteem. If a person thinks that her activities are worthless, how can she continue to have high self-esteem?

The egalitarian principle of compensatory meritocracy involves directing social resources towards ensuring that all develop their eudaimonian potential, and a consequence of this presumably would be that levels of self-esteem would be raised.

A second reason for rejecting this objection relies upon a claim about the role that social attitudes play in the amount of self-esteem that a person may gain from a particular job. At the present time, many jobs are highly esteemed because of both their high eudaimonian content and their high pay. However, the institution of compensation for non-eudaimonian work would, in all likelihood, even out the social status that particular occupations enjoy, and hence increase the possibility of all gaining self-esteem from their work. I am not alone in making this kind of point about the relationship between eudaimonian activity and self-respect. Similar claims about the self-respect generating capacities of self-developmental autonomous activity for generating self-respect have been made by other writers. For instance, Robin Attfield contends that the provision of meaningful work affords most people their best chance of obtaining the necessary good of self-respect. Attfield argues that the agent of meaningful work has standards and aims about which he or she cares and which he or she is able to apply and carry out. Attfield argues that this person's work is constitutive of its products and, therefore, if these products have the requisite qualities, the standards and aims are being satisfied. According to Attfield, meaningful work actually satisfies the requirements of self-respect itself, except where work goes badly, or alternatively, where the agent lacks a scheme of priorities for living. However, for work of this kind to go badly is often not so much a sign of lack of self-respect as of the dissatisfaction with imperfect work and again, although meaningful work does not entail that the worker has a scheme of priorities, it tends to generate rather than retard the growth of what is worth doing in life.[16] Interestingly, Attfield makes the further claim that meaningful work is, in all probability, the principal—though not the invariable—basis of self-respect. A similar claim is made by Kant concerning the relationship between meaningful work and self-respect. After distinguishing between servile and independent occupations, Kant makes the point that servile occupations are less likely to encourage people to be self-respecting.[17]

Now the observant reader will have noticed that this mechanism of generating self-respect via non-competitive self-esteem relies upon what might be thought to be an illicit psychological connection, at least on the story I have been telling. Such self-respect relies upon what I take to be the empirical fact that many persons come to be more self-respecting when they enjoy self-esteem. All of the measures outlined above involve the generation of self-respect via the generation of self-esteem. However, there is an explanation for this anomaly. While self-respect and self-esteem are *conceptually distinct*, it is also true that people often confuse the two. Of course, some critics might object that social policy should not rely for its proper functioning upon the use of what appears to be mistaken moral psychology. Given that a person should recognise her worth independently of contingent facts about herself, should she come to recognise such worth via the recognition of contingent facts? Expressed in this way it sounds almost paradoxical. There seems to be a tension between an empirical precondition of self-respect being based on self-esteem, while at the same time it being argued that self-respect is independent of self-esteem.

However, I do not think that we should be too concerned by this inconsistency. Our main concern is with ensuring that people attain self-respect, not the manner in which it is brought about. After all the primary concern of distributive theorists should not be the elimination of mistaken moral psychology.

In summary, then, four measures for encouraging equality of self-respect have been outlined in this section: these being the implementation of; i) the principle of basal interest equality; ii) the egalitarian principle of compensatory meritocracy; iii) universal citizenship and; iv) political equality. While not strictly policies which distribute the good of self-respect, they are policies which will, in all likelihood, encourage the development of self-respect for all. All measures are designed to facilitate the universal attainment of self-respect.

Non-competitive self-esteem

The other sub-category of goods in the sphere of subjectivity to which equalitarian principles can be straight-forwardly applied are the goods of non-competitive self-esteem. Earlier in this chapter I claimed that although self-esteem is an essentially comparative notion, non-competitive self-esteem is capable of being realised by all persons because it does not involve comparison between persons. Most simply put, the goods of non-competitive self-esteem involve self-esteem realised via comparison with standards that are not other people. It is self-esteem which is realised *inter alia* by the completion of tasks according to criteria set by the very nature of the task. An example of such realisation might be where a boat-builder sets himself the goal of building a fishing boat. If he successfully builds such a boat, then he may gain non-competitive self-esteem. It does not matter for the realisation of this kind of self-esteem how his activity compares with that of other persons.

Given that goods of non-competitive self-esteem do not involve interpersonal comparison, they do not (at least at first sight) generate problems for the principle of equality of subjectivity. From a logical point of view they can be distributed equally. The aim of social policy here should be to ensure that all are given the opportunity to develop skills which will enable them to complete tasks leading to self-esteem. Of course it is possible that there are some persons whose capacity for developing such skills is so low that even training cannot help them gain self-esteem. However, such persons are likely to be in the minority. The important point is that the overall aim is capable of being achieved.

Competitive self-esteem

Earlier I outlined some measures for the facilitation of universal self-respect and non-competitive self-esteem. I also noted that goods of competitive self-esteem create special problems for the egalitarian because they cannot be allocated to all equally. The problem is compounded by the fact that in the sphere of subjectivity some of the most important goods of subjectivity which social institutions distribute are competitive goods of self-esteem. Think of various honours and prizes, such as the Nobel prize and university scholarships which governments and other social institutions distribute. These are important distributive goods, and yet it would seem to be a matter of logical necessity that they be distributed meritocratically. How can these goods be distributed in a way which is consistent with the principle of equality of subjectivity outlined earlier? What principles of distribution should be applied to goods of competitive self-esteem?

Given that the goods are, in some sense, essential for human flourishing, the answer to the above question is that such goods should be distributed *meritocratically*. Prizes and honours should be distributed to those who have deserved them, according to the relevant criteria.[18] Sporting prizes, for example, should go to those who have won the competition; similarly war medals for bravery should go to those who exhibit this virtue. Goods of self-esteem are to be allocated to those who *deserve* them.[19]

One might ask how we can justify the insertion of a genuinely meritocratic principle into what is ostensibly an egalitarian project. Firstly, I think if one accepts that the competitive goods of self-esteem are in fact essentially comparative between persons, then it follows that any *particular* good of self-esteem cannot be distributed equally. If one is to distribute them, then one requires a distributive principle other than equality. However, this does not mean that we should abandon our ideal of equality. While it is true that particular goods cannot be distributed equally, it does not follow that if honours and prizes are allocated for a wide variety of fields of endeavour, that all can not realise competitive self-esteem. We could have prizes for example for sport, science, clothing design and music, as well as a large number of other activities. In so doing, it might well be possible for all to enjoy the goods of self-esteem. Our aim then becomes to ensure that a wide variety of different kinds of activities are publicly honoured.

This strategy is similar in many respects to what Michael Walzer calls 'complex equality'. In *Spheres of Justice* Walzer argues that inequality in particular goods is not incompatible with a society being more generally an egalitarian one. According to Walzer, so long as there is a wide variety of spheres of goods, it does not matter if certain people monopolise or dominate any particular sphere. Equality will be realised so long as all people are able to do well in some sphere and so long as no people are able to dominate all spheres. In a complex egalitarian society there will be many small inequalities, but these inequalities will not enable any single person to dominate in a wide variety of fields.[20] Similarly, by ensuring that a wide variety of fields of endeavour are honoured, the meritocratic distribution of particular fields will not be incompatible with a generally egalitarian approach.

The purist's objection

Let us firstly consider the objection that prizes and honours are the sorts of goods which only gain their meaning from being distributed meritocratically. Given this fact, then, *ex hypothesi* it is necessarily the case that such goods cannot be distributed equally. Now it might be argued by an egalitarian purist that rather than attempt the theoretical contortions required to justify the maintenance of prizes and honours in an egalitarian system via the use of the regulative ideal, that the proper egalitarian approach would be to rid ourselves of prizes and honours altogether. Why not eliminate these goods of self-esteem?

This is indeed a good question. Given the obvious link between self-esteem and prizes and honours, and the comparative nature of such goods, why preserve a good which leads to inequalities in the sphere of subjectivity? Moreover, a policy of eliminating prizes and honours might gain support not only from egalitarians, but also from theorists who believe comparative self-esteem to be morally vicious. It would seem that we need some good reason for keeping such goods.

I think the most convincing reason for preserving these goods is the fact that they are *integral* components of activities which are central to human flourishing. Not only is the practice of giving prizes and honours an integral element of human society as we know it, activities which have prizes and honours accorded them are essential to the human good life. Without activities such as competitive sport, or medals for bravery, human life would be greatly diminished. The world of the egalitarian purist would be an impoverished ascetic one.

However, in arguing in this way, it is also important that we not champion a world composed solely of competitive activities. While the existence of competition is an integral component of the good life—and there are also good utilitarian reasons for wanting specific activities to be undertaken under competitive conditions—this does not mean that all activities should be performed competitively. For instance, while training to be brain surgeon should include examinations and some sport should be played competitively, this does not mean that there could not be activities, such as the study of literature or bushwalking, which are pursued non-competitively. We should be careful to maintain certain areas of activity which are non-competitive. Moreover, we should be mindful at all times that the legitimacy of this meritocratic allocation of certain human goods connected to competitive self-esteem is contingent upon these particular goods being essential for human flourishing.

The objection from human nature

Some readers might object that attempting to implement the principle of equal well-being in the sphere of subjectivity is futile because of the way in which human beings are actually constructed. Human nature is such that the project of equalising our interests in subjectivity is quixotic rather than admirable. This objection may be fleshed out with the following assumptions: i) that competitive self-esteem is the overwhelmingly central component of human subjectivity and; ii) that the competitive self-esteem of all is unlikely to be satisfied by broadening the range of activities over which it is to apply. According to i) human subjectivity consists in interpersonal comparison. *Ex hypothesi* ideas of self-worth devoid of comparison with other persons have very little to do with the ways in which human beings come to understand themselves: a human person constructs her self-image and sense of worth primarily in terms of how she compares with other people. According to ii), we cannot broaden the kinds of activities which people esteem to any significant effect. Any government action which attempts to increase the range of activities from which people gain self-esteem in comparison with others will only succeed in promoting a range of activities which the majority of citizens do not value. In effect, government interference in the kinds of activities which people esteem can only demean the standing of government awards and prizes. According to this line of thought, human nature is such that there is a limited range of activities which will be esteemed.

Together these two assumptions provide the basis for an objection that human nature places constraints upon state activity in the sphere of subjectivity. If it is indeed true that human subjectivity is primarily derived from competitive self-esteem—as opposed to self-respect and non-competitive self-esteem—and that human beings will only derive competitive self-esteem from a limited range of competitive activities, then it would seem that the goal of equalising the incidence of benefit in the sphere of subjectivity is hopelessly utopian. According to this objection, we cannot meaningfully apply the egalitarian principle of equal well-being in the sphere of subjectivity.

What should be said in response to this objection to the program outlined in this chapter? To what extent might it be said that various facts about human nature conspire to prevent egalitarian outcomes in the sphere of subjectivity? In reply, we may firstly question the extent to which competitive self-esteem is the central component of human subjectivity. If we think about the lived experience of self-evaluation, is it true that when we attempt to come to an understanding of who we are and what attitude we have towards ourselves that we primarily consider our capacities and achievements in comparison with other persons? Is it true that self-evaluation primarily involves assessing our comparative status with other persons? I think that if we consider the phenomenology of self-evaluation carefully, we find that what I have termed self-respect and non-competitive self-esteem do, in fact, have a significant role to play in our lives. Whilst not wishing to deny the importance of competitive self-esteem, these kinds of self-evaluation which do not involve interpersonal comparison are also important aspects of human subjectivity.

Secondly, while there might be limits on the extent to which the range of activities from which people gain competitive self-esteem can be broadened, this does not mean that it cannot be broadened to a significant extent. We may not be able to extend the range of self-esteeming activities so that all enjoy competitive self-esteem, but that does not mean that the range cannot be markedly increased. We may conclude therefore that the objection from human nature does not negate the egalitarian strategies advocated in this chapter.

The objection from the scope of distributive justice

Finally, it might be objected that much of what has been discussed here has very little to do with distributive justice. If one considers some of the measures advocated above, such as the implementation and maintenance of universal citizenship and legal equality, at first sight they seem to be rather unconnected to the distribution of benefits and burdens. What would justify the treatment of such issues within the ambit of distributive theory?

Briefly in response, such issues are of concern for distributive theory in as much as: i) they are connected to the allocation of human goods and; ii) distributive resources can be allocated in order to ensure that these measures are properly implemented. If we take the case of political equality, here it may be said that we have an issue which is connected to the distribution of the human good of self-respect. If political equality is not enshrined in the legal codes, then the achievement of universal self-respect is far less likely. In this sense it is a distributive issue, for it concerns the distribution across a society (albeit in a rather attenuated sense) of an important human good. Secondly, legal equality is a measure which may be fostered by the provision of various funds intended to ensure that all have adequate legal representation. Therefore we may say that while it is true that many of the measures advocated in this chapter are less directly issues of distributive justice, inasmuch as they affect the distribution of various human goods across a society and inasmuch as social resources can be directed toward their implementation, they should properly be thought of as belonging within the domain of distributive justice.

Summary

The sphere of subjectivity, then, is comprised of three significant kinds of goods; goods of self-respect, non-competitive goods of self-esteem and competitive goods of self-esteem. In applying my egalitarian regulative ideal to the sphere of subjectivity I have derived the principle of equality of subjectivity. Due to various constraints upon its implementation, this principle has been divided into two component parts; the principle of equality of self-respect and non-competitive self-esteem and the principle of equality of areas for competitive self-esteem.

Notes

1. We may illustrate this distinction between *procuring* and *facilitation* by thinking of the contrast between facilitating wealth creation (for example, by the provision of a certain kind of education) and the procuring of wealth. In the one case the pre-conditions for the attainment of certain goods are provided, whereas in the other the actual goods themselves are provided.
2. It is important to note at the outset that Rawls does not really make the distinction between self-respect and self-esteem. It would appear that he uses the terms interchangeably. See Rawls, 1972, pp. 178-79 & p.234.

3. Ibid., p.440.
4. Ibid., p.440
5. The term 'organic social life' is derived from the work of the Italian social theorist Antonio Gramsci. Gramsci, in the context of various debates concerning socialist revolution, placed much emphasis on a distinction between the 'organic' and 'conjunctural' dimensions of revolutionary change. The former refers to a gradual shift in the balance of social and cultural forces. The latter refers to the momentary period of crisis in which political forces vie for control of state power. For a discussion of this see Femia, 1981, pp.52-55.
6. Op. cit., p.441.
7. Walzer, 1983, p.263.
8. Cf. Galston ,1980, p.274.
9. Op. cit., pp.441-42.
10. Ibid., p.544.
11. In this regard my account is similar to that of Gorz, who claims that citizenship involves basic income, the right to vote and the right to work. See Gorz, 1989, pp.205-6.
12. Op. cit., p.545.
13. Ibid., p.545.
14. Cf. ibid., p.234. Note that Rawls uses the term self-esteem here. It would appear that he does not distinguish between the two notions.
15. Ibid., p.440.
16. Attfield, 1984, p.144.
17. Galston, 1980, p.266.
18. This is consistent with an earlier point made in chapter eight that the proper reward for talent is admiration and the opportunity to develop that talent further, rather than excessive economic benefit.
19. This is a genuinely meritocratic principle, unlike the principle of compensatory meritocracy, which is in fact an egalitarian principle.
20. Walzer, 1983, pp.17, 19, 28.

10 Epilogue

In this book I have employed a neo-Aristotelian account of the human good and the principle of respect for persons to generate the principle of equal well-being. Additionally, by analysing distributive benefits in terms of an account of the human good, three spheres of distributive goods, to which my general egalitarian conception of justice is to apply, have been adduced. These three spheres of goods are the basal sphere, the eudaimonian sphere and the sphere of subjectivity.

By applying the principle of equal well-being to the three spheres of goods in the final three chapters, three distinct principles of distributive justice have been generated. The first principle, the Principle of Basal Interest Equality, states that:

> Distributive resources should be directed toward ensuring that all persons' basal interests are satisfied, at least to that level requisite for the pursuance of other interests.

This principle is to be ascribed *conditional priority*; thus it is to take precedence over all other possible principles of distributive justice, until such time as the levels of basal interest satisfaction are sufficient for all to pursue other interests.

In the eudaimonian sphere, application of the Principle of Equal Well-Being has generated the Egalitarian Principle of Compensatory Meritocracy which can be stated in the following manner:

> Contingent upon the existence of compensatory mechanisms which provide reparations in the form of free time, training and extra remuneration for the performance of the non-eudaimonian, eudaimonian work should be allocated to those willing candidates with the highest level of relevant comparative eudaimonian skill.

This principle is primarily concerned with ensuring that all persons enjoy eudaimonian activity, either in the workplace or in the external domain.

Finally, the application of the Principle of Equal Well-Being to the sphere of subjectivity has generated the Principle of Equality of Subjectivity. This principle, which has two main components, concerning equality of self-respect and non-competitive self-esteem and equality of areas for competitive self-esteem, can be stated in the following manner:

> With regard to self-respect and non-competitive self-esteem, social policy should be directed towards ensuring that all persons realize interests in subjectivity, via such mechanisms as the introduction and maintenance of political equality, legal equality, universal citizenship and universal training. With regard to competitive self-esteem, given its necessarily exclusive character, social policy should be directed toward ensuring that as wide a variety of fields of endeavour as is possible are honoured with the aim of achieving 'equality of areas'.

This final principle is formulated with the aim of ensuring that all persons enjoy the benefits of self-respect and non-competitive self-esteem; by widening the variety of activities from which competitive self-esteem may be achieved, we might spread the benefits of competitive self-esteem as widely as possible.

It is hoped that these three principles of distributive justice, whilst egalitarian in orientation, are not blindly so, but rather that they are responsive to the complexities of human social life. Furthermore, it is hoped that the range of distributive goods which these principles apply to, is broader than is often the case in discussions of distributive justice, and thus provides a superior basis for determining the justness of social institutions and arrangements. Of course, the distributive theory is in many ways incomplete and requires further elaboration. In order to provide a wholly satisfactory account, the principles would need to be applied to a range of real-life situations. The theory should be thought then of as a preliminary work which lays the groundwork for a more fulsome doctrine. More specifically, there are a number of other conspicuous philosophical issues which need to be addressed, including the following. Firstly, I have argued that an account of the good is a necessary condition of distributive theory. Much interesting work remains concerning various other non-constructivist attempts to derive substantive distributive principles without reference to any form of philosophical anthropology. Secondly, I have not provided any sustained defence of the *particular* account of the good employed; another area which needs to be addressed then would be how one might defend such an Aristotelian account. Of course, it may well be that the central political points can still be made without yoking my taxonomy of human interests to Aristotelian moral theory. Nonetheless, as it stands, the account needs defending against alternative views and against those who would hold that all accounts of the good are indefensible. Thirdly, there are also complex issues concerning the use of general moral principles. In recent years, a number of philosophers—the most prominent being Jonathan Dancy—have argued that we should eschew such principles because they blind us to the particularity of the moral situations we confront. Again I have not made any attempt to defend the use of such general principles. Much then remains to be done.

Bibliography

Ackerman, B. (1980), *Social Justice and the Liberal State,*.Yale University Press: New Haven, Conn.

Airaksinen, T. (1985), 'Hegel on Poverty and Violence', in Kipnis, K. and Meyers, D.T. (eds.) *Economic Justice*, Rowman and Allenheld: Totowa, N.J., pp.42-58.

Aquinas, T., (1911-42), *The "Summa Theologiae" of Thomas Aquinas*, 22v. literally trans. by the Fathers of the English Domincan Province, Burns, Oats and Washbourne: London.

Arendt, H. (1959), *The Human Condition*, Anchor: New York.

Arendt, H. (1973), *On Revolution*, Penguin: Harmondsworth, Middlesex.

Aristotle (1959), *Politics*, trans. John Warrington, Heron Books: London.

Aristotle (1969), *The Nicomachean Ethics*, trans. Ross, W.D., Oxford University Press: London.

Arneson, R.J. (1987), 'Meaningful Work and Market Socialism', *Ethics*, 97, pp.517-45.

Attfield, R (1984), 'Work and the Human Essence', *Journal of Applied Philosophy*, vol.1 no.1, pp.141-156.

Atwell, J.E. (1982), 'Kant's Notion of Respect For Persons' in Green, O.H. (ed.), *Respect for Persons*, Tulane University Press: New Orleans, pp.17-30.

Baier, A.C. (1988), 'Pilgrim's Progress' *Canadian Journal of Philosophy*, 18/2, pp.315-30.

Baier, K. (1958), *The Moral Point of View*, Cornell University Press: Ithaca, N.Y.

Baier, K. (1989), 'Justice and the Aims of Political Philosophy', *Ethics*, 99, pp.771-90.

Balbus, I.D. (1982), *Marxism and Domination*, Princeton University Press: Princeton N.J..

Barry, B. (1973), *The Liberal Theory of Justice*, Oxford University Press: Oxford.

Barry, B. (1989), *Theories of Justice*, Berkeley, University of Califorina Press: California.

Battin, M.P. (1986), 'Age-Rationing and the Just Distribution of Health Care: Is there a Duty to Die', *Ethics* 97, pp.317-40.

Baumol, W.J. (1965), *Economic Theory and Operations Analysis* 2nd ed., Prentice Hall Inc: Englewood Cliffs, N.J..

Beitz, C.R. *et al*, (eds.), (1985), *International Ethics*, Princeton University Press: Princeton.

Benn, S.I. and Peters, R.S. (1968), *Social Principles and the Democratic State*, George Allen and Unwin: London.

Bernstein, R.J. (1980), *Philosophical Profiles*, Polity Press: Cambridge.
Bradley, F.H. (1962), 'My Station and Its Duties' and 'Why Should I Be Moral?' in *Ethical Studies*, Oxford University Press: London.
Broad, C.D. (1959), *Five Types of Ethical Theory*, Adams: Littlefield.
Brown, A. (1986), *Modern Political Philospphy*, Penguin: Harmondsworth, Middlesex.
Buchanan, A.E., (1982), *Marx and Justice: The Radical Critique of Liberalism*, Methuen: London.
Buchanan, A.E. (1989), 'Assessing the Communitarian Critique of Liberalism', *Ethics*, 99, pp.852-82.
Care, N.S. (1984), 'Career Choice', *Ethics* 94, pp.283-302.
Caney, S. (1992), 'Thomas Nagel's Defence of Liberal Neutrality', *Analysis* 52/1 pp.41-45.
Casey, J. (1990), *Pagan Virtue*, Clarendon Press: Oxford.
Clarke, S.R.L. (1975), *Aristotle's Man: speculations upon Aristotelian Anthropology*, Clarendon Press: Oxford.
Cohen, G.A. (1978), *Karl Marx's Theory of History: A Defence*, Princeton University Press: Princeton, N.J..
Cohen, G.A. (1986), 'Self ownership, world ownership and equality', in *Justice and Equality: Here and Now*, Lucash, Frank S. (ed.), Cornell University Press: Ithaca N.J..
Cohen, G.A. (1988), *History, Labour and Freedom*, Clarendon Press: Oxford.
Cranor, C.F. (1982), 'Limitations on Respect-For-Persons Theories' in Green, O.H. (ed.), *Respect for Persons*, Tulane University Press: New Orleans, pp.45-60.
Daniels, N. (1977), 'Equal Liberty and Unequal Worth of Liberty', in Daniels, N. (ed.), *Reading Rawls*, Basil Blackwell: Oxford.
Daniels, N. (1981), 'Health Care Needs and Distributive Justice', *Philosophy and Public Affairs*, 10/2, pp.146-79.
Darwall, S.L. (1977-78), 'Two Kinds of Respect', *Ethics* 88, pp.36-49.
Darwall, S.L. (1980), 'Is there a Kantian Foundation to Rawlsian Justice', in Blocker, H.G. and. Smith, E.H., *John Rawls's Theory of Justice*, Ohio University Press: Athens, Ohio.
Davidson, D. (1980), 'Actions, Reasons and Causes' and 'Agency', in *Essays on Actions and Events*, Clarendon Press: Oxford.
De Marnefe, P. (1990), 'Liberalism, Liberty and Neutrality', *Philosophy and Public Affairs*, 19/2, pp.252-74.
De Vogue, A. (1983), *The Rule of Saint Benedict*, trans. John Baptist Hasbrouk, Cistercian Publications: Kalamazoo, Michigan.
Doppelt, G. (1989) 'Is Rawls' Kantian Liberalism Coherent and Defensible?', *Ethics* 99, July, pp.815-51.
Downie, R.S. and Telfer, E. (1969), *Respect For Persons*, George Allen and Unwin: London.
Dunn, J. (1969), *The Political Thought of John Locke*, Cambridge University Press: Cambridge.
Dworkin, R. (1975), 'The Original Position', in Daniels, N. (ed.) *Reading Rawls*, Basil Blackwell: Oxford, pp.16-53.
Dworkin, R. (1977), *Taking Rights Seriously*, Duckworth: London.
Dworkin, R. (1981), 'What is Equality?: Parts I and II', in *Philosophy and Public Affairs*, vol.10 no's 3-4, Spring, pp.185-246 and pp.283-345.
Dworkin, R. (1983) 'In Defence of Equality', *Social Philosophy and Policy*, 1, 1, pp.24-40.
Feinberg, J. (1970), *Doing and Deserving*, Princeton University Press: Princeton N.J..
Feinberg, J. (1974), 'Non Comparitive Justice', *Philosophical Review*, 83, pp.297-338.
Femia, J.V. (1981), *Gramsci's Political Thought*, Clarendon: Oxford.

Galston, W. (1980), *Justice and the Human Good*, Chicago University Press: Chicago.
Galston, W. (1989), 'Pluralism and Social Unity', *Ethics*, 99, pp.711-26.
Gauthier, D.P. (1967), 'Morality and Advantage' *The Philosophical Review*, 76, pp.460-75.
Gauthier, D. (1986), *Morals By Agreement*, Oxford University Press: Oxford.
Gorz, A. (1980), *Ecology as Politics*, South End Press: Boston.
Gorz, A. (1982), *Farewell to the Working Class*, Verso: London.
Gorz, A. (1989), *Critique of Economic Reason*, Verso: London.
Griffin, J. (1986), *Well-Being*, Clarendon Press: Oxford.
Gutmann, A. (1985), 'Communitarian Critics of Liberalism', *Philosophy and Public Affairs*, 14, pp.308-32.
Habermas, J. (1971), *Knowledge and Human Interests*: Heineman: London.
Hampton, J. (1989), 'Should Political Philosophy Be Done Without Metaphysics', *Ethics*, 99, July, pp.791-814.
Hardy, L. (1990), *The Fabric of This World: Inquiries into Calling, Career Choice and the Design of Human Work*, W.B. Eerdmans: Grands Rapids, Mich..
Hegel, G.W.F. (1977), *The Phenomenology of Spirit*, trans. A.V. Milller, Oxford University Press: Oxford.
Hegel, G.W.F. (1991), *Elements of the Philosophy of Right*, Allen W. Wood (ed.), trans. H.B. Nisbet, Cambridge University Press: Cambridge.
Held, V. (1973), 'Reasonable Progress and Self-Respect', *The Monist* 57, pp.12-27.
Hill, T.E. Jnr. (1973), 'Servility and Self-Respect', *The Monist* 57, pp.87-104.
Hill, T.E. Jnr. (1982), 'Self-Respect Reconsidered' in Green, O.H. (ed.), *Respect for Persons*, Tulane University Press: New Orleans.
Hill, T.E. Jnr. (1992), 'Humanity as an End in Itself', in *Dignity and Practical Reason*, Cornell University Press: Ithaca, New York.
Hobbes, T. (1965), *Leviathan*, Dent: London.
Hume, D. (1946), *A Treatise of Human Nature*, L.A. Selby-Bigge (ed.), Clarendon Press: Oxford.
Hume, D. (1975), *An Enquiry Concerning the Principles of Morals*, P.H. Nidditch (ed.), Clarendon Press: Oxford.
Jackson, J. and McConnell, C.R. (1988), *Economics: Third Australian Edition*, McGraw-Hill: Sydney.
James, W. (1950), *Principles of Psychology*, Authorised Edition, in Two Volumes Bound in One, Dover, U.S.A.: New York:,
Johnson, O.A. (1974-75), 'The Kantian Interpretation', *Ethics*, Vol.85, pp.58-68.
Johnson, O.A. (1977), 'Heteronomy and Autonomy in Rawls and Kant' *Mid West Studies in Philosophy* (2), pp.277-79.
Kant, I. (1956), *Critique of Pure Reason*, trans. Norman Kemp Smith, McMillan: London.
Kant, I. (1963), *Lectures on Ethics*, trans. Louis Infield, Harper: New York.
Kant. I. (1970), 'Theory and Practice' in Reiss, H. (ed.), *Kant's Political Writings*, trans. H.B. Nisbet, Cambridge University Press: Cambridge.
Kant, I. (1978), *Anthropology from a Pragmatic Point of View*, trans. by Victor Lyle Dowdell, rev. and edited by Rudnick, Hans H., South Illinois University Press: Edwardsville.
Kant, I. (1981), *Groundwork for the Metaphysics of Morals*, trans. James W. Ellington, Hackett Pulishing Co.: Indianapolis.
Kant, I. (1989), *Critique of Practical Reason*, trans. Lewis White Beck, McMillan: New York.
Kant, I. (1991), *Metaphysics of Morals*, trans. Mary J. Gregor, Cambridge University Press: Cambridge.
Kenny, A. (1973), *The Anatomy of the Soul*, Basil Blackwell: Oxford.
Kohn, M.L. and Schooler, C. (1978), 'The Reciprocal Effects of the Substantive

Complexity of Work and Intellectual Flexibility: A Longitudinal Study', *American Journal of Sociology*, 81, pp.24-52.
Kojeve, A. (1969), *Introduction to the Readings of Hegel*, trans. James H. Nichols Jnr., Basic Books: New York.
Kornhauser, A. (1964), *Mental Health and the Industrial Worker: A Detroit Study*, John Wiley and Sons: New York.
Kukathas, C. and Pettit, P. (1990), *Rawls: A Theory of Justice and its Critics*, Stanford University Press: Stanford, California.
Kymlicka, W. (1988), 'Rawls on Teleology and Deontology' *Philosophy and Public Affairs*, 17/3, pp.173-90.
Kymlicka, W. (1989a), 'Liberal Individualism and Liberal Neutrality', *Ethics* 99, July, pp.883-905.
Kymlicka, W. (1989b), *Liberalism, Community and Culture*, Oxford University Press: Oxford.
Kymlicka, W. (1990), *Contemporary Political Philosophy*, Clarendon Press: Oxford.
Kymlicka, W. (1991), 'The Social Contract Tradition', in P.Singer (ed.), *A Companion to Ethics*, Basil Blackwell: Oxford, pp.186-96.
Lane, H. (1976), *The Wild Boy of Aveyron*, Cambridge University Press: Cambridge.
Leiser, B.M. (1985), 'Vagrancy, Loitering and Economic Justice', in Kipnis, K. and Meyers, D.T. (eds.) *Economic Justice*, Rowman and Allenheld: Totowa N.J..
Lipsey, G. (1989), *An Introduction to Positive Economics*, Seventh Edition, Weidenfeld and Nicolson: London.
Lucas, J.R. (1972), 'Justice' *Philosophy*, 47, pp.229-248.
Luce, R.D. and Raiffa, H. (1957), *Games and Decisions*, John Wiley and Sons: New York.
Lukes, S. (1985), *Marxism and Morality*, Oxford University Press: Oxford.
Lyons, D. (1965), *Forms and Limits of Utilitarianism*, Clarendon Press: New York.
McDowell, J. (1979), 'Virtue and Reason', *The Monist* 62, pp.331-50.
McIntyre, A. (1967), *A Short History of Ethics*, Routledge and Kegan Paul: London.
McIntyre, A. (1981), *After Virtue*, University of Notre Dame: Notre Dame.
McIntyre, A. (1988), *Whose Justice, Which Rationality?*, University of Notre Dame Press: Indianna.
Marcuse, H. (1968), 'On Hedonism' in *Negations*, Allen Lane: London.
Marx, K. (1967), 'On the Jewish Question' in *The Writings of the Young Marx on Philosophy and Society*, ed. and trans. Easton, Lloyd D. and Guddat, Kurt H., Anchor Books: New York.
Marx, K. and Engels, F. (1970), *The German Ideology*, Arthur, C.J. (ed.), Lawrence and Wishart: London.
Marx, K. and Engels, F. (1975), *Manifesto of the Communist Party* in *Collected Works* vol.6, Lawrence and Wishart: London.
Marx, K. (1977), *Capital Vol.1* Penguin: Harmondsworth, Middlesex.
Marx, K. (1981), *Capital Vol.3*, Penguin/New Left Books: Harmondsworth, Middlesex.
Mason, Andrew D., (1990) 'Autonomy, Liberalism and State Neutrality', *The Philosophical Quarterly*, Vol.40 no.161, Oct., pp.433-52.
Mill, J.S. (1972), *On Liberty* and *Utilitarianism* in *Utilitarianism, On Liberty, Considerations of Representative Government,* Acton, H.B. (ed.), J.M.Dent and Sons: London.
Miller, David (1976), *Social Justice*, Oxford University Press: Oxford.
Miller, David (1992), 'Deserving Jobs' *The Philosophical Quarterly*, 42/167, pp.161-81.
Munzer, S.R. (1990), *A Theory of Property*, Cambridge University Press: Cambridge.
Nagel, E. (1961), *The Structure of Science*, Routledge and Kegan Paul: London.
Nagel, T. (1972-73), 'Equal Treatment and Compensatory Discrimination', *Philosophy*

and Public Affairs, 2, pp.348-61.
Nagel, T. (1975), 'Rawls on Justice', in Daniels, N. (ed.), *Reading Rawls*, Basil Blackwell: Oxford, pp.1-16.
Nagel, T. (1979), *Mortal Questions*, Cambridge University Press: Cambridge.
Nagel, T. (1980), 'Aristotle on Eudaimonia' in A.O. Rorty (ed.) *Essays on Aristotle's Ethics*, University of California Press: Berkeley, California, pp.7-14.
Nagel, T. (1986), *The View From Nowhere*, Oxford University Press: New York.
Nagel, T. (1987), 'Moral Conflict and Political Legitimacy', *Philosophy and Public Affairs*, 16, pp.215-40.
Nagel, T. (1988), 'War and Massacre' in Scheffler, S. (ed.) *Consequentialism and Its Critics*, Oxford University Press: Oxford, pp.51-73.
Nagel, T. (1991), *Equality and Partiality*, Oxford University Press: New York.
Nelson, W.N. (1980), 'The Very Idea of Pure Procedural Justice', *Ethics* 90, pp.502 511.
Nerlich, G. (1989), *Values and Valuing*, Clarendon Press: Oxford.
Nielsen, K. (1989), *Marxism and the Moral Point of View*, Westview Press: Boulder, Colorado.
Norcross, A. (1990), 'Consequentialism and the Unforseeable Future', *Analysis*, vol.50 no.4, pp.253-56.
Norman, R. (1976), *Hegel's Phenomenology: a philosophical introduction*, Harvester: Sussex.
Norman, R. (1983), *The Moral Philosophers*, Clarendon Press: Oxford.
Norman, R. (1987), *Free and Equal*, Oxford University Press: Oxford.
Nove, A. (1983), *The Economics of Feasible Socialism*, George Allen and Unwin: London.
Nozick, R. (1969), 'Coercion' in S. Morgenbesser *et al* (eds.), *Philosophy, Science and Method*, St. Martin's Press: New York, pp.440-72
Nozick, R. (1971), 'On the Randian Argument', *The Personalist*, 52, Spring, pp.282-304
Nozick, R. (1974), *Anarchy, State and Utopia*, Basic Books: New York.
Nozick, R. (1989), *The Examined Life: Philosophical Manifestations*, Simon and Schuster: New York.
Nussbaum, M. (1990), 'Aristotelian Social Democracy', in Douglass, R.B., Mara, G.R., and Richardson, H.S. (eds.), *Liberalism and the Good*, Routledge: New York, pp.203-52.
Ollman, B. (1971), *Alienation: Marx's Conception of Man in Capitalist Society*, Cambridge University Press: Cambridge.
O'Neill, O. (1985), 'Life-Boat Earth' in Beitz, C.R. *et al*, (eds.), *International Ethics*, Princeton University Press: Princeton, pp.262-81.
O'Neill, O. (1987-88), 'Rights to Compensation', *Social Philosophy and Policy* vol.5 no.1, pp.72-87.
Plato (1956), *Protagoras and Meno*, trans. W.K.C. Guthrie, 1st Edition, Penguin: Harmondsworth, Middlesex.
Plato (1974), *The Republic*, trans. Desmond Lee, Penguin: Harmondsworth, Middlesex.
Plato (1969), *Phaedo* in *The Last Days of Socrates*, trans. Hugh Tredennick, Penguin: Harmondsworth, Middlesex.
Pogge, T. (1989), *Realizing Rawls*, Cornell University Press: London.
Popper, K. (1945), *The Open Society and Its Enemies: Vol.1, The Spell of Plato*, Routledge: London.
Prichard, H.A. (1968), 'Duty and Interest' in *Moral Obligation and 'Duty and Interest'*, Oxford University Press: London.
Raphael, D.D. (1950-51), 'Justice and Liberty', *Proceedings of the Aristotelian Society*, vol.51, pp.167-96.

Rawls, J.R. (1958), 'Justice as Fairness', *The Philosophical Review*, 57, pp.164-94.
Rawls, J.R. (1972), *A Theory of Justice*, Oxford University Press: Oxford.
Rawls, J.R. (1975), 'A Kantian Conception of Equality', *Cambridge Review*, February, pp.94-99.
Rawls, J.R. (1980), 'Kantian Constructivism in Moral Theory', *Journal of Philosophy* 77, pp.515-72.
Rawls, J.R. (1982), 'Social Unity and the Primary Goods' in Sen, A., and Williams, B. (eds.), *Utilitiarianism and Beyond*, Cambridge Univerity Press: Cambridge, pp.159-85.
Rawls, J.R. (1985), 'Justice as Fairness: Political not Metaphysical', *Philosophy and Public Affairs*, 14/3, pp.223-51.
Rawls, J.R. (1987), 'The Idea of Overlapping Consensus', *Oxford Journal of Legal Studies*, 7, pp.1-25.
Rawls, J.R. (1988), 'The Priority of the Right and Ideas of the Good', *Philosophy and Public Affairs*, 17, pp.251-76.
Rawls, J.R. (1989), 'The Domain of the Political and Overlapping Consensus', *New York University Law Review*, 64, pp.233-55.
Reich, K. (1939), 'Kant and Greek Ethics', *Mind* 48, pp.338-54 & pp.446-63.
Reiss, H. (1970) (ed.), *Kant's Political Writings*, trans. H.B. Nisbet, Cambridge University Press: Cambridge.
Rescher, N. (1966), *Distributive Justice: A Constructivist Critique of the Utilitarian Theory of Distribution*, Bobbs-Merrill: Indianapolis, Indiana.
Rescher, N. (1972), *Welfare*, Pittsburgh University Press: Pittsbrugh.
Riley, P. (1983), *Kant's Political Philosophy*, Rowman and Littlefield: Totowa, N.J.
Ross, W.D. (1964), *Aristotle*, Methuen: London.
Rousseau, J.J. (1938), 'The Origins of Inequality' in *The Social Contract*, trans. G.D.H. Cole, J.M. Dent and Sons: London.
Russell, B. (1979), *History of Western Philosophy*, Unwin: London.
Sachs, D. (1981), 'How to Distinguish Self-respect from Self-Esteem', *Philosophy and Public Affairs*, Vol.10, no.4, pp.346-60.
Sartre, J.P. (1966), *Being and Nothingness*, trans. Hazel E. Barnes, Washington Square Press, New York.
Saunders, N.K. (1972) (ed.), *The Epic of Gilmagesh*, Penguin: Harmondsworth, Middlesex.
Scanlon, T.M. (1975), 'Preference and Urgency', *Journal of Philosophy*, 72, pp.655-69.
Scheffler, S. (1981), 'Natural Rights, Equality and the Minimal State' in *Reading Nozick*, Paul, J. (ed.), Rowman and Littlefield: Totowa N.J..
Scheffler, S. (1982), *The Rejection of Consequentialism*, Oxford University Press: Oxford.
Scheffler, S. (ed.), (1988), *Consequentialism and its Critics*, Oxford University Press: Oxford.
Scheffler, S. (1992), *Human Morality*, Oxford University Press: New York.
Schumacher, E.F. (1979), *Good Work*, Jonathon Cape: London.
Schwartz, A. (1972-73), 'Moral Neutrality and the Primary Goods', *Ethics*, 82, pp.294-307.
Schwartz, A. (1982), 'Meaningful Work', *Ethics*, 92, pp.634-46.
Sher, G. (1987), *Desert*, Princeton University Press: Prineton, N.J..
Sidgwick, H. (1967), *The Methods of Ethics*, McMillan: London.
Silber, J.R. (1962-63), 'The Importance of the Highest Good in Kant's Ethics', *Ethics*, 73, pp.179-97
Singer, M.G. (1961) *Generalization in Ethics*, Alfred A. Knopf: New York.
Skillen, A.J. (1977), *Ruling Illusions: Philosophy and the Social Order*, Harvester: Sussex.

Slote, M. (1983), *Goods and Virtues*, Clarendon Press: Oxford.
Smith, A. (1976), *An Inquiry into the Nature and Causes of the Wealth of Nations*, 2 volumes in 1, Chicago University Press: Chicago.
Solomon, R.C. (1985), *In the Spirit of Hegel*, Oxford University Press: Oxford.
Sullivan, R.J. (1974), 'The Kantian Critique of Aristotle's Moral Philosophy', *Review of Metaphysics*, 28, pp.24-53.
Sullivan, R.J. (1989), *Immanuel Kant's Moral Theory*, Cambridge University Press: Cambridge.
Sutton, A. (1979), 'The Kantian and Consequentialist Elements in Rawls's Theory of Justice', *Theoria* 45, pp.135-40.
Tawney, R.S. (1964), *Equality*, Unwin: London.
Taylor, C. (1975), *Hegel*, Cambridge University Press: Cambridge.
Taylor, C. (1979), 'What's Wrong with Negative Liberty?' in Ryan, A. (ed.), *The Idea of Freedom: essays in honour of Isaiah Berlin*, Oxford University Press: Oxford.
Taylor, G. (1985), *Pride, Shame and Guilt: Emotions of Self-Assessment*, Clarendon Press: Oxford.
Telfer, E. (1968), 'Self-Respect' *Philosophical Quarterly*, 18, pp.114-21.
Thomas, L.L. (1978), 'Morality and Our Self-Concept' *The Journal of Value Inquiry*, vol.12, pp.258-68.
Thoreau, H.D. (1983), *Walden*, Penguin: Harmondsworth, Middlesex.
Urmson, J.O. (1974-75), 'A Defence of Intuitionism', *Proceedings of the Aristotelian Society*, 75, pp.111-20.
Urmson, J.O. (1988), *Aristotle's Ethics*, Basil Blackwell: Oxford.
Waldron, J. (1986), 'Welfare and the Images of Charity', *The Philosophical Quarterly*, 36/145, pp.463-82.
Waldron, J. (1987), 'Theoretical Foundations of Liberalism', *The Philosophical Quarterly*, 36/145, pp.127-50.
Waldron, J. (1988), *The Right to Private Property*, Oxford University Press: Oxford.
Walsh, A.J. (1994), 'Meaningful Work as a Distributive Good', *The Southern Journal of Philosophy*, Vol.XXXII, no.2, pp.233-50.
Walzer, M. (1973), 'Political Action: the Problem of Dirty Hands', *Philosophy and Public Affairs*, 2/2, pp.160-80.
Walzer, M. (1983), *Spheres of Justice*, Blackwell: Oxford.
Weedon, C. (1987), *Feminism and Post-Structuralist Theory*, Oxford, Blackwell.
Wertheimer, A. (1983) 'Jobs, Qualifications and Preferences', *Ethics* vol.94, pp.99-112.
White, S..K. (1988), *Reason Justice and Modernity: The Recent Work of Jurgen Habermas*, Cambridge University Press: Cambridge.
Williams, B. (1973), 'The Idea of Equality', in *Problems of the Self*, Cambridge University Press: Cambridge, pp.230-49.
Williams, B. (1988), 'Consequentialism and Integrity' in Scheffler, S. (ed.), *Consequentialism and its Critics*, Oxford University Press: Oxford, pp.20-50.
Wittgenstein, L. (1967), *Philosophical Investigations*, trans. G.E.M. Anscombe, Basil Blackwell: Oxford.
Wolff, J. (1991), *Robert Nozick*, Polity Press: Cambridge.
Wolff, R.P. (ed.) (1977), *Understanding Rawls*, Princeton University Press: Princeton N.J..
Wood, A.W. (1971-72), 'The Marxian Critique of Justice', *Philosophy and Public Affairs* 1, pp.244-82.
Wood, A.W. (1990), *Hegel's Ethical Thought*, Cambridge University Press: Cambridge.
Wood, S. (ed.), (1989), *The Transformation of Work: Skill, Flexibility and the Labour Process*, Unwin Hyman: London.

Woolcock, P. (1984), 'An Equal Power Theory of Right', Ph.D Dissertation, University of Adelaide.
Zeller, Dr. E. (1962), *The Stoics, Epicureans and Sceptics*, Russell and Russell: London.